Discrediting the Red Scare

LANDMARK LAW CASES *&* AMERICAN SOCIETY

Peter Charles Hoffer
N. E. H. Hull
Williamjames Hull Hoffer
Series Editors

For a complete list of titles in the series go to www.kansaspress.ku.edu

ROBERT JUSTIN GOLDSTEIN

Discrediting the Red Scare

The Cold War Trials

of James Kutcher,

"The Legless Veteran"

UNIVERSITY PRESS OF KANSAS

Published by the University Press of Kansas (Lawrence, Kansas 66045), which was
organized by the Kansas Board of Regents and is operated and funded by Emporia
State University, Fort Hays State University, Kansas State University, Pittsburg State
University, the University of Kansas, and Wichita State University

Library of Congress Cataloging-in-Publication Data

Names: Goldstein, Robert Justin, author.
Title: Discrediting the Red Scare : the Cold War trials of James Kutcher,
"the legless veteran" / Robert Justin Goldstein.
Description: Lawrence, Kansas : University Press of Kansas, 2016.
Series: Landmark law cases & american society
Includes bibliographical references and index.
Identifiers: LCCN 2015044425
ISBN 9780700622245 (cloth : alk. paper)
ISBN 9780700622252 (pbk. : alk. paper)
ISBN 9780700622269 (ebook)
Subjects: LCSH: Kutcher, James, 1912—Trials, litigation, etc. | Trials (Political
crimes and offenses)—United States. | Freedom of speech—United States—
History—20th century. | Political culture—United States—History—20th century.
| Radicalism—United States—History—20th century. | United States—Politics and
government—1945–1953.
Classification: LCC KF228.K88 G65 2016 | DDC 342.7308/54—dc23
LC record available at http://lccn.loc.gov/2015044254

British Library Cataloguing-in-Publication Data is available.

Printed in the United States of America

10 9 8 7 6 5 4 3 2 1

The paper used in this publication is recycled and contains 30 percent postconsumer
waste. It is acid free and meets the minimum requirements of the American National
Standard for Permanence of Paper for Printed Library Materials z39.48-1992.

CONTENTS

Robert J. Goldstein, the author of this remarkable book on James Kutcher and a leading authority on the attorney general's "list," reminds us that the domestic surveillance program during the Cold War had many victims. The travails of Kutcher, "the Legless Veteran" whose story unfolds dramatically in the pages that follow, is also a lens through which we can examine how litigation proceeded in this contentious period; how the nation treated its veterans and the disabled; and how a person of true fortitude could find justice. Kutcher may not have been a precedent-setting litigant, yet his story is a compelling one of substantial historical significance.

Kutcher's case is an example of the heartrending, real-world impact on ordinary citizens of policies promulgated by America's leaders during the second Red Scare. When the Cold War became hot on the Korean peninsula in June of 1950, many Americans anticipated a coming conflict with an atomic bomb–armed Soviet Union. Politicians on both sides of the aisle pandered to Americans' fears. In 1947 the U.S. Congress had already passed legislation to require federal, state, and municipal workers to attest to their patriotism through loyalty oaths. Another response was to investigate certain organizations suspected of subversive activities, whether or not they actually posed a genuine threat. Even token membership in one of these groups could result in devastating consequences for an individual's pension, employment, and housing benefits. How many ordinary citizens had the courage or fortitude to fight against such odds? Kutcher was one. His plight stirred the nation's conscience at a time when too few Americans could afford to indulge their better instincts. Over ten years, Kutcher carried on his fight through administrative hearings and trials and appeals in our federal courts.

Through painstaking research in hitherto classified documents from within the government archives, access to Kutcher's legal counsels' correspondence, contemporary public sources, and not a little fortitude himself, Goldstein has presented us with a stirring tale of pain and suffering, success and setbacks, trials and tribulations, and final victory overcoming substantial odds. It is a quintessential American story. It is also an immersion into one of the darker periods of American history. We can learn a great deal from it.

In his 1953 autobiography (reprinted and updated in 1973), James Kutcher described himself as "in most respects" an "ordinary man," with "no special talents" and no especial "capacity for leadership," the type of person who "usually gets their names in the papers twice—once when they come into the world and [again] when they go out." In most respects, Kutcher does come across as quite ordinary, but he displayed absolutely extraordinary stamina, determination, and courage when, caught up in some of the most momentous historical events of the twentieth century, he successfully fought the federal government for ten years as one of the very most prominent victims of the post–World War II "Red Scare." His trials and tribulations, which became known as "the case of the legless veteran" were frequently featured on the front page of newspapers across the country.

Today Kutcher is largely forgotten. Thus, perhaps the leading history of the postwar Red Scare, Ellen Schrecker's 1998 *Many Are the Crimes: McCarthyism in America*, never mentions Kutcher, nor does the second leading account, Richard Fried's 1990 *Nightmare in Red: The McCarthy Era in Perspective* (a third leading account, David Caute's 1978 *The Great Fear: The Anti-Communist Purge under Truman and Eisenhower* gives Kutcher less than a paragraph while correctly avoiding the term "McCarthyism," since the Red Scare began well before McCarthy dominated the scene after early 1950). The purpose of this book is to literally try to revive Kutcher from the dustbin of history, to explain the importance of his case, and to put a human face to one of the leading victims of the Red Scare.

After joining a tiny and insignificant extreme left-wing group, the Socialist Workers Party (SWP), in the 1930s, Kutcher was drafted shortly before American entry into World War II. He saw frequent battle action in North Africa and Italy, and both of his legs were blown off by a German mortar shell during the American invasion of Italy in late 1943. After having both legs amputated and learning to walk with artificial limbs and two canes, Kutcher was hired in 1946 in a menial position as a Veterans Administration (VA) file clerk, with no access to national security information. However, as a result of

President Truman's March 1947 federal loyalty program, and more specifically due to the listing of the SWP on the so-called "Attorney General's List of Subversive Organizations" (AGLOSO) in 1948 as seeking the violent overthrow of the government, Kutcher was fired from his VA position. Subsequently, again essentially due to the SWP's AGLOSO listing, the government also sought to take away Kutcher's World War II disability pension and to evict him (and his ill and aged parents, whom he supported) from their federally subsidized public housing unit in Newark, New Jersey.

Primarily due to the loss of his legs fighting for Uncle Sam, the Kutcher "case of the legless veteran" became a cause célèbre, striking many Americans as grossly unfair. But Kutcher aided his own cause considerably by his dogged determination to defend himself, his skill (with the help of the SWP) in obtaining widespread publicity and support for his cause, and his understated eloquence in making his case. As noted above, Kutcher wrote an autobiography (and gave many interviews and speeches), but none of them provide significant psychological insight into what kept him motivated enough to pursue his struggle, often in the face of rebuffs from federal agencies and the courts, for ten years. In the end, the explanation seems to be the somewhat "ordinary" but still powerful one Kutcher himself repeatedly gave: he had given up his legs to defend his country, but he was not willing to give up his rights.

Kutcher not only denied that the SWP advocated the violent overthrow of the government, but also maintained (along with many others) that the loyalty program's failure to provide federal employees with details of the charges against them or to allow cross-examination of their accusers and the AGLOSO process of listing organizations without hearings, notice, or evidence were grossly unfair, and that to fire him essentially due to his SWP membership was a violation of his constitutional rights to freedom of speech and association. Moreover, the government's actions threatened to take away from him the two aspects of his life that gave it meaning: his support for the SWP and his job, which, menial as it was, gave him a sense of purpose after the loss of his legs and allowed him to support his parents, who otherwise were living solely on a small Social Security pension.

Kutcher described the decision he made to fight his case to the end as one he preferably would never have had to make, but "the gun was put to my head and I had to make it by myself." In the end, Kutcher won all of the fights for his rights, and in doing so helped to expose some of the worse abuses of the Red Scare. Because of the massive publicity given to his case by the press, the case unquestionably contributed to the Red Scare's demise, and especially to the discrediting of the federal loyalty program and AGLOSO (which, due also to other causes briefly discussed in this book, faded away rather rapidly after Kutcher's victories in 1955 in all of his legal and administrative fights). Kutcher may have been in "most respects" an "ordinary man," but for ten years he carried out an extraordinary struggle that probably would have overwhelmed most people, and in doing so, he earned the gratitude of all Americans who cared about the Constitution during a period when its central promise and premise of First Amendment freedoms were in grave danger. Above all, what made Kutcher's case so unusual is that, while most victims of the Red Scare tried to avoid publicity, Kutcher sought it out, and he was highly successful in doing so primarily because he appears to have been the only Red Scare target who had been crippled while fighting for the federal government during World War II before he was accused of being "disloyal" to that same government. Indeed, Kutcher's case appears to have attracted more publicity than that of any other federal employee caught up in the Red Scare (Alger Hiss and J. Robert Oppenheimer, two other massively publicized targets of the Red Scare, no longer worked for the federal government when they came under fire).

I am indebted to the University Press of Kansas, and especially to my editors, Mike Briggs and Chuck Myers, for their encouragement, persistence, and patience in supporting and awaiting a manuscript that took much longer to complete than originally anticipated. I also am indebted to University of Iowa history professor Landon Storrs and to an additional anonymous reviewer who read the manuscript in draft form and made numerous helpful comments and suggestions.

This book is dedicated to the memory of James Kutcher.

ABBREVIATIONS

ACLU	American Civil Liberties Union
ADA	Americans for Democratic Action
AFL	American Federation of Labor
AGLOSO	Attorney General's List of Subversive Organizations
AVC	American Veterans Committee
CIO	Congress of Industrial Organizations
CLA	Communist League of America
CP	Communist Party
CSC	Civil Service Committee
FBI	Federal Bureau of Investigation
FPCC	Fair Play for Cuba Committee
HUAC	House Committee on Un-American Activities
ISD	Internal Security Division (of Justice Department)
ISL	Independent Socialist League
KCRC	Kutcher Civil Rights Committee
LRB	Loyalty Review Board
NHA	Newark Housing Authority
SP	Socialist Party
SWP	Socialist Workers Party
VA	Veterans Administration
YPSL	Young People's Social League (SP youth group)
YSL	Young Socialist League (SWP youth group)

Discrediting the Red Scare

CHAPTER ONE

Kutcher Loses His Legs—and Then His Job (1943–1948)

James Kutcher was born in Newark, New Jersey, on December 26, 1912. According to an FBI report from mid-1948, he stood five feet, three and one-half inches, on his artificial legs, weighed 140 pounds, and had brown hair and hazel eyes. As for "distinguishing marks," the FBI reported noted, "left leg amputated above knee, right leg below knee."

Kutcher's autobiography and his subsequent writings and oral testimonies, the only sources for his early life, are almost entirely political. Thus, he never mentions the name of his parents (or his younger brother, who is referred to in passing in one sentence in his autobiography), but according to the FBI, his father's name was Hyman and his mother's name was Yetta. Especially since Kutcher mentions that his father was a fur worker who fled tsarist Russia to avoid the draft in 1909, it is virtually certain that his parents were Jewish, although Kutcher never publicly referred to any religious affiliation. (Both Hyman and Yetta were common Jewish names, there was a very high rate of Jewish emigration from Russia around the turn of the century, and the fur industry was dominated by Jewish workers.) In his autobiography, Kutcher also never mentioned any specific relationships with women, although in recounting the loss of his legs in 1943, he recalled immediately "thinking of the girls I had known, of the ones who attracted me the most but married someone else, of others whose faces had appeared in foxhole dreams," and of despairing that he could not ask "anyone to turn herself into a lifelong nurse."

Kutcher quite accurately described his life as having been shaped by three "catastrophes," namely the Great Depression, World War II, and the Cold War, three "man-made disasters" which "combined to make me into a symbol for one of the crucial conflicts of our time." Kutcher was attending Central High School in Newark when the first catastrophe that shaped his life occurred, namely the 1929 stock market crash. He recalled having wanted to become a teacher, an ambition perhaps fostered by "my parents, who had come to this country with little schooling and who had the immigrant's traditional respect for education." However, he was unable to get a steady job throughout the 1930s, aside from brief employment such as delivery boy for a butcher and scorecard seller for a summer at a local ballpark. He recalled that his "best job" was as a sales clerk in a paint store, which "paid $1 a day for six days a week, and lasted about six months, until the business went bankrupt."

Kutcher's inability to find steady employment was compounded by the fact that his father was laid off with increasing frequency for longer and longer periods. When Kutcher's allowance was cut in half and his parents told him that they could not help him attend college when he graduated high school in 1932, Kutcher recalled feeling briefly bitter about his father, "that he was a failure, that he had let me down," and that he was "selfish, thoughtless, indifferent to what became of me," although it "seems incredible now that in the third year of the depression I should really have thought that my father could get a job in another trade merely by deciding that he wanted to." According to Kutcher, he soon understood that his father's plight resulted from the fact that "rich women aren't buying as many fur coats as they used to," and he personally witnessed scenes of adults looking for food in garbage cans, people standing in breadlines, and even two men getting into a fist fight "about which one had seniority rights to the corner where both had been trying to sell apples." On another occasion, he recalled answering, along with a friend, a vaguely worded ad requesting job-seekers to report to the Newark Armory, only to find himself being recruited for the National Guard. "We got out of there in a hurry," Kutcher recalled. "My father never tired of telling how he had fled Czarist Russia in 1909 in order to escape military service and come to the land of the free, where no man had to bear arms against his will in peacetime. Anti-militarism, or anyhow non-militarism was a family as well as a national tradition, and I had no intention of ever becoming a soldier." Ironically, in what

Kutcher viewed as his second "catastrophe" (after the Depression), he was drafted in late 1940, shortly after he had signed up with a government program operated by the National Youth Administration designed to train him to become a lathe operator. Writing in 1953 (after he had been fired in 1948 from his VA job after two years and before he had legally won his reinstatement), Kutcher ironically noted that his army service "turned out to be the longest job I ever held."

By the time Kutcher was inducted into the army in January 1941, after almost a decade of more or less continuous unemployment, he had developed an increasing political consciousness. He wrote that he had observed how "demoralization and apathy were spread among workers like my father who asked nothing more than the right to earn their living by the sweat of their brow" and that "all of us who were mature or growing into maturity during the depression saw those things with our own eyes, and most of us never forgot them." Inevitably, Kutcher added, those who started by blaming themselves eventually started to doubt and blame "external conditions and institutions" and to "reconsider some of our concepts and prejudices about the role of government and the sacredness of our economic system," including the need to "look around and work together for common ends with other people in the same plight as ourselves. . . . That is what happened with me. My idealism, the love of my country and its people, and the shock of the depression, combined to convince me that fundamental changes were needed in the United States, and that it was my duty to help bring them about."

Kutcher attributed the real beginning of his political awakening to attending meetings in the early 1930s at which political figures such as Socialist Party (SP) presidential candidate Norman Thomas spoke, and to reading on his own on such subjects as the Sacco-Vanzetti affair, in which two anarchists had been executed in 1928 for a bank robbery after an extremely controversial trial that took place in a highly prejudicial atmosphere. In the fall of 1935 he began two years of attending evening classes at Essex County Junior College in Newark while still looking for work in the morning. In response to an invitation from other students, he joined the Young People's Socialist League (YPSL), the SP's youth group, in which he became active in the 1936 elections, taking on such activities as passing out leaflets and selling literature; Kutcher described the key factor in joining YPSL as seeing "millions unemployed in the depression." After joining the group, he felt an increasing sense of hope about the future, along with a growing desire to learn more about socialism and "how to get it," with additional key factors the Spanish Civil War, a conflict in which he ardently supported the democratic government of Spain against a fascist military uprising, and the Moscow Trials, in which Russian dictator Joseph Stalin purged a number of leading Russian revolutionaries in clearly faked trials. Kutcher recalled a vague understanding before then that "communism had something to do with dictatorship and I didn't want any of that," a feeling that was reinforced by the obviously staged nature of the Moscow Trials. He wrote that while he had previously thought members of the American Communist Party (CP) were "more revolutionary than I was," after observing the Russian purges and the support given President Roosevelt by the CP during the 1936 election, "I came to realize that their policies were not revolutionary at all," but rather primarily sought to "promote the interests of the bureaucratic dictators who had destroyed all democratic liberties in the Soviet Union and are concerned only with remaining in power on the backs of the people."

Kutcher soon became caught up in a major internal quarrel within the SP. Traditionally, the SP, under the leadership of Norman Thomas, had followed a "reformist" position, advocating above all electoral politics as a means of achieving socialism, and was generally considered to the "right" of the CP. However, between 1935 and 1939 the CP adopted, following Moscow's lead, a "popular front" policy in which it toned down its former revolutionary rhetoric and sought to form a grand anti-Nazi coalition, including the New Deal, the SP, and other groups that it had previously scorned as not revolutionary enough or even as "social fascist." While Thomas's dominant "old guard" faction supported the popular front, including the CP, even if that meant downplaying SP ideology, a more radical faction, known as Trotskyists (for anti-Stalin Bolshevik leader Leon Trotsky), which had largely joined the SP in 1936, viewed the popular front position to be too "reformist" and not focused enough on union organizing, and rejected the policy of cooperating on common projects with the CP. Kutcher gravitated toward the Trotskyists, who he concluded were "more serious than other members, better educated in society theory and history and more interested in spreading the socialist message among the workers, unemployed and Negroes." According to his autobiography, Kutcher was arrested and briefly detained twice while engaged in passing out union leaflets. In 1937, a final split occurred between the "old guard" and the "Trotskyists," with the former deciding not to run an SP candidate against New York City mayor Fiorello La Guardia and unwilling to condemn the CP in Spain, while the latter favored supporting an independent mayoral candidate and supporting the cause of fellow Trotskyists in Spain against harsh CP-backed repression. After the "old guard" expelled its opponents from the SP, Kutcher joined most Newark SP/YPSL members in setting up a new organization in early 1938, the SWP. Kutcher said this decision was extremely difficult, because YPSL had become "the center of my life." He described the split as due to his faction's opposition to La Guardia "because he was not a candidate of the working class" and their favoring a Spanish government of "workers and farmers" as opposed to the existing "popular front" government that could not "undertake the necessary political measures that might have assure the victory in the war against [Spanish military leader] Franco."

The SWP originated with a small group of CP members who were expelled for "Trotskyism" in late 1928 and thereafter formed in 1929 the Communist League of America (CLA) (Opposition), with about 100 members, who still viewed themselves as members of the CP. The expulsion followed similar events in the Soviet Union, where Stalin expelled Leon Trotsky and his followers in 1928, partly for ideological reasons but also due to Stalin's fears that Trotsky was his main rival for CP leadership in the Soviet Union. The key ideological elements in the splits in the Soviet Union, the United States, and other CP parties around the world were that the "Trotskyists" viewed the Soviet Union as becoming a degenerate bureaucratic dictatorship under Stalin, demanded "workers' democracy," and opposed Stalin's policy of building "socialism in one country" (the USSR), instead favoring a program of worldwide revolutionary internationalism. Although of relative insignificance in general in the United States, the

CLA did obtain some importance in a handful of labor unions and played a key role in leading a victorious Teamsters strike in Minneapolis in 1934.

In an attempt to expand their membership and influence, the CLA merged in 1934 with pacifist labor leader A. J. Muste's American Workers Party, but this union proved short-lived, and in 1936 the members of the former CLA joined the SP, where they formed a left wing as previously described. This union too quickly proved unstable, and the Trotskyists were expelled from the essentially reformist SP in 1937, as noted above, with Kutcher among those forced to seek a new left-wing home. This proved to be the SWP, which was formally organized in early 1938 with about 1,200 members. At its founding conference in Chicago, the SWP joined the worldwide Trotskyist "Fourth International" and adopted a "declaration of principles" that included demands for an anticapitalist "social revolution," called for "direct mass actions and avoidance of limitation to parliamentary activities," and, while endorsing electoral participation, warned that "at all times" the SWP would contend "against the fatal illusion that the masses can accomplish their emancipation through the ballot box."

Even as the SWP adopted this program, which along with its general propaganda clearly strongly hinted at the need for a violent overthrow of the government, the country entered a Red Scare that was to have profound consequences for the SWP and for Kutcher. Fed primarily by the red-hunting activities of the House of Representatives Committee on Un-American Activities (HUAC), led by Representative Martin Dies (D-TX), by growing concern over impending war in Europe (which broke out in 1939), and by the 1939 so-called Nazi-Soviet Non-aggression Pact between Russia and Germany, this atmosphere led to congressional passage in 1939 of the Hatch Act, which barred from government employment any member of an organization that "advocated the overthrow of our constitutional form of government," and to 1940 passage of the Smith Act, the first peacetime sedition act in American history since the 1798 Alien and Sedition laws. The Smith Act made it illegal to "knowingly and willfully advocate, abet, advise, or teach the duty, necessity, desirability or propriety of overthrowing or destroying any government in the United States by force or violence," as well as organizing groups with such purposes and related offenses. Yet another law, the 1940 so-called Voorhis Act, penalized parties that belonged to international organizations, such as the Fourth International. Faced with these laws, in 1940 the SWP withdrew its 1938 "declaration of principles" without replacing them with another set.

While the suspension of the 1938 principles was apparently an attempt to avoid, in particular, prosecution under the Smith and Voorhis acts, in 1941 twenty-nine SWP leaders were indicted on sixty counts under the Smith Act (as well as two counts under a Civil War–era sedition law), all involving allegations of conspiracy to violate a variety of its provisions, although none charged the SWP leaders with actually attempting the overthrow of the government (i.e., they were charged with, for example, conspiracy to advocate the overthrow of the government). During the trial, the government prosecutor declared that the government position was that "even though the defendants may never have done anything about overthrowing the government, the defendants can be punishing for advocating its overthrow."

Those arrested included the top leadership of the Minneapolis–St. Paul SWP/Teamsters and the SWP's top national leadership.

The indictments appear to have resulted from a confluence of factors: (1) FBI pressure on the Justice Department, reflecting the FBI's concern about spreading SWP influence in the Teamsters Union and other unions in the Midwest, which it feared might lead to strikes threatening the national security; (2) internal fighting within the Teamsters Union, rather than any real seditious conspiracy by the SWP, as the SWP Teamsters were in a bitter battle for leadership of the overall union with Teamsters president Dan Tobin and the young Jimmy Hoffa; and (3) the SWP national leadership was bitterly critical of the Roosevelt administration's increasingly interventionist foreign policy as drifting toward an "imperialist" war in Europe, even after the German invasion of Russia in June 1941 led the CP to change its post–"non-aggression" pact stance and strongly support intervention against Germany. Tobin, who had supported FDR for president in 1940, personally urged the administration to act against the SWP leadership, and the arrests came shortly after he sought to impose a receivership on the Minneapolis–St. Paul Teamsters Union and the latter abandoned its AFL affiliation and joined the CIO. Acting Attorney General Francis Biddle, apparently under the combined pressure of the FBI, FDR, and Tobin, personally authorized the federal action against the SWP, although he later wrote that he regretted doing so and had expected the Smith Act to be declared unconstitutional in its first application.

Eventually, a jury found eighteen SWP leaders guilty of the Smith Act charges (of the twenty-nine originally indicted, all were cleared of the Civil War–era insurrection charges, one SWP leader committed suicide before the trial, and ten were cleared of all charges by either the judge or the jury, which quite unusually asked for light sentences for those whom they did convict). In 1943, the convictions were upheld by the federal Eighth Circuit Court of Appeals, which unequivocally found the Smith Act constitutional and found that the SWP had conspired to "use force to overthrow the government" (an exaggeration of the actual charges) and to advocate insubordination in the armed forces. The original sentence was handed down on December 8, 1941, one day after Pearl Harbor, and following the 1943 appeals court decision the eighteen SWP leaders began serving terms ranging from six to twelve months on December 31, 1944. The trial essentially destroyed the SWP's influence in the Teamsters Union, its one stronghold, paving the way for the Tobin-Hoffa faction to assume full power.

Meanwhile, behind the scenes, the federal government established machinery to enforce the provisions of the 1939 Hatch Act (banning employment of members of organizations that advocated overthrowing the government), due not only to that law and similar provisions in a series of following appropriations acts, but also as the result of continuing, massively publicized claims from HUAC chairman Dies that the government was infested with Communists. In October 1941, for example, Dies announced he had submitted to the Justice Department the names of more than 1,100 employees who were either "communists or affiliates of subversive organizations" (in September 1942 Attorney General Biddle reported to Congress that dismissal or other disciplinary action had proven justified in only three of these cases). Biddle's report reflected that by then mechanisms had been developed to evaluate federal employees in cases in which their loyalty had been challenged, one of which was a secret attorney general's list of allegedly "subversive" groups, which included about fifty groups (the names of some of these groups were publicized by Dies, but as the press ignored Dies's listing, the existence of this forerunner of the massively publicized 1947 Attorney General's List of Subversive Organizations [AGLOSO] remained largely unknown). In a March 1943 letter to Representative John Kerr, who was chairing a House subcommittee to investigate Dies's allegations of widespread Communist infiltration of the government, Attorney General Biddle wrote that in addition to the listed groups, the government also regarded the SWP as "subversive" but had not officially included it because "no federal employee has been reported as involved at any time."

Judging by his autobiography's failure to mention the Smith, Hatch, and Voorhis acts and the 1941–1943 SWP Smith Act trial and appeal, Kutcher was oblivious—no doubt due to his own personal crisis that would lead to the loss of his legs in late 1943—to much or all of these developments, which, with their aftermaths, were to largely shape his life between 1948 and 1956.

Although Kutcher described himself and the SWP as opposing World War II as essentially a repetition of World War I struggles "over markets and raw materials and spheres of influence and not a crusade for democratic or moral principles," he went into the army without protest when he was drafted in 1940 (shortly after the initiation of the first peacetime draft in American history), partly because the SWP taught its members to accept conscription even for wars they could not support in order to "win the respect of their fellow draftees." Kutcher was inducted into the army on January 23, 1941, under armed services serial number 32057257 and was assigned to the 39th Infantry Regiment, K Company, attached to the 9th Division at Fort Bragg, North Carolina. He described the training and military discipline that ensued as above all teaching "blind obedience" backed up by coercive threats, which seemed designed to "break our spirits," such as assigning the trainees pointless and unnecessary tasks that sought to "show us that what we thought was unimportant and that our job was to obey, not reason why. We were never permitted to forget about the Articles of War or the fearful consequences of a court martial. They called this training, but I thought a better name for it was terrorization." According to Kutcher, the main topics of conversation among the soldiers, most of whom had no clear idea of what the war was about, even after Pearl Harbor, was "sports and women," and he "never ran across any soldier who fully agreed with my socialist ideas, which I did not conceal but which naturally I did not go around flaunting either."

In October 1942, Kutcher's company sailed for Europe after the completion of its training, and shortly after Kutcher was notified that his father had suffered a stroke and would probably never be able to work again. After spending a week off the British Isles, Kutcher's ship, the *Leedstown*, landed in Algeria on November 8, and his company immediately was sent into combat. Kutcher subsequently participated in battles in northern Africa at the Kasserine Pass and El Guettar, in Sicily, and on the Italian peninsula. After being transferred to the 3rd Division, 15th Infantry, he landed near Salerno on the Italian mainland in September 1943, having survived being pinned down for a half hour in Sicily under crossfire. Kutcher described his battlefield experiences as involving constant exhaustion and fear, with men around him cracking up and in some cases shooting themselves in the hand or foot to avoid further service as German resistance hardened the farther north in Italy American troops penetrated. He reported never knowing for certain if he had killed anyone "because you were hardly ever the only one firing," but he recalled in one engagement a German soldier going "over on his side after I fired" and never moving again, after which "we were driven back and I never knew for sure. I hope I didn't kill him."

In early November, Kutcher was assigned to his company's bazooka squad during the battle of San Pietro south of Rome, a battle that was the subject of front-page news coverage in the United States at the time but that today is largely remembered, if at all, because it was the subject of a short film by John Huston, who would later become a legendary film producer. Kutcher, who was given the task of carrying bazooka ammunition, recalled coming under German strafing and artillery and mortar fire as American troops sought either to drive the Germans off a nearby mountaintop or to bypass them. He reported "digging in" with another soldier from Brooklyn named Schulman, who had recently married and desperately missed his wife. After taking an afternoon nap on November 9, 1943, Kutcher reached for some food, then heard a mortar shell landing and felt a "sharp blow on the back of my legs, roughly the same" as if "someone hit you there hard with a baseball bat." Schulman was fatally wounded by the shell, while medics responding to Kutcher's cry for help told him, "Well, they'll take you back to a hospital where they'll amputate your legs and then when get back to the States the Army will give you a new pair." Two doctors at a nearby field hospital confirmed that his legs required amputation, and Kutcher gave his approval. He reported subsequently reading a newspaper item about a woman who missed her husband terribly and had asked the army to send him home for a visit. According to Kutcher's autobiography, she soon received a telegram "announcing that her husband had been killed in action. That was Schulman."

After ten days in a field hospital, Kutcher was sent to an army hospital in Naples in time for Thanksgiving dinner, but he could not keep any food down due to an attack of jaundice, which required a series of blood transfusions. Although his immediate reaction upon realizing that the war was over for him was one of joy, his feelings soon turned to despair as he tried to picture a life without legs and recalled a legless veteran who used to sit in a wagon and sell pencils outside a Newark store. While his parents depended upon him, now he would be an extra burden to them as a "cripple" for the rest of his life, and he would have no hopes for "many of the normal joys" that he had already missed at age thirty-one. "Now I can say good-bye to all of that," Kutcher recalled thinking. "They amputated not only my legs but all my hopes of ever having a normal personal life."

After a month at the Naples hospital, Kutcher was flown to another hospital at Bizerte, Tunisia, where he was awarded a Purple Heart and underwent some procedures to help prepare him to ultimately receive artificial legs. After another four months, he was shipped to Clark General Hospital in South Carolina, and then in the spring of 1944 to Walter Reed Hospital in Washington, D.C., where he remained for eighteen months and was outfitted with artificial legs. He was also given a pair of canes and gradually learned how to walk, reporting that the first time he was able to walk out to the hospital corridor from his room, "I felt prouder than a parent watching their first-born make the transition from crawling to toddling." Kutcher recalled receiving visits from his parents and friends and learning the lesson from the courage of other patients that "No matter how badly off personally you were there was always someone else who seemed to have it worse." By the time he was released from the hospital, Kutcher had become proficient at walking. He was honorably discharged from the army with the rank of private first class on September 27, 1945, and was able to walk into his home in a scene of joy.

Such feelings were short-lived, however, since Kutcher soon realized that he needed to have something to do with his life. He began reading, doing clerical work for the Newark SWP branch (which elected him secretary), and riding around town in an especially equipped car furnished by the government, but increasingly he was seized by a feeling of separateness and differentness from others. "I wanted to be a whole man," Kutcher wrote, "to think with a whole mind" and not to see "the world through my stumps." He felt "wholly comfortable" only when watching a movie in darkness and driving alone in his car, but increasingly realized that a "preoccupation" with a desire to "work out a relationship of equality with the rest of the world" made clear that he not succeeded in "rehabilitating" himself simply by "learning how to walk." A growing sense of aimlessness was compounded by his realization that his government disability pension of a $325 check monthly was not enough to support himself and his parents, who were living on a Social Security pension of only $33 a month. The solution, Kutcher decided, was to get a job, which would "solve all my problems, psychological and financial, at one strike" by allowing him to "stand on my own, like everyone else." After almost a year of his drifting aimlessly, one day a representative of the VA visited him at home and asked him about his plans. Kutcher asked if there might be a VA job and the representative said he thought so, although he told Kutcher that he would be better off going to school to train for a "good job." Kutcher wasn't interested in going to school and preferred even a VA job that "wasn't too good," to which the VA representative told him that he "was making a mistake." In the end, in August 1946 he got a VA job as a filing clerk with "ridiculous ease" and without any help from anyone else by passing a civil service exam. He took the exam after filling out an application for federal employment ("standard form No. 57") in which he indicated that the lowest salary he would accept was $40 per week. Kutcher provided five references, all residents of Newark, and stated that both of his parents were "completely dependent" upon him. Without further elaboration, he claimed a job preference as a "disabled" veteran whose service had terminated with his September 27, 1945, army discharge. In response to questions on the form, Kutcher stated that he had never been arrested, indicted, convicted, fined, imprisoned, or even "summoned into court as a defendant" in connection with "any violation of any law or police regulation or ordinance whatsoever" and also that he had never "advocated" or belonged to "any organization that advocates the overthrow of the Government of the United States by force or violence." Kutcher's application was subsequently referred to the Veterans Administration, which received it on July 19, 1946, and scheduled a job examination for Kutcher for 9 AM in Newark on July 29. On that day, Kutcher specifically applied for a temporary appointment to a VA clerical position, noting that he had been "disabled in combat in Italy, Nov. 9 1943--I suffered loss of both legs through enemy mortar near San Pietro Nov. 9, 1943." Kutcher was informed that same day, after filling out a multiple choice test, that his resultant score of 89, including a ten-point military preference as a "disabled veteran," made him eligible to serve as a clerk; the "notice of rating" form included the handwritten statement by a VA official that he was a "double amputee--legs." Kutcher was told that his application and rating would be "kept on file, and as soon as there is a suitable vacancy, you will be notified to report for a personal interview."

On August 13, 1946, Kutcher was hired on a temporary basis by the VA's "Loan Guarantee Division" office at 20 Washington Place in Newark, partly based on his ten-point military disability hiring preference. In a form filed that day, Kutcher described the position as "clerical work in connection with guarantee of loans to veterans," with an annual salary of $1,954. The form also indicated that he was then receiving a government pension for "disability incurred in military service" and that he had a "physical defect or disability," namely "amputation both legs lost through enemy mortar fire." In a written oath sworn that day before VA official Lilia D'Ambrosio, Kutcher declared that he had not offered anyone anything to obtain his position, that he would "support and defend the constitution" against "all enemies, foreign and domestic," that he neither advocated nor belonged to "any political party or organization which advocated the overthrow of the Government of the United States by force or violence" and that while a federal employee he would "not advocate nor become" a member of any such group, and that he would "observe the provisions of the Civil Service laws and rules and Executive orders concerning political activity, political assessments, etc."

In a separate written oath, Kutcher also affirmed that he was not engaged in "any strike" against the federal government and not a member of "an organization of Government employees that asserts the right to strike" against the government and would not "while a government employee become a member of such an organization." Although he had already been hired on a temporary basis, on August 13 the VA sent requests for information to at least two of Kutcher's references; one of them, a Newark restaurant owner named Milton Goldstein, responded with a letter (received by the VA on August 26), which termed Kutcher "honest, reliable and industrious." According to an October 4, 1946, Civil Service Commission (CSC) directive to the VA, Kutcher's position required him to serve a "probationary period of one year beginning on the effective date of his appointment" and was subject to "check of records and such investigation as is necessary"; the following day the VA converted his job from "temporary" to "probational" status, with the notation that he had been "serving satisfactorily during his trial period."

In a series of subsequent efficiency ratings, Kutcher's performance was repeatedly rated high on standard VA forms. Thus, on January 14, 1947, he was rated "very good," and on June 13, 1947, his evaluation was "excellent." On March 31, 1948, the last VA efficiency rating before Kutcher was fired on "loyalty" grounds, his performance for the entire year was rated "very good." The VA efficiency reports included thirty-one separate subcategories subject to evaluation as "adequate," "weak," or "outstanding." Kutcher never received a single "weak" rating, while he was repeatedly categorized as "outstanding," with such traits as "industry," "cooperativeness," "dependability," and "attention to pertinent detail." In a detailed April 23, 1947, assessment of his work, supervisor "M. D'Arcangelo" supported these evaluations, terming Kutcher "punctual, cooperative, and rated by supervisor as doing an efficient job." D'Arcangelo described Kutcher's duties as involving checking and arranging folders, extracting information from files, and typing "charge out cards," duties which did not require him to "move from his desk" and did "not overtax the physical capacity of this disabled veteran." D'Arcangelo added that Kutcher finished his "not very heavy" workload "to a satisfactory degree and in ample time" and thus could be given "more work and still do a competent job," but "inasmuch as a better placement could not be made at this time," Kutcher should be "retained in his present capacity." Apparently due to such high ratings, on August 24, 1947, Kutcher's annual salary was increased to $2,020. On November 7, 1947, he was transferred to the VA's "accounts, control and records section" in the Loan and Guarantee Division at that salary. In March 1948, Kutcher was transferred to a position as "mail and records clerk" in the Registration and Research Section of Newark VA's Vocational Rehabilitation and Education Division, and his posting was changed from "probationary" to "permanent." On July 11, 1948, a month before the government sought Kutcher's firing on "loyalty" grounds, his salary was increased to $2,350 due to a general federal pay raised approved by Congress.

Kutcher described his first job as filing claims for veterans under the GI bill to buy a house or start a business. During his first "loyalty" hearing in September 1948, Kutcher described the job as having "no discretion" and limited to stamping documents to show that certificates of eligibility had been issued to "veterans who wanted to get a loan under the GI bill and to buy a house or for business" and then giving "it to the typist to type up." After he was transferred, he filled a similar position filing contracts between employers and veterans who were receiving on-the-job training. While such jobs might seem like "nothing to brag about, routine, even dull," Kutcher wrote this was not true for him. "No corporate president was more content with his job," he declared, as for the "first time in my life, I had a sense of security" and a "real job," one that allowed him to feel not "socially useless after all, that despite my disability I could hold a job like other people, that in certain ways I was even better than before I was drafted! All in all, this was the happiest time of my life since my school days. . . . And then on August 16, 1948 came a bombshell more stunning than any I ever experienced in the war." This was what Kutcher termed the "third catastrophe."

What in retrospect can be seen as the first portent of a potentially dark cloud looming over Kutcher's horizon appeared in a CSC standard form 84 request of January 30, 1948, from the Newark VA office to the Federal Bureau of Investigation for a "loyalty" report on Kutcher. This request, stamped received by the FBI on February 21, 1948, listed Kutcher's "aliases and nicknames" as "Jimmy," "K.O." and "Killer," and reflected President Truman's initiation of a sweeping federal employee loyalty program in March 1947. The program never gave a positive definition of "loyalty," but all federal employees were to be screened and six criteria were listed to be considered as potential indications of disloyalty, by far the most important of which for Kutcher (and most other federal employees charged with "disloyalty") was a finding that an individual had

> membership in, affiliation with or sympathetic association with any foreign or domestic organization, association, movement, group or combination of persons designated by the Attorney General as totalitarian, fascist, Communist or subversive or as having adopted a policy of advocating or approving the commission of acts of force or violence to deny other persons their rights under the Constitution or the U.S., or as seeking to alter the form of Government of the U.S. by unconstitutional means.

The institution of the March 1947 federal loyalty program to some extent reflected a continuation of the World War II screening program, but far more the development of the postwar Red Scare, which in turn was a product of the development of the early Cold War and continuing claims by Republicans and other conservatives (including especially HUAC, the FBI, the Catholic Church, and the U.S. Chamber of Commerce) that there was widespread Communist infiltration of the federal government. Such claims were considerably bolstered by the 1946 arrest in Canada of a Russian spy named Gouzenko, who claimed that the Russians had a widespread spy network in both Canada and the United States, as well as the leaking of U.S. documents in 1946 to a left-wing magazine, *Amerasia*. Perhaps even more important were the 1946 elections, in which many Republicans used the "communist infiltration" against the Truman administration (using the slogan "communism vs. republicanism") and won control of both houses of Congress for the first time since 1930. As a direct result of the elections, Truman, who had previously resisted pressure to take further action to protect the federal government against "subversive infiltration," two weeks later established the "President's Temporary Commission on Employee Loyalty" to study the subject. The commission's report, submitted in early March, provided the blueprint for Truman's establishment of a sweeping federal loyalty program on March 21, 1947. In testimony to the commission, FBI director Hoover reported that under the existing World War II loyalty program, the FBI had made over 6,000 investigations and that 101 dismissals of federal employees had resulted. (Other sources give the number of World War II dismissals as 1,300.) The commission reported that it could not "state with any degree of certainty how far reaching" the threat of subversive infiltration of the government was, but that the presence of "*any* disloyal or subversive persons" must be dealt with "vigorously and effectively."

Unlike the World War II program, which investigated federal employees only in response to specific allegations of "disloyalty," the Truman program provided for investigating the loyalty of all federal employees, with the FBI authorized to undertake a "full field investigation" in all cases where preliminary inquiries raised questions about federal employees. In cases in which the full field investigation warranted it, federal employees would then be subjected to hearings by loyalty review boards established in each federal agency, subject to a final agency determination by agency heads and a subsequent appeal to an all-government Loyalty Review Board (LRB). Although employees facing loyalty charges were entitled to hearings and counsel and to notification in writing of the allegations against them "as specifically and completely as, in the discretion of the department or agency, security considerations permit," in practice the FBI refused to disclose to either the agency or the individual the sources of its information or to allow its agents to appear at hearing. Therefore, federal employees charged with disloyalty effectively could neither know nor cross-examine those whose information was the basis of the allegations.

In December 1947, Attorney General Tom Clark issued the first listing of "subversive" groups, with no advance notice to them, no evidence or specifications, and no opportunity to contest the Justice Department's finding. This listing soon became universally short-handed as the Attorney General's List of Subversive Organizations (AGLOSO). The SWP was on this list, without further specification, but in subsequent lists, beginning in September 1948, the SWP was specifically categorized as "communist," "subversive," and seeking the unconstitutional alteration of the government. The SWP repeatedly challenged its AGLOSO listing and asked for a hearing on it, but was ignored by the Justice Department. Although the SWP was massively infiltrated by FBI agents and subjected to repeated illegal burglaries, bugs, and wiretaps, no evidence of criminal behavior by the SWP was uncovered subsequent to the 1941 Smith Act trial. Nonetheless the FBI opened a formal program of sabotage directed against the SWP in 1961, citing its voicing of dissident opinions and its practice of "openly espousing its line on a local and national basis through running candidates for public office."

Although the Truman administration repeatedly declared that links to AGLOSO would be considered as only "one piece of evidence" concerning individual disloyalty and not be considered conclusive without considering other evidence, the Loyalty Review Board (LRB) established as the ultimate administrative authority under Truman's loyalty program publicly declared in a finding of December 17, 1948, that it was "mandatory" that all members of groups listed as seeking to unconstitutionally alter the government be denied government employment. This finding was based on the 1939 Hatch Act, which banned from government employment anyone with "membership in any political party or organization which advocated the overthrow of our constitutional form of government." The December 1948 public LRB finding was in strong contradiction to its earlier advice to government agencies, for example a March 9, 1948, memo that declared that AGLOSO membership or links should not be considered as "per se establishing disloyalty," but determinations should be made "upon the entire record in the case." However, the LRB also required that Justice Department determinations concerning AGLOSO-listed groups "must be accepted" for the purpose of all administrative hearings, and agency determination boards should not seek to challenge the "controlling conclusion reached by the Attorney General in such lists," as the issue of AGLOSO inclusion would be for the "Attorney General to decide and not for the [agency hearing] board and the board should permit no evidence or argument before it on the point." At one point, Kutcher was asked to list all organizations with which he was "affiliated other than religious or political organizations or which show religious or political affiliations." Kutcher named two Newark groups, the Disabled American Veterans and the American Veterans Committee (AVC); the latter group came under attack during the then-emerging Red Scare as left-wing but was never listed on AGLOSO.

Compelling evidence exists that the introduction of the Truman administration's loyalty program, and AGLOSO in particular, was overwhelmingly based on political, rather than security, considerations. (Although U.S. government interceptions and decoding of Soviet communications under the so-called VENONA program had revealed by early 1947 a widespread spy network inside the United States, Truman was unaware of these findings as they were kept highly secret by the American intelligence agencies involved for fear of letting the Soviets know that their code had been broken. Along with the opening of Communist files in Russia forty-five years later following the collapse of communism and the Soviet Union, VENONA indicated that the Soviets were supervising more than 300 spies in the United States, many of them CP members, including at least three espionage agents at Los Alamos, where the atomic bomb was developed during World War II. However, the files and VENONA also indicated that by 1947 the Soviet espionage program in the United States, which had been run in cooperation with the American CP leadership, was shut down after the Soviets learned about the defection of two of their top agents, Whittaker Chambers and Elizabeth Bentley.) In late February 1947, a month before he instituted the loyalty program, Truman wrote to the governor of Pennsylvania that "people are very much wrought up about the Communist 'bugaboo,' but I am of the opinion that the country is perfectly safe so far as Communism is concerned—we have too many sane people." In his memoirs, White House counsel and top Truman aide Clark Clifford declared that his "greatest regret" from decades of government service was his failure to "make more of an effort to kill the loyalty program at its inception," while in a 1978 interview, Clifford said his own feeling was that "there was not a serious loyalty problem" and that the "whole thing was being manufactured." He added that Truman felt it was a "lot of baloney" but acted because "we had a presidential campaign ahead of us and here was a great issue, a very damaging issue, so he set up this whole kind of machinery." Truman biographer David McCullough's conclusion is echoed by most other students of the subject: he writes that by "acting first on the loyalty issue" Truman hoped to head off HUAC and "also, importantly, he wanted no accusations of administration softness on communism at home just as he was calling for a new hard approach to communism abroad [in his 'Truman Doctrine' speech to Congress of March 9, 1947, followed twenty days later by announcement of the loyalty program]."

Attorney General Tom Clark made clear in public statements that AGLOSO reflected concern less that the listed groups were a real security threat than that they posed an ideological threat, and was intended to destroy political dissent by "isolating" such organizations. Thus, Clark told Congress in early 1948 that the major goal of AGLOSO was to reduce listed groups to "impotence" by exposing their purposes to the "vaccine of public opinion," so that they could longer be "used for subversive propaganda" to promote "alien philosophies," which he repeatedly made clear was their perceived primary offense rather than plotting the overthrow of the government. He added that the government's "strategic objective" was to "isolate subversive movements in this country from interfering with the body politic." Although AGLOSO was supposedly aimed solely at helping to implement the Truman loyalty program, Clark listed as two *separate* ways of accomplishing this the "continuous study and public listing" of AGLOSO groups and the "complete elimination of subversive persons from all Government positions."

AGLOSO quickly became a test utilized throughout the country not only by the federal government but by state and local governments and even private organizations, such as the Columbia Broadcasting System. According to the most comprehensive studies available, by the mid-1950s 20 percent of the entire workforce was being subjected to one kind of loyalty test or another, and AGLOSO and similar listings (HUAC had their own more extensive list, for example) were used to blacklist individuals in a wide variety of occupations, especially in the government, educational, and entertainment fields. Thus, in December 1947, shortly after AGLOSO was first publicized, leading Hollywood producers announced they would not hire any person accused of Communist affiliations who did not deny it, following the massively publicized HUAC "Hollywood Ten" hearings into alleged Communist infiltration of the film industry (based largely on FBI leaks to HUAC).

There is no evidence that Kutcher was in any way singled out for "disloyalty" proceedings, as he was an active SWP member, and, as previously noted, the SWP was subjected to massive FBI surveillance. Between 1947 and 1953, about 4.7 million federal employees were investigated under the Truman loyalty program, and more than 26,000 were subject to full field investigations after preliminary reports (almost always involving AGLOSO affiliations, sometimes of friends, relatives, and even parents) raised questions in the mind of the FBI. More than 17,000 full field investigations led to formal charges and hearings by agency loyal boards, and ultimately about 550 federal employees were fired. About 6,400 federal employees resigned during the course of loyalty investigations, in many cases presumably to avoid facing further proceedings against them, while more than 16,500 were cleared following loyalty board hearings. In every known case where formal hearings were held, the sole basis of charges against federal employees was FBI reports, which were often vague and never supported by any testimony, so those charged could never find out details of the allegations or cross-examine their "accusers."

In response to the apparently routine January 1948 VA request concerning Kutcher's loyalty, on May 24, 1948, FBI director J. Edgar Hoover ordered the Bureau's Newark field office to open a "full field investigation" on Kutcher, based on 1946 reports that indicated that, according to "confidential informants" (a term sometimes used to disguise FBI illegal wiretaps or burglaries or both), Kutcher "had been visiting the SWP headquarters daily and performing clerical duties" there, as well as "participating in meetings and other functions of the SWP." Hoover's memo reported that FBI information indicated that Kutcher was then (in 1946) "negotiating" for a VA position, and, in addition to his directive to Newark, requested the FBI Washington, D.C., field office to "review the files of pertinent Government agencies and report the results thereof" and asked the St. Louis office to examine Kutcher's army personnel records. Correctly anticipating that the Kutcher case might prove highly sensitive and reflecting his notorious sensitivity to criticism, Hoover noted that Kutcher had "lost both legs in action in Italy" and cautioned that due to his "physical condition" resulting from his wartime service "this case should be assigned to an experienced Agent" and "each interview should be conducted in a discreet and circumspect manner so that no criticism can be directed at the Bureau." Hoover's memo no doubt reflected a May 14, 1948, memo about Kutcher written by an agent (whose name is redacted in the version declassified in 1980) to assistant FBI director D. Milton Ladd, which noted the reports about Kutcher's relationship to the SWP had drawn Ladd's attention "to the fact that Kutcher lost both of his legs in action in Italy" and therefore "the case presents a rather anomalous situation, in that a young man who lost both of his legs in defending his country, should now be the subject of an investigation because of questionable loyalty to it. This is the sort of situation which might cause some criticism of the Bureau. I wanted to call your attention to it specifically before it was sent to the field for investigation."

In response to Hoover's May 24 request, the St. Louis field office confirmed on June 16, 1948, basic information about Kutcher's military service, including his September 27, 1945, honorable discharge due to "amputation of both legs due to enemy action." The FBI's Newark field office provided a nine-page single-spaced June 17, 1948, typewritten memo on Kutcher's SWP-related activities, which largely elaborated on Hoover's May 24 report. The Newark memo summarized Kutcher's VA personnel record, which had been made available to the FBI, reported that Kutcher's parents were "born Russia," and stated that "confidential informants" had indicated that Kutcher attended "meetings and social functions" of the Newark SWP branch "almost daily" in 1945 and 1946 and had been "performing clerical duties there," and that in 1945 and 1947 Kutcher had attended a Grass Lake, Michigan, SWP "Midwest Vacation Camp." According to one informant, Kutcher had taken "care of the door" at Newark SWP functions "from 1945 to 1948." The report indicated that the FBI informants reported that Kutcher had typed SWP speeches and reports, that Kutcher was both an SWP member and a member of the Newark SWP executive committee, and that SWP members thought Kutcher "had great potentialities" as a party member and leader inasmuch as he was "well read." An April 7, 1949, memo makes clear that the 1948 Newark memo was based on multiple informants as well as "microphone and technical [i.e., telephone wiretap]" surveillance of the SWP's Newark office.

The Newark memo reported that one informant reported that Kutcher had pledged $10 to the *Militant*, the SWP's newspaper, and that the *Militant* had a picture of Soviet dissident Leon Trotksy on its masthead, along with a quotation from Trotsky, which declared that "only the world revolution can save the U.S.S.R. for Socialism, but the world revolution carries with it the inescapable blotting out of the Kremlin [i.e., existing Stalinist] Oligarchy." In addition to the reports by FBI informants, the Newark memo added that FBI agents had personally observed Kutcher at the SWP Newark office in 1945 and at the Michigan camp in 1947 had noticed a car with New Jersey license plates, which New Jersey motor vehicle records indicated was licensed to Kutcher. The memo added that three references listed by Kutcher in his federal job application were characterized by informants as "members and chief contacts" of the SWP Newark branch and that one of them was affiliated with the AGLOSO-designated Walt Whitman School of Social Sciences. However, the report added that over a dozen of Kutcher's VA supervisors, colleagues, neighbors, and landlords "state employee loyal American," that the Newark VA personnel records had "no information" that "reflected on the employee's loyalty," that Kutcher's credit record reflected no "information concerning loyalty," and that files of the Newark police, HUAC, and the FBI's identification division all had no information on Kutcher. On June 30, 1948, FBI Washington field office head Guy Hottel confirmed that HUAC and FBI files contained no information on Kutcher, as was also true of other files that were consulted.

On July 21, 1948, Hoover transmitted four copies of the St. Louis and Newark reports to CSC Investigations Division head James E. Hatcher and requested to be informed of any "ultimate disposition which is made of this case." Hatcher, in turn, forwarded the material to VA Personnel Relations Division chief R. G. Beers on July 30, with a request that the enclosed information be "referred promptly to the appropriate agency loyalty board" and with the notation that any consequent action had to be reported to the CSC LRB, which had overall supervision of the federal loyalty program. In response to a telegram from VA headquarters, Newark office manager Joseph O'Hearn telegrammed back on August 10 that Kutcher was still employed there "in capacity of mail and record clerk, CAF-2 [Kutcher's civil service rank], $2350 per annum." As the result of the FBI report the VA Philadelphia office sent Kutcher a "personal and confidential" letter, signed by Philadelphia branch loyalty board chairman Benjamin Hinden, which requested O'Hearn to "personally" deliver the letter and to obtain a signed receipt for it, also to be marked "personal and confidential." The letter, which Kutcher signed for on August 16, was captioned "notice of proposed removal action." It informed Kutcher that, in accordance with Truman's March 1947 loyalty order, as well as provisions of two other laws, including the Hatch Act, charges were being presented "for your proposed removal from employment with" the VA "to become effective" in "thirty (30) calendar days from receipt of this notice."

The "charges of record" were stated to be evidence of Kutcher's Newark SWP membership, given the late 1947 AGLOSO listing of the SWP, as well as evidence of his "employment" at the Newark SWP branch headquarters and of his financial pledge to the *Militant*, and "evidence of record of your association and activity with persons, associations, movements and groups designated by the Attorney General as subversive in nature." None of the charges indicated that Kutcher had either personally advocated or participated in any illegal or violent activities in connection with the SWP. Kutcher was advised that he had the right, within ten days of receiving the charges, to respond to them in writing and to request an administrative hearing before the branch loyalty board, which would include the rights to a personal appearance, to present witnesses and evidence, and to be represented by counsel and to examine all publicly available regulations concerning administration of the loyalty program. Kutcher was further advised that for the removal notice period of thirty days, "you will be carried in an active duty and pay status."

According to Kutcher's autobiography, that evening he met with George Breitman, his closest friend and a fellow SWP member, who told him that he had been a "casualty in the last war and now you are a casualty in the cold war." Kutcher related that Breitman brought along a stack of newspaper clippings and notes, which led him to conclude that the Truman administration, in implementing the loyalty program, had decided to "outdo" Republican critics who claimed the administration was "soft" on Communism, an allegation that Republicans had used in their 1946 congressional elections to help win control of both houses of Congress for the first time in sixteen years. According to Kutcher, Breitman warned that the cards were stacked against him under the loyalty program, because "they don't have to follow legal process, they don't have to prove that you are disloyal; on the contrary, you have to prove that you're not disloyal." Moreover, Breitman added, AGLOSO was the "worst part of the whole thing," allowing the persecution of individuals solely for their associations and granting the attorney general a power no American had "ever held before" of designating groups as subversive without any legal process or hearing : "Bang! The Attorney General comes out from behind closed doors and suddenly announces that such-and-such organization is 'subversive' and the organization can do nothing about it under the executive order." Breitman characterized AGLOSO and the entire loyalty program as designed to allow the government to punish "anybody" whose ideas it "doesn't like."

According to Kutcher's account, Breitman told him the SWP had determined to fight its AGLOSO listing "in every way it can," but that in the meantime Kutcher had only ten days to decide upon one of three possible courses of action: (1) to chalk things up to bad luck and "go and look for another job before any formal finding of disloyalty" had been made; (2) to deny the charges and ask for a hearing, for example by saying he had left the SWP months earlier; or (3) to "make a really principled fight against this whole witch hunt and help to strike a counter blow at those who are trying to destroy democratic traditions and proceedings" by admitting to SWP membership while denying that the party was subversive and challenging "their right to fire you merely because of your socialist views and associations." Breitman termed the first course the "easiest" as it would cause the "least trouble and controversy," while adopting the second course would probably not work and also would mean "you will have to give up all connections and activities" as long as he worked for the government. The third course, admitting SWP membership while denying disloyalty, Kutcher recalled Breitman telling him, would be the "toughest" and involve a "public fight" leading to "publicity or notoriety, depending upon how the press handles it," especially because "I know how sensitive you are about your legs, but that would become a big feature of the case, like it or not." Breitman warned such an approach would cost Kutcher his privacy, lead to public stigmatization as disloyal, and perhaps make it impossible to find another job while the case was being contested, all without any certainty of winning. However, he added, it would also be a "great contribution to the fight to preserve civil liberties" and a "courageous example of resistance to tyranny." Kutcher reported that he told Breitman that evening, "The main thing I am interested in right now is keeping my job."

Kutcher first responded to the August 13 "notice of proposed removal action" with an August 17 letter, hand-drafted before being sent in typewritten form to VA Philadelphia branch loyalty board chairman Hinden (with a copy to VA branch manager O'Hearn), in which he simply asked to examine copies of Truman's March 1947 loyalty order and other relevant documents referred to in Hinden's letter "so that I can decide what course of action to follow." He also noted that he had received Hinden's letter only when Newark VA office manager O'Hearn had handed it to him on August 16, "which I believe affects the [time] period" granted him to take "advantage of the rights and privileges referred to" by Hinden. In an August 20 response to Kutcher, Hinden reported that the documents Kutcher had asked to examine were available for inspection at the Newark VA office and suggested that he request O'Hearn to grant him access to them. On August 23 Hinden sent O'Hearn a letter requesting that he make the documents available to Kutcher; two days later O'Hearn responded that upon handing Kutcher Hinden's August 13 letter he had informed Kutcher that the documents would "gladly" be made available, that he had again informed Kutcher of this upon receiving a copy of Kutcher's August 17 letter to Hinden, and that "during the latter part of last week Mr. Kutcher did avail himself of the opportunity to thoroughly review all regulations covering this matter."

Kutcher reported in his autobiography that between the August 16 notification of loyalty charges against him and his formal response of August 25, he thought long and deep about how he should respond to the allegations. He rejected out of hand Breitman's second alternative, seeing no reason to lie about his affiliations as "I had done nothing wrong, nothing I was ashamed of, so why should I lie or try to deny what I believed in? I'll see them in hell first." He recalled that the next few days were "agony" as he avoided spending time with other people, instead driving to parks and sitting in his car while he tried to make a decision "on which my entire future might depend." Kutcher wrote that the "thought of losing his job" and the sense of "contentment and security" it had provided "gave me a physical pain in the stomach"; there were only two other times in his life when he had felt so angry, both highly politically tinged: when a "gang" of hoodlums tried to break up an SP rally in Jersey City in 1938 and when Trotsky was assassinated on Stalin's orders in Mexico in 1940.

Aside from anger, Kutcher wrote, he was flooded by feelings of "self-interest, moral values and political considerations," and he recalled weighing the "pros and cons of each possible course of action dozens of times, balancing them one against the other, debating them over and over." In the end he decided that there was "no real conflict between self-interest and my moral and political duty. I had to fight to keep both the job and the right to hold my political convictions." Even if he lost the fight, Kutcher reported reasoning, he would have openly challenged the "witch hunt" and encouraged others to act similarly, and while he considered the argument why should he "stick" his "neck" out instead of letting someone else do so, he concluded that if everyone thought that way "no one would take the first step and the witch hunt would proceed without hindrance." Although realizing that the press would make a great deal out of his injury, Kutcher ultimately decided that the injury was not his fault and therefore he had "no right to exploit it, but I also had no right to let it dominate me. Once I thought that it didn't dominate me any longer. . . . As long as you make it clear that you are fighting for a principle and not for special privileges because you are legless, than you have no cause to be sensitive about it." Kutcher recalled telling himself that having a job "without liberty" would yield little satisfaction as it could be bought only "at the price of acquiescing in a conspiracy to make a police state out of this country."

Having reached his decision, Kutcher informed his parents about his situation, with his mother warning about "rash" action and his father declaring that the entire matter would be found to be a "mistake" since Kutcher was not "disloyal." Kutcher also discussed his decision with Breitman, who introduced him to George Novack, a New York City SWP member who had been highly involved in a variety of defense cases, including the 1941 SWP Smith Act trial. Novack suggested setting up a defense committee, the Kutcher Civil Rights Committee (KCRC), to coordinate and raise money for the case, with the specific aim of getting support from people of "all convictions," most of whom "will not share your political views." Novack declared that the case was sure to attract widespread attention and perhaps could strike a "mortal blow" against the loyalty program, as it would be the first "real test" of the program. Novack promised to help teach Kutcher how to speak in public about the case and warned him that it would involve considerable time and work, especially as "our adversary was the administration of the most powerful government on earth." In the meantime, Novack suggested that Kutcher begin to write his response letter to the VA loyalty board and to prepare for a press conference at which Kutcher would "break your story to the public."

In an August 25 letter to Hinden that presumably was drafted in consultation with the Newark SWP, Kutcher formally "challenge[d]" the VA's right to fire him "on the grounds of my [SWP] membership" and requested a hearing, while terming "the entire procedure" one that was "illegal and unconstitutional." Portending what would become a highly publicized ten-year struggle, Kutcher demanded that his hearing be open to the press "since I feel that this issue concerns the American people as a whole," adding that "for the same reason, I cannot restrict the defense of my job to these channels alone, and serve notice on you that I will take such other measures as I may find suitable." Kutcher declared that he "never denied" and "make no secret" of his SWP membership and support. "On the contrary, I proudly affirm it," he added, while denying "the false accusation" that the group was "subversive" or "advocates the overthrow of the government by force and violence." Declaring that "I am opposed to witch hunts and attacks on civil rights," Kutcher noted that the SWP had publicly demanded a hearing to gain removal from AGLOSO but that this request had been denied and that instead the Truman administration was "proceeding to punitive and discriminatory measures" against SWP members, in violation of "my constitutional and civil rights" and in a manner smacking of the "worst practices employed in police states." He voiced his support for "political organization and action by the working people, who represent the great majority of the population, to put an end to these evils" and said that because "socialism is the only system that can bring humanity peace and freedom" he would vote "next November, whether approved by the government or not," for the SWP presidential ticket.

First voicing what would become his most publicized and eloquent mantras, Kutcher declared he had never advocated force or violence to achieve socialism and that "the only time in my life I ever practiced force or violence was under the orders given me in the Army by the U.S. Government," and that his political views had not been queried before his draft board conscripted him, the Germans fired a mortar shell at him in Italy, or American military surgeons amputated his legs. He added, "The Army did not ask me about my political views or the party to which I belonged when it gave me the purple heart." Kutcher declared that it had taken a "long time" to learn how to use his artificial legs but he did so in order to gain employment because he had to "contribute to the support of my aged and sick parents." He continued:

You understand that it is not too easy to get a job when you have no legs. But two years ago this month I went to work for the Veterans Administration, and have filled my job satisfactorily. Now you propose to deprive me of that job, solely because of my political views and the party to which I belong. This is political persecution and I intend to fight against it with all my vigor, because my job is at stake, because a great principle involving my own rights is affected, and because it concerns thousands of other government employees, many of them veterans, whose rights are similarly threatened by this dictatorship procedure. . . . You have the right to disagree with my views, but not to deprive me of my job for holding them, or for belonging to a party and associating with people who share them or contributing my money to support of a newspaper that defends them. I contend that I have the same right to a government job as . . . any other American, and that not a single shred of real liberty will remain for anyone in this country if I and other political opponents of the [government] are to be hounded out of our jobs because of the principles we believe in. I have already been deprived of both my legs and my freedom of movement. I do not propose to have any government official deprive me of my freedom of thought and expression and my right to earn a living. The methods employed against me are those of totalitarianism and not of democracy.

In response to Kutcher's letter, on August 26 Philadelphia VA loyalty board chairman Hinden informed him that a hearing on the proposed firing had been scheduled for September 10, 1948, in Philadelphia. In the meantime, on August 19, FBI director Hoover informed his Newark field office that a photograph taken in July 1947 at the Grass Lake, Michigan, SWP camp included Kutcher, according to an August 18 identification by an employee of the Newark VA division where Kutcher worked. On August 26, Hinden informed Newark VA manager O'Hearn about the September 10 Philadelphia hearing, noting that Kutcher was entitled to be paid for traveling to Philadelphia for the hearing "under established regulations," and requesting that Kutcher be granted "ample" opportunity to participate since "an estimate of the amount of time required to hear the case cannot be determined at this time." Such authorization was granted to Kutcher in an August 27 memo from O'Hearn, which informed him that he would be listed as absent from his duties due to "official business" "for conference purposes" at the Philadelphia's VA office for September 10, as well as for September 13–14 "if necessary." An August 30 memo written by Philadelphia VA branch loyalty board chairman Hinden reported that he had "emphatically" rejected a request that the Philadelphia hearing be open to the public, which had come from George Novack, the SWP official who also served as the secretary of the newly formed Kutcher Civil Rights Committee (KCRC); Hinden stated that the board was bound by regulations requiring that "all hearings be private." Kutcher also requested an open hearing in an August 30 letter to Hinden, which declared that "I have nothing to conceal in this matter, either about myself or the political ideas for which my employment in the Veterans Administration is threatened." In a bizarre coincidence resulting from congressional action entirely unrelated to Kutcher personally, on September 3 he was notified by the VA that his annual salary had been increased from $2,020 to $2,350 (over 15%) as of July 11, 1948.

Although Kutcher's request for an open hearing was denied, the developments leading up to the September 10 Philadelphia hearing led to the emergence of the Kutcher affair into the public arena in late August 1948 in a manner that was carefully stage-managed by the SWP and KCRC, heavily covered by the press (although at first only locally), and thoroughly monitored by the FBI. Even before Kutcher formally dispatched his August 25 letter to Hinden requesting the loyalty hearing that would be scheduled for September 10 in Philadelphia, his backers began to publicize Kutcher's case. Thus, in an August 23 letter to the city editor of a Newark newspaper, New Jersey CIO official Arthur Burch declared that "the most sensational case in the series of 'disloyalty' discharges of government employees" would "break" at an August 25 Newark press conference concerning the Kutcher matter, to be attended by Kutcher himself along with several "prominent public figures," including New Jersey CIO president Carl Holderman. Burch's letter described Kutcher as a "Purple Heart veteran" who had "lost both of his legs in Italy in 1943" and who was being "discharged because of membership in one of" the AGLOSO organizations. It further declared that "beyond the personal circumstances," the "unusual aspect" of the case was that

Kutcher did not deny membership but "says that he intends to fight his case as a question of principle, holding that he cannot be discharged solely because of his political views." Burch never specifically referred to the SWP but stated that Kutcher "definitely is not a communist."

Burch's letter was followed up by an August 25 "immediate release" press statement on the letterhead of the New York headquarters of the SWP that summarized and quoted from Kutcher's same-day hearing request letter but that, oddly, failed to mention that day's Newark press conference. This peculiar omission may have been an attempt to foil feared FBI surveillance (Burch's letter had included the request that its information be held "confidential until the time of the press conference"), but, if so, it failed: an August 25 teletype message from the Newark FBI office to Hoover reported that the Newark SWP was forming a "Kutcher Civil Rights Defense Committee," had scheduled a press conference on the case that day, and was seeking to organize on a "national scale." Hoover responded to Newark with an August 26 teletype directing that Kutcher-related developments be followed in a "discreet fashion through confidential sources" and that FBI headquarters be "fully advised by teletype of all pertinent activities in connection therewith."

The Newark FBI office responded to Hoover's August 26 teletype the same day with a memo that enclosed press clippings from the substantial coverage that the August 25 Kutcher news conference attracted from August 26 New York/Newark area newspapers, including front-page stories in the *New York Star*, the *New York Daily News*, and the *Newark Star-Ledger*, as well as less prominent coverage in the *New York Times* and other papers. All of the press accounts declared that the VA was seeking to fire Kutcher solely for his SWP affiliation. At least three of the stories, including the *Daily News* account, included headline references to Kutcher as "legless," thus introducing a popular appellation that would be endlessly repeated during the next ten years. At least three included pictures of Kutcher, including a front-page *Star-Ledger* photograph of him trying, with obvious difficulty, to navigate a small flight of steps, aided by his canes.

The news accounts of the press conference indicate that Kutcher gave reporters copies of his August 25 letter to Hinden, and several quoted extensively from it, including Kutcher's comments that neither his draft board, the Germans who blew off his legs, nor the army surgeons who amputated them had inquired of his political opinions. The *New York Star* described Kutcher as a "mild-mannered, sparse-haired man who seemed older than 35," while the *Daily News* account reported that the SWP "hates Stalinism as much as it hates capitalism," and that support for him had been voiced by the national and New Jersey CIO, the American Veterans Committee, and the New York Civil Rights Defense Council, all of whom emphasized "that they are not in sympathy with his political views, but feel that he is being undemocratically booted from his job." The *Star-Ledger* and *New York Times* accounts quoted Kutcher as declaring that "this witch hunt in government offices has gone far enough," that it was time "for someone to stand up and fight back," and that while he was opposed to both the American Communist Party and the Soviet Union "because they are Communist in name only," he would "defend any Communist Party member in the same situation as I am at present." New Jersey state CIO president Holderman was quoted as terming the government's loyalty program "a very infectious business that is spreading beyond the confines of government service into labor" and calling for an end to "this totalitarian policing."

In his autobiography, Kutcher termed the press conference a "success" and expressed special pride about the support from Holderman, declaring that "to have the support of the New Jersey CIO, with a quarter million members, on the very day that the case was presented to the public, and to have hopes for support from the national CIO and its millions of members was evidence enough for me that at the very least my voice would not fall on deaf ears." He recalled that after the press conference was over "almost everybody crowded around to shake my hand and wish me luck" and that while his fellow VA workers had all read about the story, "I did not hear a hostile comment from anyone" when he went to work the next day. He adds in his 1953 autobiography, "I keep running into people in all parts of Newark who remember those first newspaper articles and want to know how I am getting along. All my fears about how people might react proved groundless. Nobody said anything unpleasant to me."

Kutcher's scheduled September 10 Philadelphia VA loyalty hearing led both the FBI and Kutcher's supporters to step up their activities. An August 26 FBI memo summarized developments regarding Kutcher, declaring that a "supplemental report" on the case was being forwarded to the CSC and directing the Newark FBI office to "follow this matter closely and keep the Bureau informed." In apparent response to what was perceived as widespread adverse publicity concerning the case, the memo noted that Kutcher's "physical handicap" had been especially called to the attention of FBI assistant director Ladd and that "subsequently a pink memorandum summarizing the situation was prepared for the attention" of FBI director Hoover. A September 9 memo from Ladd to Hoover focused on "publicity which has recently been attached" to the Kutcher case due to the "controversy which Kutcher has created," with lengthy excerpts from an August 26 *New York Post* article, which had quoted extensively from Kutcher's August 25 letter to Hinden.

In the meantime, the formal creation of the KCRC was announced in a September 5 press release reporting that Harold Russell, an armless World War II veteran who had gained considerable prominence and won an Academy Award for his appearance in the movie *The Best Years of Our Lives*, had agreed to serve as national chairman of the organization. The news release stated that Russell had occupied a bed adjoining Kutcher's for five months at the army's Washington, D.C., Walter Reed hospital. (Perhaps inevitably, this led to headlines such as "Armless actor aids legless vet" in the September 8 *Newark Star-Ledger*.) The press release added that prominent cartoonist and Pulitzer Prize winner Bill Mauldin and New Jersey CIO president Holderman had also agreed to serve as KCRC members and that George Novack was serving as the group's national secretary. The September 5 announcement also reported VA Philadelphia Loyalty Board chairman Hinden's rejection of Novack's request for an open hearing, reporting that Hinden had stated that only private hearings were permitted in order "to protect the individual from adverse publicity," but that Novack responded that Kutcher "considers his best protection is the greatest possible publicity." The release noted that Kutcher's SWP affiliation was the cause given for his proposed dismissal and complained that the SWP had been "placed on [Attorney General] Clark's blacklist" without hearings, without any specification of charges, or submission of evidence and that "all demands later made for a hearing have been turned down."

In early September letters to the New Jersey CIO Council and the American Veterans Committee, Novack declared that the Kutcher case "dramatically symbolizes the present witch hunt directed against labor and the democratic rights of the American people" and urged that "all labor and liberal organizations" rally to Kutcher's defense, because "if the administration succeeds in discharging a legless veteran from his job as a clerk for his political beliefs, there will be no limit to the government's 'disloyalty' purge" and "no one will feel safe from the reactionary witch hunt now sweeping the country." In response to the growing publicity on the Kutcher case, former first lady Eleanor Roosevelt expressed her concern directly to Attorney General Tom Clark on September 3, leading Clark to respond to her in a September 7 letter that "the recourse of the individual in such cases" was to appeal to federal loyalty boards. Clark also maintained that he would be "glad" to arrange for the SWP to have "one of its representatives" present to the Justice Department "any material which it may wish to submit relative to its [AGLOSO] designation," and added in a handwritten note, "I would be happy to talk with Mr. Kutcher if he desires." (However, AGLOSO organizations which sought to gain reviews or hearings concerning their designations were repeatedly rebuffed by the Justice Department until it issued administrative hearing procedures for such cases in 1953 in response to a 1951 Supreme Court decision.) On the morning of the September 10 hearing, the *Philadelphia Bulletin* quoted Kutcher as declaring, "This is a test case. Someone has to make a stand against persecution. I'm determined to fight, not only for myself but for any government employee."

According to Kutcher's autobiography, many people who were personally sympathetic were "reluctant to join a committee or sign their names to a letter of protest," so that "in the first stages, especially, it proved much easier to get organizations to endorse my fight, pass resolutions or contribute money toward legal expenses than it was to get individuals to join our committee." Kutcher reported that eventually, however, a "large committee of some of the most prominent labor, liberal, religious and education figures in this country was assembled to help me," and the "sponsoring letter produced wonderful results."

Although Kutcher's September 10 hearing before a three-person VA loyalty board, which lasted three hours including a lunch break, was closed to the press and public, a sixty-two-page double-spaced typed transcript survives in KCRC and other files. The transcript strongly suggests that an unfavorable outcome for Kutcher was preordained by his prehearing acknowledgment and defense of his SWP ties, although Kutcher probably did himself little good by elaborating on his SWP affiliation and socialist beliefs, and occasionally by undercutting, in a somewhat fuzzy way, his previous disavowal of any advocacy of violence to overthrow what he depicted as a predatory and unjust capitalist regime in the United States. The "case" against Kutcher, described by presiding loyalty board chairman Benjamin Hinden as charging him with "disloyalty to the government of the United States" (a phrase that, oddly, was never used in the August 13 statement of charges against him), was presented by VA "management representative" George Merker. Kutcher was accompanied by New York attorney Arthur Burch, KCRC secretary Novack, and his lead attorney, Chicago lawyer Michael J. Myer (who ultimately billed the KCRC in connection with the Philadelphia hearing for $700, a very substantial sum in 1948. There is no documentary evidence that Myer personally prepared Kutcher for the hearing.). The government's "case" against Kutcher essentially consisted of Merker's reading of the August 13 statement of charges: no evidence or witnesses were provided to support or elaborate upon them, with Merker adding to the statement only that in Kutcher's August 25 response he had "proudly" affirmed his SWP membership.

In response, Myer launched a series of objections to the proceedings and motions for their dismissal, essentially based on the contentions that they violated Kutcher's constitutional rights to freedom of speech, freedom of association, and due process and that, because they solely rested on Kutcher's SWP affiliation, they violated repeated statements by President Truman and other federal officials that AGLOSO affiliations would be regarded as only "one piece" of evidence and that no federal employees would be discharged absent evidence of their individual disloyalty to the United States.

Among Myer's specific contentions were that the Hatch Act provision referenced in the August 13 charges, which absolutely barred federal employment to members of organizations that "advocated the overthrow of our constitutional form of government," was unconstitutionally vague and violated constitutional rights to freedom of speech and association; that Truman's 1947 loyalty order was also unconstitutionally vague and additionally violated the constitution by establishing AGLOSO without providing an opportunity to listed organizations to challenge their designations and authorizing federal dismissals based on "the doctrine of guilt by association"; and that the specific proceedings against Kutcher violated his rights by seeking his dismissal based solely on his SWP ties while barring him from challenging the SWP's AGLOSO designation and by proceeding on the basis of "guilt by association which is a violation of fundamental concepts of constitutional law," because "it is fundamental law of this country that guilt is a personal matter." On this latter point, Myer maintained that the charges and the hearing presented "no evidence whatever attributing personal disloyalty" with regard to "Kutcher's own belief, his own conduct, his own activities" and since Truman's March 1947 loyalty order standard was whether "on all the evidence, reasonable grounds exist to believe that the person involved is disloyal," rather than "membership or non-membership" in an AGLOSO organization, "there is not a proper charge framed here with which he has been presented which would be a violation of the Executive Order."

Hinden quickly dismissed all of Myer's challenges, declaring that the allegations concerning Kutcher's SWP affiliations in the August 13 statement of charges "would bring him within the purview" of Truman's loyalty order "if proven" and that the board was barred by its authorizing directives from going "into questions relative as to whether or not" the SWP "should be" AGLOSO-designated (Hinden subsequently refused, on this basis, to allow testimony concerning the nature of the SWP from the party's 1948 presidential campaign director). When Myer requested a "bill of particulars as to what association, what persons, what groups, etc., [so that Kutcher] will have something specific to meet," Hinden again denied the motion, on the grounds that the charges were based upon a "complete"

FBI investigation "and for security reasons the information contained in these reports as to sources cannot be disclosed," although the board would "take into consideration the fact that the employee has been handicapped in his defense by non-disclosure to him of confidential information."

Following Hinden's dismissal of all of Myer's challenges to the proceedings, Kutcher took the stand. After describing his educational background and early military service, he described, in an extremely laconic manner, being hit by the German mortar shell that destroyed his legs at the 1943 battle of San Pietro. According to Kutcher, "I was in a hole with a fella" at about "about three o'clock in the afternoon, and I said I was hungry, so we decided to get up and reach for a can of rations. That's the time I was wounded. The other fella died." He related that upon his calling for first aid assistance, a medic "started to put tourniquets on my legs" and "said 'We'll take you back and amputate your legs—(just told me just like that)—and when you get back to the states the Army will give you a new set.'" Kutcher thereupon briefly described having his legs amputated at an army field hospital and ultimately being evacuated to the United States and spending "about a year or so recovering" at Walter Reed hospital in Washington, D.C., where "they fixed up my legs—gave me artificial legs and then discharged me" in September 1946. Kutcher then described his job history with the VA, reporting that it originated when a VA representative visited his house and "asked me what I intended to do now that I was out of the service, and I asked him whether or not it was possible to get a job with the Veterans Administration. He said 'yes.'"

In response to Myer's questions, Kutcher reported that he had been an SWP member since 1938 (after belonging for two years to the youth group of the Socialist Party), that the SWP did not advocate the violent overthrow of the government but rather advocated democratic methods and sought positions on "the [electoral] ballot every time they get the chance," that "we are presently opposed to the government of Stalin [in the Soviet Union] and we think that the government of Stalin should be done away with," and that he personally viewed Stalin's government as "dictatorial, totalitarian, it's undemocratic." Kutcher added that although he felt that World

War II "was not a war to bring four freedoms [a reference to President Roosevelt's statement that the United States sought to bring about freedom of speech, freedom of association, freedom from fear, and freedom from want]," both in the military and as a VA employee he had never engaged in any kind of conduct intended to impede or undermine governmental efforts. At one point, after he described his current VA position, VA "management representative" Merker declared, "We will admit" that Kutcher's VA job "is not sensitive [in terms of national security concerns] for the purpose of the record if that is what you are establishing."

With respect to the SWP's AGLOSO listing, Kutcher said that he had learned of it in "October or November [1947] when the Attorney General first issued the listing [which in fact was not published until early December]" but that he did not view the group as subversive and felt that the "party had been done an injustice since they had not been given any prior notification and since they were not permitted a hearing." Kutcher flatly denied that he had ever "associated with or participated in activity" that he considered "subversive," had ever committed or advocated "any acts of treason or sedition," had ever disclosed any confidential information obtained through his employment, or had ever committed any "act of disloyalty to the government of the United States" or been involved with "any act of sabotage, espionage or attempts to do so." In response to Myer's (and later Merker's) questions about his "social views" about the American government, Kutcher responded that he felt it did not serve "the best interests of all the people" and that he preferred a "socialist society" controlled by a "workers and farmers government that would proceed to socialize the means of production" and create a society "more democratic than the one we have," based upon the "principle of production for use rather than for profit."

In response to Myer's questions, Kutcher flatly declared that he did not "advocate the violent overthrew of the present form of the government" to achieve such a system, that he believed in the "concept of rule by the majority of the people," and that his desired form of society could be attained only by convincing "the majority of the people that such a society is necessary and that it should be established by constitutional amendment." However, in subsequent responses to questions from loyalty board chair Hinden, Kutcher muddled his political waters by suggesting that violence would inevitably be necessary to overthrow the "minority" rule of American capitalists because they would never peacefully accept being democratically ousted from power and because, in any case, the electoral system was so rigged in a manner that a democratic change was impossible. Thus, Kutcher said that violence might be needed if the "minority of the capitalists" currently wielding power refused to "accede" to democratic change and that there was "no example of history of the minority group in power consenting to a change that was necessitated" by changing "social conditions," giving as an example the refusal of the southern slaveholding minority to accept "the decision of the majority when they elected Abraham Lincoln president of the United States." Thus, Kutcher continued, the SWP advised the "working class that although we don't advocate violence, it's not wrong to protect yourself against violence if it used by the minority to prevent the carrying out of the majority decision." Moreover, he added, "the minority parties, or the capitalist parties, are the ones that pick the candidates, and whichever candidate the working class votes for, the capitalists are still in control of the government" and had enacted laws "which make it very difficult" for other parties to "get on the ballot," and that they "pass laws in the south forbidding Negroes to vote" and had in the past (presumably referring to the 1919–1920 Red Scare) refused to seat socialists who had won legislative elections. Kutcher seemed to sum up his position by stating that democratic change could be achieved "if the minority of capitalists consent to it" but otherwise "then the majority must use force in order to enforce its will" and that even if groups espousing his viewpoint failed to win elections force "may be necessary."

Kutcher described his SWP activities in response to questions from Merker and Hinden as purely volunteer work, including selling party literature and "performing clerical duties" such as "setting up the mailing list and taking minutes of meetings." Alluding to the list of SWP-related activities that were included in the charges against him, Kutcher also stated, generally in response to leading questions from Merker, that he was in "full agreement" with statements in the *Militant*, the SWP paper, that he had "fairly extensively" read the writings of Leon Trotsky and was "in full agreement with it" and that he had attended SWP national conventions in 1944 and 1948 (although Kutcher had previously stated that he was hospitalized for his war injuries in 1944). Sensing that Kutcher's unnecessarily expansive answers were probably not aiding his cause, Myer objected that, because Trotsky had written "I imagine, 20 to 30 books and probably 100 times that much in unbound material," Kutcher's statement of "full agreement" was "almost meaningless," with the result that Kutcher agreed, in response to a rephrasing by Merker, that he was "in accord" with Trotsky's "political theories" and "method of accomplishing his political beliefs."

Clearly sensing that Kutcher's comments concerning the possible need to use force to bring about change had not served him well, Myer asked a leading question that resulted in Kutcher stating that it was "right" that the SWP "believed it could come to power constitutionally," and a few minutes later Kutcher responded to a query from Hinden by agreeing that if the SWP were in a minority, he would not advocate violent change. Following a brief appearance by a New Jersey clergyman active in the Newark American Veterans Committee who testified that Kutcher was "one of the best loved members of the chapter" and that he had never heard "of any discredit" or "blemish" concerning Kutcher's character, Myer stressed this theme almost exclusively in his closing statements. With regard to Hinden's refusal to allow the testimony of the SWP's 1948 presidential campaign manager, on the grounds that the board could not inquire into the validity of the SWP's AGLOSO designation, Myer declared that the barred testimony would have established that the SWP "is not a subversive organization" and had been listed "without a hearing, without any opportunity to be heard, and that it has since asked for a hearing and has been denied."

He added that the board seemed to be "most concerned" about whether Kutcher "advocated a change from capitalism to socialism" by unconstitutional means, and he maintained that Kutcher "certainly made it clear that he does not advocate any minority taking arms in hand and, being in the minority, going out and trying a coup," but only favored the use of "constitutional methods," including the passage of constitutional amendments, as there were no grounds to believe that the Constitution "guarantees once and forever the capitalist system," just as slavery had not been permanently guaranteed although it existed when the Constitution was adopted. Kutcher's main point, Myer declared, was that "everybody, the vast majority of the people would be better off under socialism" and "he doesn't want to force that on anybody who doesn't want it, not until, at least, the majority" feels that "this would better serve their interest." Myer concluded by maintaining that Truman's loyalty order required a determination concerning Kutcher's loyalty based "not simply on that part of the evidence" concerning the SWP's AGLOSO designation but "rather on the basis of all the evidence whether or not this man is disloyal" and thus upon "his whole conduct" and "what he has actually done against what his views are," especially since, despite his SWP membership, regarding his time in the army and working for the VA there was "not a shred of evidence" demonstrating that "his political views in any way endanger the United States" or affected his conduct as either a "good soldier" or a highly rated federal employee. "There is no evidence here," Myer declared,

> that he was guilty of any sabotage, any treason or that he was in a position where he did or could give aid or comfort to the enemy or give them information. This isn't that kind of case at all. If there ever was a case in my humble opinion where a person is being prosecuted—yes and even persecuted for his thoughts—that's all—for his views and his belief I say this is one. . . . [W]eighing all the evidence this board cannot determine that this man has been disloyal and should therefore be retained in the service.

Although Myer consumed five double-spaced typed pages in delivering his closing remarks, the closing statements of an apparently confident Merker took up only one page. Merker declared that Kutcher had "admitted" not only to membership in the SWP, but "also activity, sympathetic association, I submit," leaving the board with "no alternative" but to find Kutcher "disloyal to the United States" as he not only did "not forgo his [SWP] membership but continued active therein" despite "full cognizance" of the group's AGLOSO listing, thus intentionally avoiding the "requirements pertaining to employment." Following Merkel's closing argument, Hinden closed the hearing by stating that the board would "consider all of the facts and evidence" and noted that if it ruled against Kutcher the latter was entitled to appeal further to the head of the VA. Clearly reflecting the widespread publicity given to the case, Hinden declared that the hearing panel was not a "callous, unsympathetic board" and that it would consider the war record "of the employee and the fact that he lost his legs in action." Before adjourning the September 10 hearing, Hinden agreed to Myer's request that he be sent a transcript and allowed fifteen days afterward to submit a written brief. Noting that the August 13 charges had suggested a decision should be reached within thirty days, Hinden said, "We couldn't possibly reach a decision within that time limit," even absent allowing the filing of Myer's brief, and therefore, "Mr. Kutcher will remain on active duty and pay status pending the board's ruling."

Following the conclusion of the hearing, Myer summarized his arguments before the board to ACLU lawyer Clifford Forster in a gloomy September 14 letter that asked for suggestions in connection with his wish to submit a "brief on the constitutional questions." Myer informed Forster that "of course" and "needless to say" all of his motions had been denied by the board and that the government had "rested its case" entirely on the SWP's AGLOSO listing and Kutcher's "admitted membership therein" while refusing to hear arguments "going to the question of whether the SWP should or should not be on the Attorney General's list." In his autobiography, Kutcher also recalled feeling that the hearing been unfair in refusing to question the AGLOSO listing, as well as in refusing all of Myer's motions for clarification of the charges and in the manner of his cross-examination, which he described as "designed to make me contradict myself" and "just trying to trip me up." He wrote that early in the hearing he felt "we might as just pack up and go home" as it would be "impossible to get justice from this Board." Kutcher wrote a similarly gloomy account to actor Harold Russell, his former hospital roommate at Walter Reed, who had been announced as KCRC national chairman, in which Kutcher related "I never thought I would be writing you in the situation that I am in now," as he thought he had "settled down in a groove for the rest of my life" after getting his VA job. Instead, he lamented, "it looks as though I am going to lose my job and called all sorts of false names and I don't know what's coming next." Kutcher told Russell, "I am a socialist and no matter what happens I always will be because I think that's the only way to prevent more wars," adding, "I swear to you, Harold, that I am as good an American as anyone else, and that my party is not subversive and never has been," but the "people in Washington" were "so worked out about the communists that they are ready to crack down on anybody who wants to fight for a better world." Noting that the SWP's AGLOSO listing could not be contested at the hearing, Kutcher declared, "If that is the American way, then I am a monkey's uncle," and that if people could not obtain a "fair trial in this country" then "things will get as bad here as in Russia."

In an October 3 letter to KCRC officials, Russell clearly sought to minimize his role with the group, in what appears to have been a clear reflection of the growing fears of "guilt by association" (also perhaps of the Hollywood "blacklist," which leading movie producers had announced the prior December, almost simultaneously with the publication of the Truman AGLOSO list, after the notorious HUAC "Hollywood Ten" hearings). Russell declared that he wished it "completely understood" that his interest in the Kutcher matter was solely limited to "his right to a hearing before his peers" and his plight "as an individual and not as a member of a particular party," that he had "no sympathy" with the SWP's "tenets and principles," and that therefore his KCRC participation "does not in any way involve me or constitute any sort of an association" with SWP activities. Additionally, Russell listed numerous "conditions" for his continued participation, which seemed designed in fact to force the KCRC to cease any further reference to him, including that "no stationery be printed up bearing my name," that "no publicity, promotion, membership drives or press releases be made in my name without my approval," that he be notified of all KCRC cosponsor members, that no KCRC activities appear under SWP "auspices or letterhead," and that his "interest" be terminated "when a hearing has been obtained for Kutcher." Russell concluded, "I expect a reply from you to this letter agreeing to all the conditions I have made."

Although a KCRC appeal for support dated October 6 went out over Russell's signature as "chairman," it was almost certainly written and likely dispatched before his October 3 letter was received. While stating that the signers, which also included other KCRC officials, "do not necessarily agree" with the views of Kutcher and the SWP, "we do agree that the right of free speech, the right of unrestricted political activity and the right to hold public and private employment regardless of belief must be upheld" and that "all these rights are being violated in Kutcher's case." The letter especially denounced AGLOSO as a "subversive blacklist" issued without hearings, charges, or evidence, termed it a "cruel abuse of official power to cut off the livelihood of a war-crippled veteran who supports aged and sick parents," labeled the Kutcher case the "most dramatic symbol of the witch-hunt sweeping through our country," and said that it indicated that no American "is safe from persecution."

Both the SWP and the KCRC focused during September and early October on publicizing Kutcher's case and denouncing what they viewed as the unfairness of the hearing while they waiting for the VA loyalty board to make its ruling. Thus, the SWP sent a September 18 letter to all of its local branches which termed the board's procedures a "one star-chamber hearing before the [VA's] purge board," and urged all SWP branches to establish local KCRC chapters "on the broadest possible basis," including participation "of the broadest possible sections of the trade union movement, of Negroes and other minority groups, of veterans' organizations, of the youth, of liberals, and so on." The letter urged gearing up for a "long drawn out struggle" against the "current red-baiting witch hunt, the government purge of civil service employees, the administration subversive blacklist and the rest."

The KCRC also kept up a flurry of letters, press releases, and requests for endorsements, which habitually referred to Kutcher as the "legless veteran who faces dismissal" from his VA job "solely because of his political opinions." Thus in letters sent to supporters in late September that requested financial assistance and urged the establishment of local chapters throughout the country, the KCRC declared that it regarded the matter as "the test case in the fight against the witch-hunt now sweeping the country" and that it intended to contest it "through all the administrative steps and legal channels up to the Supreme Court, if necessary." Private correspondence and press releases from the KCRC and supportive organizations in September and October reported growing backing for Kutcher, including from the United Automobile Workers, the national CIO, the American Veterans Committee (AVC), and several prominent figures, including philosopher John Dewey, sociologist Lewis Mumford, and author Norman Mailer. Thus, the AVC, in a September 27 letter to KCRC national secretary Novack, reported that its National Planning Committee had adopted a resolution declaring that the Kutcher case "symbolizes the present dangers to the democratic rights of the American people," that "if an administration may discharge a legless veteran from his job as a clerk for his political beliefs, there may be no limit to the current 'disloyalty' purge," and that "no one will feel safe from the reactionary hysteria now sweeping the country."

On September 22 (one day after Kutcher received another positive, if somewhat less enthusiastic, VA efficiency rating, evaluating his work as "good," as opposed to past ratings as "excellent" or "very good"), the KCRC issued a press release with the text of a letter from Kutcher to President Truman asking Truman to personally intervene on his behalf, to meet with him to "discuss this case further," and specifically to "halt the dismissal proceedings against me until such time as you have called a public hearing at which my party can defend itself and me against the subversive charges." Kutcher opened his letter by reporting that he had read with "considerable interest" newspaper accounts that morning about Truman's visit to a Denver army hospital in which the president was quoted as declaring, "Nothing is too good for these men." He then discussed his wartime experience and the "disloyalty" charges lodged against him "because I belong" to the SWP, due to its AGLOSO listing, adding, "I am as proud of my membership in this party as you are of yours in the Democratic party. What I do deny and what my party denies, is that it is 'subversive' or advocates force and violence in order to achieve socialism." Kutcher noted that the SWP was a legal political party that appeared on electoral ballots and that it had been AGLOSO-designated without an opportunity to "prove that it does not belong on this list," thus denying it the "elementary democratic right to defend ourselves." In his peroration, Kutcher wrote:

I ask you, Mr. President, is this the democratic way? Would you like to be charged with a crime, and not told exactly what the crime is, or when you committed it, or where, and not permitted to face your accuser or examine the evidence, or have a lawyer or a trial and then be told you are guilty? What is the difference between such a procedure and the one followed behind the iron curtain? . . . [At the Philadelphia hearing] my attempts to discuss the main issue—is my party subversive or not—were ruled out of order as irrelevant and immaterial and the questioning was confined to something I had already publicly admitted—am I or am I not a member of the Socialist Workers Party. I see no reason to expect justice from such a set-up, and I ask you, Mr. President, to intervene. . . . As one of those about whom you said, 'Nothing is too good for these men,' I think I am speaking for most when I say that we don't want special privileges, we just want a square deal.

On September 28, the KCRC issued another press release, which reported that thanks to the intercession of Eleanor Roosevelt, Attorney General Clark had agreed to meet with Kutcher in Washington on September 30 and that Kutcher planned to "point out that if my political views did not disqualify me from employment by the government in the army for 4½ years during the war, they should not disqualify me from employment by the government in the VA today." During a press conference following the meeting with Clark, Kutcher termed himself "one of the casualties of the 'subversive' blacklist," and referring to his wartime injury, declared, "this is not the first time I have been listed as a casualty." His "petition" to Clark declared that both he and the SWP "indignantly" objected to the AGLOSO designation, "as well as to the arbitrary and unprecedented manner" of the listing, and demanded a "bill of particulars" and a public hearing, which alone "can rectify a horrible miscarriage of justice in the case of my party" and could "enable me to save the job to which I believe myself as much entitled to as you are entitled to yours. . . . I ask you to halt the dismissal proceedings against me and to immediately call a public hearing at which my party can defend itself, and me, against this false 'subversive' charge." Kutcher told reporters that in response to his request for a hearing on the SWP's AGLOSO designation, Clark had responded that "unlike others [an apparent reference to widely publicized congressional hearings into alleged Communist infiltration of American government society] the Justice Department does not conduct its hearings under the klieg lights and amid great fanfare."

In an October 4 letter to New Jersey CIO president Holderman, KCRC general secretary Novack reported that Clark had told Kutcher at the meeting (which Novack reported that he had attended) that he would personally speak to VA administrator Carl Gray about "Jimmy's case, and to review the record," but that "it remained his department's policy not to hold public hearings or to specify charges" with regard to AGLOSO listings, although designated groups "could submit any material to him refuting this accusation." In his petition to Clark, Kutcher had characterized such an offer as totally inadequate and equivalent to asking someone to "defend himself against a charge of murder, without letting him know whom he is charged with murdering, or when, or under what circumstances." Kutcher described Clark as being "courteous" during the half-hour meeting, but totally unyielding on the issue of allowing a hearing for the SWP on its AGLOSO designation. He also quoted Clark as stating the AGLOSO list published in late 1947 was "essentially the same" as a secret World War II listing developed by then attorney general Francis Biddle (which it was, with considerable additions) and that its intent was not to "harass any political parties" but simply to eliminate "undesirables" from the federal service. According to Kutcher, Clark promised to "personally study" Kutcher's record and assured him that the LRB "can be depended upon to give an impartial decision in your case." According to Kutcher, Clark cited as evidence of the fairness of the loyalty program that Kutcher had been the first person to directly protest to him although "hundreds" of employees had been fired under it. Clark added that if Kutcher was "just trying to make a political issue" out of his case by "seeking all this publicity," then "I won't have anything to do with it," and suggested that "you're acting too much under the influence of a political group." Kutcher's account has Clark closing the meeting by putting his arm around Kutcher and declaring, "What we're trying to do with it is protect all the things you boys fought for." Clark himself told a reporter that Kutcher's activities "must have been motivated by a political standpoint" and "prompted by persons with political interests," but Kutcher's "war record is very much in his favor" and "if it can be shown he was not actually subversive I'm sure he won't be moved [i.e., fired]."

While the KCRC concentrated on bolstering public support for its cause, the Philadelphia VA loyalty board was considering Kutcher's fate. Myer, Kutcher's lawyer, was provided a transcript of the September 10 hearing on September 20, and although he filed a list of "exceptions" involving minor corrections to the transcript, he did not file the brief that he had been given permission to submit. Myer explained in a October 7 letter to KCRC official Arthur Burch that "it would be a waste of time, and would serve no purpose as far as affecting the result," especially as "in a number of instances I am afraid the transcript of the Record may actually be correct, and there either Kutcher or I did not express the thought involved as well as it should be." In an October 6 letter to the VA board, Myer said he had decided not to file a brief because Kutcher's position had been "adequately set forth in the motion to dismiss [made at] the proceedings, the motion for a finding at the close of the Government's case, the statements made by me in support of those motions, and in my summation at the close."

Myer's obvious expectation that the VA board would rule against Kutcher came to fruition on October 11, 1948, when the three-person board unanimously ruled that "reasonable grounds exist for the belief" that Kutcher "is disloyal to the government of the United States" and that Kutcher should therefore "be removed [from his VA job] on the grounds of disloyalty." This decision was transmitted to Kutcher in a "personal and confidential" letter from Philadelphia branch deputy VA administrator Robert Wilson dated October 11, which was hand-delivered to Kutcher on October 12 by Newark VA manager O'Hearn and for which Kutcher signed an acknowledgment. The letter informed Kutcher that he was entitled to appeal the ruling to the head of the VA within ten days and would thereupon be granted a personal hearing from the VA Loyalty Board of Appeals in Washington, but would otherwise be removed from his post at the close of business on October 25, 1948, and that in the meantime, he was being suspended without pay. Newark VA acting manager A. T. Curley informed Philadelphia branch deputy VA administrator Wilson in an October 12 letter that "the suspension of Mr. Kutcher, pending final decision to remove, has been effected as of 10:00 a.m., October 12, 1948." An October 12 VA "notification of personnel action" document, standard form 50, records Kutcher's suspension as "not to exceed 14 days" and as "being effected under provisions of Veterans Administration Technical Bulletin 5-85, dated June 29, 1948, pending removal of employee"; a copy of this form was forwarded on October 12 to the Washington VA Loyalty Board of Appeals.

CHAPTER TWO

Kutcher Loses Two More Rounds (1948–1949)

On October 13, 1948, Kutcher told a news conference that he would appeal the adverse VA Philadelphia branch loyalty board decision to the central VA appeals board, and to higher boards and the U.S. Supreme Court if need be. He termed himself first a casualty of World War II and now a "casualty in the battle for civil rights and freedom of speech." In a prepared statement, Kutcher pledged to "spend the rest of my life proving the falsity of the charges against myself and my party. I intend to prove that we are not subverting the democratic process, but that they are persecuting us in an unconstitutional manner." He added, "If anyone knows of a job for a slightly used veteran, rewarded for the loss of his legs with a stigma of 'disloyalty,' I wish you would refer him to me as I am now in the market for a job that will help me support my parents." Kutcher formally notified Philadelphia VA deputy administrator Wilson on October 14 that he wished to appeal the decision of the branch loyalty board. Myer followed up with an October 16 letter confirming to Wilson that Kutcher wished "to appeal the decision of the branch office Loyalty Board removing him" from his post to the central VA Board of Appeals and that, "in view of the importance of this case and the wide public interest which it has aroused," the appeals hearing "be before the entire board" rather than just a subpanel, as was usually the case.

The September 10 Philadelphia VA loyalty board hearing, Kutcher's September 20 appeal to President Truman, his September 30 meeting with Attorney General Clark, and, especially, the October 11 Philadelphia ruling to dismiss Kutcher from his job and Kutcher's October 13 news conference initiated an extensive new burst of press coverage, although it was almost entirely limited to East Coast newspapers, especially in the Newark, New York City, and Philadelphia areas. Perhaps 80 percent of the stories included the phrase "legless vet" or "legless veteran" to describe Kutcher in their headlines, and virtually all did so within the text of their articles, with the result that by late 1948 Kutcher's name and case was almost uniformly tied to this appellation. Thus, the September 10 *Newark Evening News* headline was "Legless Veteran Protests," and its story began by referring to "James Kutcher, 35-year-old legless Newark Veteran"; the September 22 *New York World-Telegram*'s Kutcher story was headlined, "Legless Vet Asks Truman Job Aid," and its article began with the phrase, "A legless veteran asked today to meet with President Truman"; the September 29 *New York Star* had a story headed, "Legless Veteran, Facing Job Loss, to See Tom Clark" (which, quite unusually, characterized Kutcher as "disabled" in its first sentence); and the October 14 *New York Times* carried a story with the headline, "Legless Veteran Dismissed as VA Clerk" (with a first sentence that said he had "lost both legs" due to German shelling during World War II). The SWP newspaper the *Militant* carried a story about Kutcher as its September 20, 1948, lead article, with an all-capitalized one-inch-high headline that screamed, "LEGLESS VET DEFIES WITCH-HUNTERS."

In general, the news coverage was straightforward, but simply by publishing stories about the case the press accounts suggested that something was very peculiar about it. Not surprisingly, accounts in the Trotskyist press made their editorial feelings clear: the *Militant* account just referenced termed the Kutcher affair a "great outrage" against American civil liberties and the Philadelphia hearing a "star-chamber proceeding" that was "only going through the farcical procedure provided by Truman's administrative order." Similarly, the French Trotskyist labor journal *La Lutte Ouvrière* (Workers' Struggle), in an October 14 article under the headline, "L'Affaire Kutcher," referred to Kutcher as "our comrade" and declared that by leading the campaign on his behalf the SWP was in the "forefront of the American workers struggle to defend the workers' movement against the military and pro-fascist tendencies of Wall Street."

Although editorial comment about Kutcher was relatively sparse, it appears to have been universally hostile to the VA's attempt to fire him. Thus, the highly conservative *Brooklyn Daily Eagle* declared that "no one has been more vigilant or critical of the Communist movement in America than we have," but "we deplore this incident," because Trotskyists were "deadly adversaries" of the CP, because "there is nothing unconstitutional about a man subscribing to a philosophy of Socialism, Communism or any other radical idea" so long as he did not join "with others in conspiracy to carry his ideas into action," and because "there are plenty of leaders in the real Communist movement who still roam about freely and who should be attended to first before making a national issue of some unfortunate victim of local hysteria." The September 24 *Trenton Evening Times* declared that there was "nothing unreasonable" about Kutcher's demands for a public hearing on his case, and, in light of his having "established his loyalty to his country beyond question" during World War II, "he has also earned, it seems, an exceptional consideration regardless of his membership in an organization of questionable character." The October 2, 1948, *New York City New Leader* expressed "a sense of shame" for "this country when, in the name of ferreting out the disloyal, we hit at a legless veteran who makes no effort to conceal his political beliefs" and who "has sacrificed a large portion of his anatomy in his country's service" and "had nothing to do with secret documents."

Columnist Gerald Johnson, writing in the October 20 *New York Star*, sarcastically declared that Kutcher's firing from his VA post had "saved" the country, so that "we can once more sleep easy at night." Having served the nation "faithfully and at great cost," Johnson concluded, Kutcher could now "trundle his wheel-chair down the years wearing alongside his Purple Heart the yellow badge of disloyalty, both gifts of his country," which would "certainly" not "give his legs back and probably not give him his job back, nor lift the stain it has put upon his name." Writing two days later in the same paper, columnist I. F. Stone declared, under the heading, "The Case of the Legless Veteran," that Kutcher's ordeal demonstrated that "basic civil liberties and basic procedural standards" were threatened by the operation of Truman's loyalty program, which was clearly going "beyond any supposed necessity for protecting secrets so vital they justify the abandonment of traditional liberties," as was apparent from that fact that "hardly a job in the whole federal service" was "further removed from vital secrets" than Kutcher's post as a VA file clerk.

Clearly, he concluded, Kutcher was being punished purely "for his ideas irrespective of his conduct or his record," but this was especially nonsensical because, given the SWP's vehement anti-Stalinism, party members could hardly be suspected of seeking to "steal the atom bomb and ship it to the Kremlin except perhaps with a mechanism attached to make it go off when Stalin turned the spigot on the office samovar." Stone declared that President Truman's loyalty order and its procedures were ultimately responsible for the Kutcher case, and "more pitiable than a man without legs is a President without firm principles."

In an October 23 national ABC radio broadcast, Dorothy Fuldheim, in a commentary by the Brotherhood of Railway Workers, asked, "How many legs does a young American have to sacrifice to prove that he is a loyal American?" while a late 1948 *Los Angeles Times* article termed Kutcher the "national symbol for those protesting the wave of witch hunting." The July 1, 1949, *Los Angeles Sentinel* said that while a "good case can be made out for the error of Mr. Kutcher's views," nobody had inquired into them "when he was sent to Italy where he lost his legs," and his firing showed the loyalty program "at its worst, the penalizing of a citizen" for holding an unpopular view and "the loss of a job where the kind of views he held made no difference" and "could not possibly have affected national security. The democracy that Mr. Kutcher fought for in Italy won't be served until he is restored to his position." According to Kutcher's autobiography, articles on his case also appeared in France, England, Germany, and Italy.

On October 20, Philadelphia deputy VA administrator Wilson forwarded Kutcher's entire file to VA headquarters in Washington in connection with Kutcher's pending appeal to the VA Loyalty Board of Appeals and on the same day also directed Newark VA manager O'Hearn to, in the meantime, extend for up to thirty days Kutcher's suspension from duty without pay (scheduled to otherwise expire on October 25 and result in his termination). In the meantime, on September 17, Attorney General Clark published a "consolidated" list of AGLOSO organizations, now specifically designating the SWP as "communist" and "subversive" and seeking the unconstitutional overthrow of the government. In the wake of this revised listing, on

October 18 the all-government LRB declared that all six groups, including the SWP, listed as seeking the unconstitutional overthrow of the government required the "mandatory" exclusion of their members from government employment under the Hatch Act. Although this decision was not publicly announced until December, it was clearly reflected in a November 1 letter to Myer (with copies to Kutcher and the Philadelphia VA branch) sent on behalf of VA administrator Carl Gray by his executive assistant, O. W. Clark. The letter strongly urged that Myer waive Kutcher's right to a hearing by the VA Loyalty Board of Appeals and accept instead a ruling by Gray (to whom an adverse appeals board ruling could be appealed) in order to avoid "further delay" in what Clark essentially described as a clearly hopeless situation for Kutcher.

Thus, Clark suggested that "it may be in Mr. Kutcher's best interest" for Gray to make a decision "without the delay necessarily involved in the holding of any further [VA] hearing" so that "the appeal may be taken more properly" to the LRB, the final administrative authority in loyalty cases, given that the results of further VA consideration were essentially foreclosed by a combination of factors: Kutcher's admitted SWP membership; the recent AGLOSO designation of the SWP as an organization seeking the unconstitutional alteration of the American form of government (a copy of which was enclosed in the letter to Myer); long-standing directives from the LRB directing agency loyalty boards to refuse to entertain any challenges to the accuracy of AGLOSO listings; and the text (which Clark quoted) of the 1939 Hatch Act (and similar subsequent federal laws) barring federal employment of members of organizations that "advocate the overthrow of our constitutional form of government." If Myer chose to pursue the VA appeals board route, moreover, Clark rejected Myer's request that the full board membership (rather than the normal procedure of a hearing by a subpanel) hear Kutcher's case as it was not "in the best interest of Mr. Kutcher or of the Veterans Administration" to contemplate the delay that would "inevitably be required to get together all of the members of this board." Clark asked Myer to let the VA know of his decision concerning pursuing the VA appeals board route "as soon as possible."

In a November 3 letter to KCRC national secretary Novack,

Myer correctly assessed Clark's letter as "almost stating, in so many words, that they will deny the appeal" and indicated his inclination to therefore pursue a direct appeal to VA administrator Gray, although the hearing route nonetheless "might be worthwhile" "from the point of publicity and public interest." Novack responded to Myer on November 11 by asking him to notify the VA that "we accept their suggestion that we waive the hearing before the panel and submit the appeal [directly to Gray] on the basis of the record," as "we don't think there's much to be gained by insisting on this particular hearing" and "we'll get the publicity on Gray's decision which, from the [November 1 Clark] letter appears to be a foregone conclusion." In a November 15 letter, Myer notified VA executive assistant administrator Clark of the decision to waive the VA loyalty appeals board hearing, although he reiterated "all of our objections and exceptions to the legality of the proceeding, including those complaining of the violation of Mr. Kutcher's constitutional rights of free speech, assemblage and due process," and stated that the VA "has not proved its case against Mr. Kutcher." In sending a copy of the letter to Novack the same day, Myer expressed pleasure that the "case is getting more and more support" and asked to be sent "copies of the main publicity items." In the meantime, a November 12 KCRC letter to its local committees made clear that it did not expect to win the case in further administrative appeals, but was planning to take it "into the federal courts" and fight "all the way to the Supreme Court if necessary."

Despite Kutcher's waiver of the VA appeals board hearing, a November 22 VA document indicates that nonetheless a three-person board subpanel was in fact convened to consider the Kutcher case and was furnished a complete file on it in order to prepare a "formal recommendation" to VA administrator Gray. As the VA and, subsequently, the all-government LRB considered Kutcher's appeals, his suspension without pay was extended on November 24, 1948, and again on December 27, 1948, January 11, 1949, and January 24, 1949, each time for up to an additional thirty days. Each such extension was accompanied by a blizzard of government paperwork, which became so cumbersome that on January 28, 1949, VA Loyalty Board of Appeals executive secretary R. G. Beers directed that henceforth the extensions simply be made "until final determination is made in the case" in order to "reduce the amount of paper processing in the handling of the suspension." However, Beers's directive apparently had no impact, and a subsequent extension of Kutcher's unpaid leave was processed on February 24, 1949.

On December 29, 1948, Gray's assistant, O. W. Clark, informed Kutcher (with copies to Myer and to VA officials in Newark and Philadelphia) that, acting on Gray's behalf, he had concluded, after "careful analysis," that "there is no choice but to affirm" the Philadelphia loyalty board decision, given that Kutcher had "admitted" to being an SWP member, considering the SWP's AGLOSO categorization as seeking to "alter the form of Government of the United States by unconstitutional means," the binding nature of that finding on the VA, and the explicit terms of the Hatch Act making it "mandatory" to ban members of such groups from federal employment. Clark informed Kutcher that he had twenty days to make a final administrative appeal to the LRB, and that in the meantime his status as suspended "from duty and pay" was being continued.

Clark's letter to Kutcher included a copy of LRB chairman Seth Richardson's December 17, 1948, "Memorandum 32" to LRB members, informing them that Attorney General Clark had classified the SWP as an organization seeking to "alter the form of government by unconstitutional means," which Richardson reported the LRB had "construed" to bring all SWP members within the mandatory dismissal requirements of the 1939 Hatch Act banning federal employment of anyone belonging to organizations that advocate the "overthrow of our constitutional form of government." Richardson's memo declared that finding of current membership in such an AGLOSO-designated organization required the "mandatory" firing of such members. Gray's decision was made public on January 4, 1949, in a KCRC press release that quoted Kutcher as demanding a public hearing on the "real" and "crucial" issues of the validity of the SWP's AGLOSO designation, which he declared that Attorney General Clark had "arbitrarily denied," thus establishing a "bureaucratic witch-hunt method," which was the same kind "used by Hitler and Stalin against their political opponents," one that would "lead to a police state if not stopped." In his autobiography, Kutcher similarly bitterly complained that Memorandum 32 effectively "changed the rules in the middle of the game," since originally he had been told that AGLOSO listing was to be considered "one factor" in determining loyalty, but now SWP membership required "mandatory" dismissal. "This put an end, once and for all, to any pretense that my case was to be judged solely on its merits," Kutcher lamented, especially since the VA's December 29 letter had declared that the SWP designation was binding on the VA.

Myer advised KCRC national secretary Novack on January 3, 1949, that LRB chairman Richardson's October 18 memo suggested that even the LRB was "taking the position that they cannot" challenge AGLOSO designations "and that as far as they are concerned the only possible question is [SWP] membership," so that "the matter is cut and dried as far as the Loyalty Review Board is concerned." Therefore, he concluded, the "only purpose of a hearing" would be "the news value involved" as well as to put on the record as the basis for a subsequent court suit arguments that sought "to prove the absence of disloyalty on Kutcher's part, as well as the [SWP's] nonsubversive character" and to demonstrate "the refusal by the Attorney General of a public hearing."

Novack responded, in two separate January 5 letters, that "we should by all means go ahead" with the LRB appeal, both for the reasons Myer had suggested and to establish a "definite objective for the next stage of our campaign." Novack declared that the "most significant feature" of Richardson's October 18 memo was that "it casts aside completely any consideration of cases on individual circumstances" if those charged with disloyalty belonged to the Hatch Act category of AGLOSO organizations, contrary to "assertions of the lower loyalty boards that each case would be considered on its merits" and thus "absolutely" established "the principle of 'guilt by association.'" Novack urged Myer to "press and develop this argument" at the LRB hearing and thus to challenge Richardson's interpretation as being "not only contrary to all rules of equity and justice" but rendering "the whole loyalty review procedure farcical." Myer formally requested an LRB hearing in a January 14, 1949, letter, which was acknowledged by LRB executive secretary L. V. Meloy on February

16 (with no explanation for the delay). Meloy informed Myer that the hearing could be held in either New York or Washington, and asked for Myer to suggest which place and date would be "most acceptable to you and your client."

Upon receipt of Meloy's February 16 letter, Myer reported to Novack on February 18 that Kutcher was slated for hospitalization in early March (following early February surgery during which, according to a February 7 letter from Kutcher to Novack, surgeons "took about an inch and half of bone and some tissue that the doctor said was not healthy"). Myer therefore suggested that a delay in the hearing should be requested and that New York would be preferable to Washington as the hearing venue (since Kutcher lived in Newark). Following consultation with Kutcher and Novack, on February 24 Myer formally requested an LRB hearing for the week of March 28, preferably on March 30 or March 31, in New York City. Myer reported to Meloy that he was requesting a delay from the LRB's preferred earlier hearing date because his own work would make it "almost impossible" to attend an early March hearing and because Kutcher "has just recently undergone his sixth amputation operation" and wished to attend the hearing, but "his physical condition will not permit him to do so at the time you suggest." Meloy responded with a March 1 letter setting the LRB hearing for March 30 (subsequently changed to March 31 following a March 21 phone conversation between Meyer and Meloy) in New York City. On March 22, LRB chairman Richardson appointed a three-man subpanel of the twenty-member board to hear the case and forwarded copies of Kutcher's file to them. Appointed panel chair was John Harlen Amen, a prominent New York lawyer who had served at the Nuremberg German war criminals trial; John Kirkland Clark, another well-known Manhattan lawyer; and Boston lawyer Henry Parkman, a former member of the Massachusetts State Senate.

According to surviving notes and a partial transcript of the March 31 LRB board hearing, the session was apparently quite brief and heard testimony only from Kutcher and from SWP national chairman and 1948 presidential candidate Farrell Dobbs, with both their statements and Myer's argument focused on denying that the SWP was a subversive organization. According to handwritten notes that appear to have been taken by an LRB panel member, Myer asked at one point whether the "only question" was whether Kutcher was an SWP member or if the issue was his individual loyalty, to which panel chairman Amen responded that the board's "jurisdiction extends to both."

Dobbs testified that the SWP sought to "replace the capitalist economic system with a socialist system" but that his party worked to "make this change in accordance with the constitutional procedures of this nation" and participated in elections "whenever and wherever we can." He declared that SWP membership would not lead to the commission of sabotage, espionage, treason, sedition, or advocacy of the unconstitutional alteration of the American government, since "you can change a social system only when you have convinced the majority of the need for change" and such actions would "only isolate" the party. However, echoing Kutcher's Philadelphia loyalty board testimony, Dobbs added that if "the capitalist minority seeks by force and violence to subvert the will of the majority, we will say to the majority, use force and violence to defend yourself. . . . We are fully aware . . . that throughout history the ruling minority has always sought by force and violence to prevent . . . fundamental change, and the majority, when it has decided to establish socialism in America, must be prepared to defend itself." Dobbs also testified that the SWP opposed the Communist Party's "program and tactics" as "detrimental to the interests of the working people" and "directed primarily by the interests of the Stalinist government in the Kremlin," which had "imposed a police state dictatorship over the people."

According to Kutcher's autobiography, he testified for only five minutes, but the board did not seem to "have much interest in their own questions," most of the session was devoted to "arguments on constitutional aspects of the case by Mr. Myer," and it was "plain" that "Memorandum 32 was" the "chief consideration" of the LRB. In particular, Kutcher quotes LRB member Clark as asking "what possible course" would allow the board to disregard Attorney General Clark's AGLOSO designation and categorization of the SWP, as Clark was the federal official "deputed" to consider such matters.

Following the hearing, Myer told reporters that "evidently this great government is afraid to take the risk of employing James Kutcher as a $42-a-week clerk" because it "disagrees with his political opinions," yet Kutcher had risked and "lost his legs" to fight for a government "he did not agree with." He reiterated that if Kutcher lost the appeal that he intended to "carry the case into the Federal courts, and up to the Supreme Court if necessary" in order to rectify "this undemocratic procedure which deprives Kutcher of his rights of free speech and opinion." Kutcher added that the "real issue" in his case was, "Does the political party in power have the right to blacklist other parties?" He maintained that he was fighting not only for himself but also "for the thousands of other government workers and everyone else facing this kind of inquisition by the present administration" and that "more and more people in the labor movement, in the colleges and everywhere are coming to realize that my case has become the test of civil rights in this country" and a "symbol of the whole fight to halt the loyalty purge which is so clearly a violation of the Bill of Rights." Declaring that he had been "counted out" but "only for a short time" upon losing his legs during World War II, Kutcher said that Attorney General Clark was "trying to count me out again," but "this, too, will be only for a short time" as "too many liberty loving Americans" would support his "fight to preserve democracy and freedom of thought."

Despite LRB chairman Richardson's October 18 Memorandum 32 holding that AGLOSO organizations categorized as falling under the Hatch Act required automatic termination of their members from federal employment, surviving documents make evident that one or more members of the New York LRB panel were uncomfortable with the case and either resisted upholding Kutcher's dismissal or wanted the panel to state that it had made no finding concerning individual disloyalty on Kutcher's part. This is clearly evident from an April 1, 1949, letter from Richardson to panel member John Kirkland Clark, which clearly expressed irritation in response to a query from Clark and essentially directed the panel to uphold Kutcher's firing on the basis of his SWP membership, without getting into any other matters, although Truman's order seemed to require a finding regarding individual loyalty. Thus, Richardson wrote Clark that Attorney General Tom Clark had ruled that members of organizations "described" under the Hatch Act "must be separated from the service," that the "only purpose of the loyalty program is to recommend dismissal from the service because of improper connection" with AGLOSO organizations, and that "Kutcher clearly falls within this rule, and I see no reason why you cannot end the Kutcher case by finding that he is a member of an organization described in the Hatch Act. . . . I would see no reason why there is any necessity for you to mention the question of [individual] loyalty in your recommendation. If a man is a member of such an organization as is defined under the Hatch Act, he must be found ineligible . . . [and that] alone requires his separation from the service."

Subsequent to Richardson's letter, the New York LRB panel met and unanimously concluded that given Kutcher's admission to "active" SWP membership and his stated intention to continue his membership "regardless of consequences," and in light of Clark's Hatch Act AGLOSO classification of the SWP, there was "no alternative, under existing law" to finding that Kutcher's removal from his VA job was "mandatory." "Under these circumstances," the panel added, "it is unnecessary to consider or pass upon the question of whether there are reasonable grounds to believe that appellant is disloyal to the government of the United States." This decision was transmitted to LRB executive secretary Meloy on April 20 and communicated to Myer, with a copy to Kutcher in an April 25 letter from LRB chairman Richardson. (The letter was somewhat oddly and without explanation sent over the signature of panel member Parkman rather than Chairman Amen, but this apparently did not reflect any sympathy to Kutcher on Amen's part, as a few days later, on April 30, 1949, Amen telephoned the FBI's Washington headquarters to suggest that the Bureau "cover" a New York City SWP May Day rally that he "understood" that Kutcher would address and that would also reportedly feature a Soviet film entitled *Road to Life*.) Richardson's letter omitted any reference to the issue of Kutcher's individual loyalty, simply reporting that the LRB panel had determined that Kutcher "has been and continues to be" an SWP member, and, since the SWP was "an organization within the purview" of the Hatch Act, Kutcher's removal was "mandatory" and the LRB panel "therefore affirmed the decision of the Administrator of the Veterans Administration."

In a separate "confidential" April 25 letter to VA Personnel Relations Division chief R. G. Beers, Richardson directed him to remove Kutcher from the VA "rolls at once" and to "please advise this office promptly of the effective date of Kutcher's separation." This directive was transmitted to Newark VA manager O'Hearn in an April 28 letter from VA assistant administrator for personnel G. H. Sweet, and implemented by a notification of Kutcher's "removal" on CSC standard form 50 filed on April 29, 1949. The form listed Kutcher as holding position 3009-3921 with an annual salary of $2,423.04 and informed Kutcher that "if any annual leave is found due you, pertinent leave date will be indicated" on "your final check." Newark regional VA personnel officer L. C. Pautler informed Sweet of this action in an April 29 "personal and confidential" letter. A CSC standard form 98, dated May 18, 1949, from the VA and captioned "Agency Report on Closed Loyalty Case," with a copy sent to the LRB, confirmed that Kutcher had been "removed effective cob [close of business] April 29, 1949."

In a truly bizarre coda to this flurry of paperwork, Sweet urgently telexed O'Hearn on May 6 to inquire about the "circumstances surrounding dismissal of James Kutcher from your office," to which O'Hearn responded on May 10 that he had acted "in accordance with a letter you enclosed from the chairman of the Loyalty Review Board," which stated that, as an SWP member, Kutcher "must be removed from the rolls of the VA." On June 6, 1949 LRB executive secretary Meloy wrote to VA Loyalty Board of Appeals executive secretary R. G. Beers that "since you have advised that Mr. Kutcher has been removed from the service the case has been closed in this office and the file is returned herewith." The LRB advised the CSC of Kutcher's removal in a June 8 memo, while Richardson wrote FBI director Hoover with the same news in a June 17 "confidential" memo, noting that Hoover had requested to be notified about the "disposition of the case": his memo featured two xx's typed in a check-box next to the category reading "ineligible and dismissed on loyalty."

Between the September 10, 1948, Philadelphia VA panel ruling against Kutcher and the final administrative holding against him in the aftermath of the March 31, 1949, New York LRB hearing, the KCRC considerably stepped up its efforts on Kutcher's behalf, issuing a steady stream of letters, news releases, sample speeches to be given and resolutions to be passed on Kutcher's behalf, along with appeals for funds, news coverage, organizational and individual backing, and the creation of local KCRC chapters.

According to a March 1, 1949, KCRC bulletin, by then at least twenty locals had been formed, geographically ranging from Boston to San Francisco, and between October 20, 1948, and January 31, 1949, the group had collected slightly over $1,000 and expended over $1,350; these figures apparently do not include about $425 that Kutcher reported having spent as of March 1, 1949, primarily in connection with travel, restaurant, postage, and telephone expenses (Kutcher was reimbursed $100 on March 14 as a "first installment"). The group had considerable success in seeking increased support in all of these areas during late 1948 and early 1949, especially in winning increasingly nationwide press coverage, which largely resulted from a series of speaking engagements by Kutcher and Novack.

In an obvious effort to gain broad support, KCRC statements, such as in November 1948 and January 1949 press releases, repeatedly cited various groups and prominent people who were supporting their efforts, while stressing that the organization "does not subscribe to Mr. Kutcher's political views" but felt "he has the same right to have them and his job as he did when he lost his legs with the infantry during the war." The KCRC repeatedly termed Kutcher the "legless Purple Heart veteran" fired from his VA position solely due to his SWP affiliation and labeled his case "nationally recognized" as a "critical test of the restrictions on democratic rights involved in the current loyalty purge procedures."

On January 8, 1949, shortly after VA administrator Gray had turned down Kutcher's appeal from the October 1948 adverse Philadelphia VA branch loyalty board finding, the KCRC kicked off a petition campaign asking President Truman to restore Kutcher's job and "grant a public hearing to his party at which he can clear his name of the stigma placed upon it." The petitions, which were headed "Help the Legless Veteran James Kutcher," featured a picture of Kutcher in a standing position supported by his two canes. While the KCRC and other Kutcher supporters repeatedly stressed his "legless" condition, at least one supporter expressed opposition to this strategy: in a March 3, 1949, letter to the KCRC, which enclosed a $50 donation, Mechanical Educational Society of America national secretary Matthew Smith said he couldn't understand this argument since "discrimination for political opinions is stupid in all conscience and the studied repetition of Mr. Kutcher's injuries leads to a slight inference that if he had not been dismembered in the war no claim for job restoration would be made." However, Smith conceded, "you probably think it is good propaganda and you may be right." (The KCRC was apparently not convinced by Smith's argument: as of its March 30, 1949, press release, it began referring to the matter as "The Case of the Legless Veteran--James Kutcher," a terminology that Kutcher later used in his 1953 autobiography. But even Kutcher may have felt some ambiguity about the stress on his disability: he concluded a thank-you letter to supporters published in the September 29, 1948, *Newark Star-Ledger* by declaring, "I am not asking for any special privileges or pity because my legs were amputated; I am asking only for a square deal in the democratic way.")

Among those cited by the national KCRC and local chapters as supporting Kutcher, or whose support is recorded in KCRC files, were scores of prominent academics, including over 100 University of Chicago professors (among them psychologist Bruno Bettelheim, sociologist C. Wright Mills, political scientist Hans Morgenthau, and Nobel Prize–winning chemist Harold Urey), philosopher John Dewey, labor historian Selig Perlman, and noted civil liberties experts and professors Thomas Emerson and Alexander Meiklejohn. Other prominent KCRC supporters included New York City councilman Eugene Connelly, lawyer Arthur Garfield Hays, and many well-known authors, including Carey McWilliams, Alfred Kazin, Lewis Mumford, Edmund Wilson, and Norman Mailer. Mailer, who agreed to sign twenty copies of his book *The Naked and the Dead*, which had made him famous overnight, to help with fundraising, issued an October 15, 1948, statement that characterized Kutcher's "persecution" as "hideous" and termed the government's actions against Kutcher part of a program of "attack and persecution of men of any left-wing political persuasion," designed to "silence finally even the mildest liberal conceptions," which indicated "the strength of fascism in America."

The KCRC also gained formal endorsement or other support from many local and national unions (usually, but not always, affiliated with the CIO), a variety of civil liberties and public interest groups, and other organizations. Thus, an Illinois UAW local sent $25 and a Youngstown United Steelworkers local enclosed a check for $10 (while expressing sorrow that "we are unable to afford much more" as current contract negotiations created a "very big problem financially"). George Bass, head of an Ohio local of the United Rubber, Cork, Linoleum and Plastic Workers of America, which claimed 15,000 members, asked President Truman to restore Kutcher to his job, declaring that it was a "cruel abuse of official power to cut off the livelihood of a war-crippled veteran who supports aged and sick parents" and terming the case "the most dramatic symbol of witch-hunting that is now sweeping through our country" and leaving no one "safe from persecution." The secretary of a St. Paul, Minnesota, UAW branch sent an April 6, 1949, letter reporting his union's endorsement of the KCRC and a denunciation of the procedures used against Kutcher as a "travesty of our ideals" and "a terrible commentary on these times in which the United States now occupies the place once occupied by Czarist Russia—the citadel of world reaction."

Other (more restrained) endorsements of Kutcher's cause came from groups as diverse as the Newark chapter of the NAACP, the ACLU, the AVC, Americans for Democratic Action, the Slovene National Benefit Society, the Commission on Social Justice and World Peace of the New Jersey Conference of the Methodist Church, the Pittsburgh branch of the Women's International League for Peace and Freedom, the Pittsburgh and Newark Baptist Ministers Conference, and the New York City chapter of the National Lawyers Guild. Most of the organizations that supported the KCRC, however, were (generally CIO) unions, including the Ohio, Rhode Island, Illinois, New Jersey, Minnesota, and Connecticut state CIO councils; CIO city councils in Detroit, Newark, Philadelphia, and Minneapolis; the International Union of Marine and Shipbuilding Workers of America; and scores of other individual union branches, including at least thirty UAW locals, over a dozen locals of the United Electrical Workers, the textile workers, and a broad scattering of other locals, including a few AFL groups such as the New Jersey State Federation of Teachers and the New York City locals of the dressmakers and milliner workers unions, and the Oakland railroad workers local of the AGLOSO-listed radical Industrial Workers of the World. According to a highly sympathetic account published in the April 13, 1949, *Newark Jewish Ledger*, which quite unusually featured a picture of a bedridden Kutcher in pajamas covering what were clearly the stumps of his amputated legs, the number of groups supporting him was "almost endless and is constantly growing."

Frequently, endorsing groups provided financial donations to the KCRC and adopted resolutions that, while typically disavowing Kutcher's political views, denounced his firing and the perceived procedural deficiencies of the Truman loyalty program, notably the SWP's AGLOSO designation in the absence of a hearing. Thus, the Brotherhood of Sleeping Car Porters, a black union long dominated by its president, A. Philip Randolph, an extremely visible leading civil rights activist, termed Kutcher's firing a "disgraceful act, a miscarriage of justice and mockery of our country," as well as an action that had disregarded the "basic political liberties and basic procedural safeguards necessary to protect the welfare of the very people who have given so much to protect that very government that now destroys [Kutcher's] personal freedom."

Even the notoriously conservative American Legion denounced the government's handling of the Kutcher affair in a September 1948 publication, terming it a "paradoxical" and "almost perfect example of bureaucratic bungling in how not to handle a doubtful loyalty case," as while "highly placed Commies" who had "never served a day in the armed forces" remained entrenched in "extremely sensitive [federal] positions" and "not a single Stalinist Communist has been identified by name as having been ousted from the government," Kutcher, "a legless Trotskyite working on a little $40.00 a week clerical job" that was "definitely non-confidential or sensitive," was being fired solely for "cheerfully" admitting his ties with an "insignificant sect." (After a copy of this statement was supplied to the KCRC, which publicized it, resulting in its quotation in a prominent article in the March 11, 1949, *Christian Science Monitor* and other newspapers, the director of the Legion's National Americanism Commission wrote to the KCRC on March 30, 1949, to complain that the Legion report was "not for general publication" but was "restricted to the key Legionnaires then receiving it" and did not reflect the Legion's "official policy.") At least a scattering of individuals also wrote directly to government officials to denounce Kutcher's firing: thus, a New York man wrote on November 30, 1948, to the VA Loyalty Board of Appeals terming it "ludicrous—if it weren't so pathetic—that this government should show such fear of this veteran and the party to which he belongs" after the "sacrifice which the war demanded of him."

On the other hand, some people and groups (such as the American Legion, as just discussed) declined to support, or expressed at best limited support for, the KCRC or Kutcher, apparently at least partly for fear of being linked with the SWP. Thus, the well-known author James T. Farrell wrote KCRC national secretary George Novack on October 18, 1948, that he was resigning from the organization as he felt the group should "not be an adjunct of SWP policy, and, at all events, I don't want to be on the Committee." Author Barrows Dunham agreed to issue a statement in support of Kutcher personally, but declined to join the KCRC because "active members" of such groups typically "pass beyond the limits of the case itself" and the KCRC "would probably want to do things and say things with which I would profoundly disagree but which would become attributable to me if were a member." Similarly, a man named Murray Bacon wrote to the KCRC on March 8, 1949, with a donation accompanied with a request to withdraw his name from the KCRC because while "the bulk of your committee meets with my whole-hearted approval," there were also some people "connected with it whose devotion to democracy and attitude toward communists and communism is open to question in my mind."

The SWP, in fact, clearly focused considerable efforts on collaborating with the KCRC and always exercised major, if perhaps not absolute, control over it, clearly viewing the Kutcher campaign as a means of increasing its visibility and influence. Thus a November 11, 1948, letter from national SWP headquarters in New York directed all SWP branches to "concentrate their efforts in the next period around the Kutcher case and carry this campaign to all the organizations in their localities, urge them to pass resolutions and to send money" to the KCRC. A similar January 8, 1949, SWP letter reported that the organization's December 26–27, 1948, national plenum in New York had concluded that the "entire party must be mobilized behind this case to secure the support of every local union, veterans' organization, student and youth organization" and that "the case should be on the agenda of every branch meeting," as only with "all-out support" for the KCRC "can the proper job be done." It added that the Kutcher case "is a challenge to . . . [the SWP to] break through routine methods of functioning and to organize its force for the biggest campaign we have yet carried out. We can be even bolder in blazing new avenues of publicity and support than in any previous political or defense campaign."

In publishing its January 1948 petition to President Truman in support of Kutcher, the KCRC informed local committees that it was inaugurating a "nation-wide campaign to extend our support to secure justice for James Kutcher into the rank and file of sympathetic organizations and among the bulk of the American people," foreseeing a "prolonged" struggle in the federal courts in anticipation of Kutcher losing his final administrative appeal to the LRB following VA administrator Gray's late December 1947 rejection of his appeal from the October Philadelphia VA loyalty board finding. A critical weapon wielded by the KCRC in its campaign was Kutcher himself, who gave numerous public talks about his struggle, including many speeches in the Newark area, and addresses to the January 15, 1949, Connecticut state CIO convention and the May 1949 Pennsylvania state CIO convention. Beginning with the June 1949 Minneapolis CIO convention, Kutcher undertook a nine-month speaking tour with stops along the way including Flint, Detroit, Chicago, Cleveland, Toledo, Pittsburgh, Seattle, San Francisco, and Los Angeles. According to his autobiography, the demand for his talks in Los Angeles was so great that a planned two-week stay turned into three months, while during his two weeks in Detroit Kutcher reported receiving over seventy speaking invitations and averaged six to eight meetings per day; in Youngstown, Ohio, he was interviewed by three different radio stations on the same day. Kutcher's talks essentially hammered home the same points that he and the KCRC had already repeatedly stressed, but they provided a focus for extensive press coverage in local newspapers as he toured the country. Thus, he told the Connecticut CIO in January 1949 that he had gotten a "raw deal, instead of a fair deal [a reference to the Truman administration's slogan]" from the VA and termed the SWP's AGLOSO listing without a hearing "not a democratic procedure but an imitation of police-state methods." In Minneapolis, Kutcher was introduced by a local minister who, commenting on Attorney General Clark's Texas roots and the Truman administration's campaign to deport "subversives," termed Clark the "greatest subversive in the United States," who "ought to be deported back to Texas." In Chicago, he was introduced by labor scholar and activist Sydney Lens, who termed his case "like a hole in the dike holding back the waters of reaction and thought control," which unless plugged up threatened a "witch hunt" that "can submerge all the rights of labor." During a post–speaking tour engagement in New York City in December 1949, Kutcher stressed that he didn't want any "special sympathy" simply because a "mortar shell and my legs happened to meet in the same place in Italy in 1943"; rather "all I want are the rights that belong to any man or woman. The significant thing about my case is not that I lost my legs but that I lost my rights, which are infinitely dearer and more precious to me."

Kutcher's speaking tour was supplemented by a six-week tour in the Midwest in March and April 1949 by KCRC secretary Gorge Novack, which Kutcher, in his autobiography, termed a "great success," with demands for Novack to speak "morning, noon and night," resulting in a "stream of resolutions, letters and financial contributions." Eventually, overwhelmed by the demands of the trip, Kutcher reported, Novack collapsed and had to cancel the rest of his engagements. Kutcher quoted Novack as saying that while he had participated in speaking tours earlier on other cases, "I've never seen anything like what I saw these last few weeks" and "nothing compared to the reception and interest that met me this time."

Kutcher related in his autobiography that overall each legal setback in his fight with the federal government led to new "victories in the battle for public opinion," and "each administrative defeat, stripping away illusions about the intentions of the witch hunters, seemed to create new areas of interest and to open new avenues of support for us." Thus, the LRB's rejection of Kutcher's appeal in early 1949 and the speaking tours of Kutcher and Novack generated considerable additional publicity across the nation. For example, the March 14 *Cleveland Plain Dealer* reported that Novack had told a gathering of more than fifty people there that the Kutcher case was "a most dramatic and extreme symbol" of the federal loyalty "witch hunt," which was subjecting government workers to a "reign of terror," while the January 20, 1949, *Los Angeles Sentinel* and the April 30, 1949, *Los Angeles Times* each carried a brief report on talks there by local speakers sponsored by the Southern California KCRC (which was particularly active). A brief February 23, 1949, *New York Times* dispatch clearly reflected both the diversity of the KCRC's efforts and its success in obtaining publicity: under the heading, "Concert Aids Kutcher: Trio Appears Here to Further Cause of Legless Veteran," the article reported on a KCRC-sponsored evening of classical music at Carnegie Hall, which featured "Haydn's Trio No.6 in D, Dvorak's 'Dumky' Trio, Beethoven's Trio in C Minor, Op. 1, No.3, and Tcherepnine's Trio in D, Op. 34."

On May 9, 1949, the SWP *Militant* published an editorial cartoon depicting LRB members at a desk on which sat a letter from "Tom Clark" that declaimed, "Nothing wrong with his work, but he wants socialism!" and informing Kutcher, "You're still fired!" The same issue included an essay containing a May Day speech delivered by Kutcher to a New York City SWP meeting (publicized in a brief advance notice in the *New York Times*) that declared that the "capitalist class is trying harder than ever to intimidate our party" as part of preparation for "the third world war," just as "every dying ruling class has tried to stave off its inevitable doom by spending its last fury on the revolutionary opposition." The *Militant* also engaged in a spat with the Communist Party, which it accused in a March 7, 1949, article of "six months of criminal silence" about Kutcher followed by "a poisonous attack" filled with "Stalinist slanders." The *Militant* specifically referenced a February 18 *Daily People's World* article, which termed Kutcher a member of a "little group" that "devotes itself to combating the Communists and the Soviet Union and has not caviled to cooperate with the most reactionary and anti-labor forces to achieve this end"; it complained that Kutcher had received "favored treatment" from "right-wing labor leaders and some liberal publications," which sought a "convenient escape from the battle, a safe civil liberties case in which they can speak up without fear of being targeted as Communists themselves," while "ignoring or apologizing for the persecution of Communists whose defense is now the first line of defense of all civil liberties."

Throughout the period between the first bringing of VA charges against Kutcher on August 13, 1948, and the New York LRB adverse panel finding of April 1949, the FBI continued to closely monitor the case, with about a dozen memos dispatched between the Newark and New York field offices and director Hoover during this eight-month period. Although some of the memos simply forwarded newspaper clippings to Hoover, others clearly establish that the FBI intensively investigated and surveilled both Kutcher and the SWP's campaign to defend him. Thus, a September 14 Newark memo to Hoover stated that a "confidential informant" had reported that the local SWP branch had discussed the Kutcher matter recently, that the SWP was "going to make a big campaign out of this incident," and that it was "soliciting the help of trade unions, veterans organizations and fraternal organizations" in the hopes of "really" making the party "well known nationally" and getting itself removed from AGLOSO, obtaining pardons for SWP members jailed as a result of the 1941 Smith Act prosecution, and getting "Comrade James Kutcher his job back." The memo also reported that "considerable publicity is being given to the Kutcher case in the New York press" and summarized the *Militant*'s coverage of related matters. The information in this memo was forwarded by the FBI to the CSC investigations division on October 12, and from that office to the VA on October 19. An October 8 memo from the Newark FBI office to Hoover reported that the SWP was planning to print up letterhead stationery captioned "A Non-Partisan Citizens Group formed to win Justice for James Kutcher," which would bear the "names of five officers, not yet chosen, along with a list of organizations backing Kutcher," and that although the "exact use to which this letterhead will be put has not been learned," it "is probable that letters soliciting assistance will be directed to prominent persons and possibly Government officials."

An April 7, 1949, FBI memo reported that "there has been a great deal of newspaper publicity" concerning Kutcher. Bizarrely, the

FBI apparently did not learn of the LRB panel's adverse decision on Kutcher's appeal until it was reported in a May 2 *New York Times* article, which was summarized in a May 9 FBI memo. In the meantime, an FBI informant's account of Kutcher's New York City May Day speech (which LRB member Amen had alerted the FBI to, but which was also publicized in advance by the *New York Times*), sent by "urgent" May 2 teletype to Washington, related that Kutcher had delivered a brief, "almost purely sentimental" talk about "his experience with Army in Africa and Italy during war and lonesomeness caused by separation from Party at that time and lack of news of its activities." The informant added that other speakers at the rally, reportedly attended by about 200 people, including "thirty to fifty non-party members," denounced American schools for infecting "minds of youth with capitalist propaganda" and lacerated "American science as aiding U.S. war mongering and imperialism instead of improving the lot of workers. . . . After speeches refreshments were served until six PM."

During the three and a half years between the adverse April 1949 LRB finding and Kutcher's October 1952 federal appeals court victory (discussed below), the FBI continued to monitor the case, but recorded very little additional information. Although an "urgent" May 2 teletype on Kutcher's May 1, 1949, SWP meeting address had already been filed, as just noted, FBI director Hoover requested "all pertinent information in detail" about the "speech delivered by Kutcher as well as other activities at meeting" in a May 10 teletype to his New York office "so that same can be transmitted" to the CSC. New York responded the same day with a three-page single-spaced account of the meeting based on the report of a "confidential informant," who, among other items, related that the May Day "celebration" began with a "dull, long-drawn out and poorly executed" film entitled *The Road of Life*, which "executed treatment of the problem of juvenile delinquency and reform schools." The report then recounted the speech by a "teen aged youth" who had denounced American schools for "distorting the minds of youth and filling them with false capitalist propaganda" before providing a detailed summary of Kutcher's presentation, which the informant declared was "calculated to rouse the sympathies of the audience," with a "great deal of fuss about his rising from his crutches." The account said that, contrary to the earlier report to Washington, Kutcher's speech was "not almost purely sentimental" but included attacks on "capitalists today" who were "trying harder than ever to intimidate the Party, for they see the handwriting on the wall," and, like "every bankrupt and ruling class" in history were attempting "to stave off its inevitable doom by spending its last fury on the revolutionary opposition." According to the informant's account, Kutcher compared the persecution and perseverance of the SWP to that of the Bolsheviks in tsarist Russia and proclaimed that "no subversive lists, no loyalty purge" could destroy the party's "correct, scientific ideas" and that "so long as we understand this, no campaign of intimidation can stop our march to victory." The revised report did agree with the earlier account that about 175 to 200 people were in attendance, including up to 50 non-SWP members, and also that "the celebration broke up about 6:00 PM after the serving of refreshments."

Yet another, virtually identical, account of the meeting was sent to Washington by the New York office on May 18, and May 24 and May 26 FBI memos document that four copies of the May 18 report were forwarded to LRB head Richardson and that the FBI thereupon changed the status of its Kutcher investigation to "closed." According to a June 10, 1949, letter to Hoover from Assistant Attorney General Alexander Campbell, the Justice Department had also terminated an investigation of Kutcher because its examination of FBI reports had failed to disclose "any available evidence" indicating that Kutcher had violated any federal statutes. Hoover, who was notoriously sensitive to any possible hint of criticism of himself or the FBI, seems to have taken Campbell's letter as a rebuke, as he responded with a June 15 letter that declared that the FBI's function was "solely that of a fact-finding agency" and that when it conducted loyalty investigations it furnished its findings to the "appropriate agency for whatever action that agency considers proper" and did not "participate in the adjudication of the matter and in no instances does the Bureau make a recommendation as to whether a federal employeé should be retained or discharged." A note typed on Hoover's copy of the letter referred to the fact that Kutcher's case had been "widely publicized" due to his having "lost both legs in the Italian campaign of 1943."

Despite the official closing of the FBI Kutcher file in May 1949, the Bureau continued to gather information about Kutcher thereafter, although on a minimal basis until Kucher's 1952 federal court victory touched off a subsequent explosion of massive surveillance of Kutcher. Thus, the FBI files include a July 4, 1949, ACLU "weekly bulletin" reporting that the ACLU was filing a brief in support of Kutcher's impending court challenge to what it termed his "shocking dismissal" based solely on his SWP affiliations, which it stated would be based on the fact that AGLOSO had been compiled without any hearing to determine if the SWP "actually advocated overthrow of the government." A few FBI documents also very briefly report between 1949 and 1952 on the KCRC and Kutcher's court suits.

At least one letter in support of Kutcher was sent to the FBI. In a June 8, 1949, letter from a self-identified Republican disabled veteran, to Hoover, the author suggested that Kutcher's army service was "proof enough that he is as good an American as anyone else" and that his case "should be taken up more seriously because he fought for the right to choose whatever party he desires."

CHAPTER THREE

Kutcher Loses in Court at First, but Then Wins (1950–1952)

Although the KCRC originally prepared a press release in anticipation of a January 23, 1950, filing in the Kutcher case in federal
district court, ultimately attorney Myer's complaint was submitted
on February 9, 1950. The KCRC reported in late January that the
additional delay was due to the withdrawal of one of their attorneys,
but that the committee "has been exceptionally fortunate in securing
the services of one of the outstanding attorneys in Washington—Mr.
Joseph L. Rauh Jr., of the firm of Rauh and Levy." Rauh was president of the leftish but extremely anticommunist Americans for Democratic Action (ADA), which had earlier endorsed Kutcher's cause,
and one of the nation's leading civil liberties attorneys. Rauh was
clearly brought into the case because a federal court filing required
someone with more experience than Myer; also, because the suit had
to be filed in Washington, the services of a Washington lawyer were
highly desirable. Rauh repeatedly made clear that he disagreed with
Kutcher's politics but strongly opposed the government's attempts to
punish Kutcher for them. When Kutcher wrote his autobiography,
Rauh asked (and Kutcher agreed) to include language stating that
Rauh had "worked diligently" on the case because he believed that a
"real infraction of civil liberties and a grave injustice is involved," that
he agreed with "few, if any, tenets of the SWP," and that he consented
to give "his time and energy . . . all without compensation" in order
to preserve Kutcher's "right to free speech and free association without losing [his] government job." In connection with oral arguments
on the case, which were not scheduled until June 1951, Novack wrote
to Myer on June 21 that he and Kutcher would go to the hearing and
that in his last conversation with Rauh, "I agreed with him that there
was no need for you to be present and I assume that you do not feel

the urge. I am quite sure that [Rauh] and his assistant will handle the opposition and the argument competently and that it is sufficient for you to confer with him by phone and letter from now on."

The key points in the twenty-page double-spaced complaint filed on February 9, 1950, in federal district court in Washington were that: (1) in violation of the terms of Truman's March 1947 loyalty order, Kutcher had been dismissed in violation of his First (free speech) and Fifth (due process) amendment rights, because there was no evidence presented of any personal "disloyalty" or showing of a "clear and present danger to the security of the government of the United States or to any other public interest resulting from anything the plaintiff said or did"; rather, he was fired "solely" due to his SWP membership and activities as a result of the government's wrong and unconstitutional categorization of SWP under AGLOSO and the Hatch Act; (2) Kutcher had been deprived of a fair administrative hearing because he was not informed of the basis of the charges against him, allowed to publicly rebut them or subpoena, cross-examine, or confront adverse witnesses, or contest the government's SWP's AGLOSO classification and its categorization as an organization falling under the 1939 Hatch Act ban on federal employees belonging to groups deemed to advocate the overthrow of America's constitutional form of government; (3) the SWP, an organization dedicated to "lawful means" of bringing about social change, which had repeatedly run candidates for elective office, had been wrongly and unconstitutionally AGLOSO-designated and deemed a Hatch Act organization without any evidence or charges or the opportunity for a hearing, despite repeated requests for one, in alleged violation of the Hatch Act; and (4) the Hatch Act and Truman loyalty program were facially unconstitutional because they violated guaranteed First Amendment and due process rights of Kutcher and all other federal employees by establishing standards that were "so vague and indefinite" that they provided "no prior guide" for their conduct, lent themselves to "arbitrary and discriminatory application by administrative officials," and authorized punishment based solely on "guilt by association." The suit, which named VA administrator Gray, Attorney General J. Howard McGrath, the three CSC commissioners, and the twenty-one LRB members as defendants, asked that the

Hatch Act and loyalty program be declared unconstitutional, that McGrath be ordered to "suppress and destroy" all AGLOSO lists designating the SWP, and that Kutcher be reinstated to his position, which, the lawsuit stressed, he had performed "efficiently and satisfactorily," and which the government agreed gave him no access to "sensitive" information that could threaten the nation's security.

According to the complaint, which was written in a legally unsophisticated style (for example, completely lacking in citations to any court rulings that might bolster or provide precedent for its arguments), "no evidence" was presented at Kutcher's VA loyalty appeals hearing, "nor was there any suggestion at the hearing, that the plaintiff had ever wrongfully disclosed any information to any person, that he had ever been criticized for the performance of his duties or that he had ever evidenced any 'disloyalty' to his country or any allegiance to any other country." Thus, according to Myer, the Hatch Act, Truman's loyalty order, and Kutcher's firing had "no relationship to the security of the United States" but were "solely for the purpose of punishing" the SWP for its members' views "in violation of the plaintiff's constitutional rights under the First and Fifth amendments." Because Kutcher's discharge was solely based upon his SWP ties "rather than upon his own acts, beliefs or state of mind" and because he could not challenge the SWP's AGLOSO designation, Myer continued, Kutcher effectively "had no hearing whatsoever on the question of his loyalty to the Government of the United States" or whether he belonged to a Hatch Act organization. Nonetheless, it maintained, as a result of his firing Kutcher had "become blacklisted as a 'communist,' 'subversive' and 'disloyal' person for private as well as government employment" and, as "his reputation has been destroyed, it became impossible for him to obtain any employment, and he has in fact become far more unemployable by reason of the defendants' actions herein complained of, than by reason of the loss of both his legs in the war."

When his lawsuit was filed on February 9, 1950, Kutcher and Rauh stressed to reporters at a widely covered press conference that the SWP's orientation was anti-Stalinist and nonviolent and that Kutcher's battle was being fought on behalf of the civil liberties of all Americans. Thus, Kutcher declared, "I am not only on Mr. Truman's blacklist, I am on Stalin's blacklist, too," and Rauh added that his client was "as opposed to Soviet Russia as anyone in this room." Kutcher said his party sought to gain its objectives only "by the ballot and peaceful means," and repeated his earlier comment that he had never practiced violence "except when in the Army—and then at the behest of the United States government." Rauh stressed his personal abhorrence of "everything" the SWP believed in "except freedom" and characterized the Kutcher case as "an almost perfect example of what's wrong with the loyalty program." Kutcher added that he felt "the loss of my civil liberties more keenly than the loss of my legs."

Shortly after Rauh agreed to serve as cocounsel in early 1950, he wrote Novack on April 3 that he was "troubled" by the "association" of Kutcher in the "public mind of people who are essentially [Communist] fellow travelers and whose sole deviation [from the CP "line"] is in the field of civil liberties for Trotskyites," a development that he termed "the one thing that can ruin the Kutcher case." Thus, he said that the KCRC had "lost most of the force" of the recent statement by fifty-nine Harvard professors in support of Kutcher "by the inclusion of Harlow Shapley," a well-known astronomer who was often accused of being a Communist sympathizer. Although, Rauh continued, "I know this is a difficult problem for you," in the "long run the cause of civil liberties will be served best by sticking to the principle that we want as our allies only those who really believe in civil liberties at home and abroad."

Novack responded on April 11 that although the issue Rauh raised was "difficult," it involved the "important principle" that "a case or committee which seeks to organize the broadest possible support for its work" could not "justifiably refuse aid from people simply because of their political views or associations," especially since the KCRC's goal "from the beginning" was to "mobilize as many diverse trends of opinion as possible against the violations of democratic rights and fair legal procedures involved in the loyalty program." Should the KCRC abandon that principle, Novack argued, it would have to determine how to "discriminate among potential supporters or introduce loyalty tests," which would inevitably negate "the whole concept of united action in defense of civil rights"; therefore the only proper "loyalty test of civil rights" should be their "attitude with regard to the Kutcher case." Thus, in what amounted to a dig at Rauh's ADA (and many other liberals who had bitterly and repeatedly attacked the CP, and had either turned their back entirely or, at most, offered tepid support in the numerous cases of government harassment and persecution of the CP in the post–1947 period), Novack declared that even if some KCRC backers "would not support the civil rights of Communists" and were thus "incorrect and inconsistent and to that degree ineffective defenders of civil liberties," he would not "thereby refuse to request or receive their help in the Kutcher case." Novack reminded Rauh that the ADA's attempts to distance itself from the CP had not really succeeded, since "not a few politicians in Washington and elsewhere believe that association with the ADA can injure their careers and any cause they claim to be interested in," and "this fear-and-smear technique of the reactionaries is the handiest weapon for dividing, isolating and cutting down forces that should unite in common defense of things worthwhile. All my experience teaches that it is fatal to yield to such pressure in the field of civil liberties."

The ACLU also expressed reservations, although ultimately it did support Kutcher. In June 1949, ACLU staff counsel Herbert Levy informed the KCRC that his organization's board of directors had voted to file a legal brief on their behalf, but one carefully delimited to back only "Kutcher's contention that he was found guilty of belonging to an organization advocating the overthrow of the government, without the organization having been granted a hearing by the Attorney General" on this issue. (The ACLU repeatedly refused to challenge the government's right to publish lists of "subversive" organizations, instead only demanding that the listed groups be granted hearings on their designations.) In a June 11, 1951, letter to Novack, Levy declined to furnish the KCRC with a letter "to be circulated in conjunction with your appeal for funds," although he indicated it was "completely agreeable to us if you want to include the phrase you read to me over the telephone to the effect that the ACLU is filing a brief as a friend of the court in this case."

A week later, Levy wrote Novack to complain that the KCRC stationary was listing the ACLU as having "endorsed" the organization, but in fact, "although we, of course, offered the committee any help we can give in fighting the case and publicly offered to cooperate" with the KCRC, the ACLU had never approved of the "Committee itself" and had "never endorsed any organization." Levy therefore requested the KCRC to "change your letterhead appropriately to indicate that we endorse your purpose rather than the Committee itself." Novack responded on June 21 that there was "no intention on our part to convey anything misleading in citing the ACLU as an endorser" and that he had already changed future KCRC materials before having received "your official communication," but that "we are in no position to immediately scrap all of the material on hand printed in the old style." Whether by coincidence or not Levy's "friend of the court" brief in connection with Kutcher's June 1951 filing requesting a federal district court summary judgment in his favor was dispatched "too late to be filed," according to a June 26 letter to Levy from Rauh, who added that he was "dreadfully sorry" this had happened as "I would have liked to file it."

The *Washington Post*, in a lengthy February 23, 1950, editorial, strongly supported Kutcher, vehemently declaring that the lawsuit had revealed "very grave defects of the loyalty program," which had imperiled "cherished safeguards of individual liberty" and made Kutcher "the victim of a dual arbitrariness," first by designating the SWP without a hearing as an organization "held to advocate what it denies advocating," and second by imputing to Kutcher the group's alleged views "by mere fact of his membership," a concept "repugnant to American law." The *Post* added that the nation needed "no protection against a legless [VA] clerk," that his punishment served no interest aside from "vindictive[ly]" retaliating against him "solely because he entertains certain unorthodox and unpopular political opinions," and that the "cost of a loyalty program that can produce such results" included granting "absolute discretion" to "a single political appointee, the Attorney General, to proscribe voluntary associations of American citizens; the stigmatization of individuals as disloyal by a star chamber administrative tribunal" and "the restriction of the rights of advocacy guaranteed by the First Amendment, as least as far as Government employees are concerned" was too high.

Shortly after the filing of the lawsuit, which attracted considerable national publicity, similar attention was attracted by a March

1950 statement in support of Kutcher by sixty Harvard University professors, including the vehemently anticommunist Pulitzer Prize–winning historian Arthur Schlesinger Jr., leading sociologist Pitirim Sorokin, American Association for the Advancement of Science president-elect Kirtley Mather, and Harvard Observatory director Harlow Shapley. They declared that the "loyalty purge" firing of Kutcher and attacks on other federal employees "create a frightening atmosphere that cuts the nerve of independent thinking," involved procedures that violated the "basic decencies of notice and hearing that are part of our due process of law," and placed enormous punitive power in the hand of "administrative officials and other non-judicial bodies" who proceeded on the basis of "arbitrarily defined" doctrines of "guilt by association" and "subversion" that were "inconsistent with genuine freedom of association and freedom of thought."

According to a May 5, 1950, letter from Myer to Novack, the federal government responded to his filing in late April. Although copies of the federal brief do not appear in any records obtained by the author, there is no reason to doubt the accuracy of Myer's summary: he told Novack that the government largely admitted most of the "facts set forth in [our] complaint and raises the question of whether these facts entitled us, as a matter of law, to any of the relief requested." According to Myer, the "main theme" of the response was that the attorney general was obliged under the Hatch Act and Truman's loyalty order to prepare lists of "subversive" organizations, and having placed the SWP in such lists "that determination is conclusive; also, that the loyalty boards have a right to rely" upon secret FBI reports and "that this constitutes a sufficient hearing" under Truman's order. While Kutcher's lawyers contemplated filing a request for summary judgment in response to the government's filing, a decision was made to delay the filing in the hope that two cases pending before the Supreme Court might settle matters. These two decisions, *Joint Anti-Fascist Refugee Committee v. McGrath* and *Bailey v. Richardson*, were both handed down in April 1951, but ultimately had no impact upon Kutcher's case (although at first it seemed that they might).

In the *McGrath* case, three AGLOSO-designated groups sued the attorney general on the grounds that their listing violated their rights to free speech and due process, especially due to the lack of any hearing or evidence before groups were listed. Although the Supreme Court upheld the organizations, 5–3, terming the attorney general's procedures "patently arbitrary," the Court failed to declare AGLOSO unconstitutional, limiting its ruling to holding that the three organizations were entitled to some kind of hearing (in court or by an administrative body was not made clear), and not even striking the three groups from the listing in the meantime. In the *Bailey* case, the Court upheld by a 4–4 tie (with newly named Justice Tom Clark recusing himself in both cases given his previous involvement in them as attorney general) the government's right to withhold classified information and the right to cross-examination for individuals in loyalty cases.

Although Kutcher reported in his autobiography that he felt like "dancing with joy" upon hearing of the *McGrath* ruling, feeling that the attorney general would have to "withdraw" the entire AGLOSO list and perhaps "withdraw all actions based on the list, including my discharge," the Justice Department failed to establish any AGLOSO hearing procedure for two years, and in the meantime, as Kutcher wrote, "acted as if it hadn't heard the news." Moreover, the *Bailey* case, involving individual discharges as opposed to organizational listings, was more directly relevant to Kutcher's case, and it clearly offered no support for his position.

Rauh wrote Novack on May 3, 1951, that he didn't believe the two rulings would require amending the planned request for summary judgment by the federal district court, although he felt "as you do, that the Supreme Court's actions in those cases enhance the importance of the Kutcher case." He added that he would need a "few more days to figure out just what our next step should be," but that both decisions were "shrouded in doubt." Since *McGrath* had seemingly required AGLOSO hearings, Rauh added, then "certainly" Kutcher could not be fired "on the basis of a listing without a hearing and our cases would be exceedingly strong." However, he noted that the three *McGrath* dissenters had "held no hearing was necessary" and that the Court's controlling opinion "seemed to think the organization would get the hearing in the District Court" rather than by administrative loyalty boards. Thus, he added, it is possible to argue that the [*McGrath*] Court was again split 4–4, just as in *Bailey*, on the key "question of the necessity for hearing before the Attorney General," and thus the Kutcher district court "might very well deny any motion for summary judgment and then we would have a long trial" about exactly what the SWP "did or didn't advocate." In any case, Rauh concluded, he intended to "sound out Government counsel very soon on their intentions," which might consist of requesting dismissal of either the entire Kutcher case or the KCRC's request for summary judgment on the basis of *Bailey*, motions that, if granted by the district court, "would be an initial defeat for us" but provide a "way of getting up to the Supreme Court" during its fall 1951 session.

In a May 8 letter to Novack, Myer reported having "discussed the strategy as thoroughly as possible" in a lengthy phone conversation with Rauh in which the latter was "very anxious" to avoid the possibility of a district court trial focused on the SWP's views, "primarily, I believe, because of the length of time which it would take and also, I suspect because of what he saw take place in the Communist Party trial" (referring to the 1951 trial of top CP leaders under the Smith Act, which ended with convictions of the CP leaders and contempt of court citations against their lawyers). He told Novack that he and Rauh agreed to focus on seeking to "get the Kutcher case into the Supreme Court as quickly as possible," as it "squarely" posed the issue of whether the high court "having said A in the [*McGrath*] case is prepared to say B [i.e., require the government to grant the SWP an AGLOSO hearing] in the Kutcher case." Myer said that Rauh would talk to the "Attorney General's office in the next few days to see whether he can find out what their views are regarding a motion for summary judgment or other disposition in the Kutcher case" and that "unless they have some very definite and acceptable suggestion, we will probably file a motion for summary judgment and take our chances on the possibility of the judge ordering a trial."

In a separate May 8 letter to SWP official William Warde, Myer told Warde that he felt it would be a "mistake" to immediately file a lawsuit demanding that the attorney general "delist" the SWP, since such action "might practically compel him to resist" and also because it "might complicate the Kutcher case in that a judge might possibly say that he will delay deciding" pending "outcome of the delisting suit." Myer added that Rauh advised against the alternative approach of simply making a "formal demand" to the attorney general for the SWP's delisting because "even this should not be done at the present time" by the SWP but "should preferably be made by some other [AGLOSO] organization." Myer concluded by advising that "no decision should be made" at present; instead, a "reasonable length of time" should be waited to "see what the Attorney General will do" on the AGLOSO hearing issue in the light of *McGrath*.

Rauh told Myer in a May 9 letter that he had had a long telephone discussion with Justice Department attorney Edward Hickey, who was "handling all the loyalty and the subversive organization cases now in the courts," and that Hickey had related that following the *Bailey* and *McGrath* rulings the Kutcher case was the only dispute "now in the courts involving the federal loyalty program." According to Rauh, Hickey had asked for "a week or two, at which time he would tell me what their [legal] position is going to be" concerning *McGrath* organizations and Kutcher, but had indicated that the government "would also like to avoid a lengthy trial if that were possible" and "asked me what suggestions we had on this." Rauh related that he had responded that "we might move for summary judgment" on the basis of *McGrath* and that the government might move for dismissal or summary judgment, partly on the basis of *Bailey*, and that "if the judge granted the motions of either side, we could avoid a trial" (and presumably immediately appeal to a higher federal court). Rauh concluded that "we are starting work here on a motion for summary judgment" (reflecting that Myer, who had drafted such a motion months earlier, had been effectively replaced as the lead Kutcher attorney), with the "thought of "having it ready for filing in mid-June and having the argument [before the district court at] the end of June."

Rauh informed Myer on May 31 that Hickey had informed him on May 29 that the Justice Department had still reached no decision concerning its legal strategy "insofar as the subversive lists were concerned" and had therefore asked for "more time." Rauh reported that he had responded that "we would not move for summary judgment this week or next" and that Hickey had "promised to try and let me have the Department's answer the end of next week." Rauh added that he had just received notification of a pretrial conference set for June 6 in the Kutcher case and that it therefore might be possible "to try the case before the summer recess and thus avoid some of the problems that we are worried about." He concluded that in any case "we should oppose any continuance of the pretrial conference which the Government might seek," absent governmental assurances that "any such continuance would not affect the trial of the case next month," and that the Kutcher lawyers should not "have too much trouble getting ready for the trial, as we have already agreed that our strategy should be one of putting Kutcher on the stand and resting."

In a series of letters and phone calls during the first half of June 1951 between Rauh, Myer, Novack, and Levy, Kutcher's team made final plans to file for summary judgment, following the June 6 pretrial conference. The conference was convened by federal district court judge Edward Curran in what was designated Civil Action 636-50, and attended by Rauh and Justice Department official Joseph Kovner, an assistant to department attorney Hickey. Myer informed Novack in a June 4 letter that, following the pretrial conference, Rauh remained "very anxious" to have the "case tried as soon as possible, which probably would mean in about two or three weeks," since "if the case goes over until fall, we might not be able to get through the Court of Appeals into the Supreme Court in time for a decision next year." Myer added that he understood that the government wished a postponement "despite Rauh's efforts to force an early trial" and that as a result "there may nonetheless be a postponement until fall." Myer concluded that there would be "no need" to file for summary judgment if the case was set for trial in June, but if it was postponed until fall "we will then consider the advisability of making such a motion in order to hasten" its disposition.

Rauh reported in a June 6 letter to Myer that Kovner had requested a week's postponement of the pretrial conference, as the government was still finalizing its legal posture in the case in the light of the recent Supreme Court rulings and that he had responded by stating that "we had no desire to embarrass the government by insisting" on a hearing before "their position was fully determined, but that we were extremely anxious to have a trial before the summer vacation." Rauh added that he had noted that Kutcher had been unemployed for "a long time due to the delays inherent in this proceeding" and had maintained that it was "unfair to protract the litigation if there was any possibility of a trial this June," whereupon Judge Curran had indicated "grave doubt" that a June trial could be held and suggested that Kutcher's lawyers petition the district court's chief judge to "advance the case" while in the meantime postponing the next pretrial conference until June 14. According to Rauh, in response to a query "on the way out," Kovner "kept repeating" that the LRB had in fact ruled "on all the evidence" and "on the basis of Kutcher's personal views and actions," thus making "our case just like the *Bailey* case," and therefore effectively maintaining that Kutcher was suspended "after a valid hearing on his personal loyalty and that the court could at most only grant Kutcher "the right to a new [administrative] appeal" while he remained under suspension. Rauh said that Kovner had conceded that if he was wrong, and the LRB had "actually decided" to fire Kutcher solely due to his SWP ties, "we have a valid argument" that the loyalty hearings "were decided wrongly" and that Kovner had "tentatively" stated that the government "position was likely to be" that failure to grant the SWP a hearing in such a situation had violated the Hatch Act. Rauh concluded that he proposed to file a motion to "advance the case for trial at the end of this month" and if that were denied, a motion for summary judgment should be filed "late next week and try to get that heard" by the end of June.

Myer reported to Novack on June 7 that Rauh had reported the government had no objection to trying the case at the end of June, but this "still depends upon whether the district court can place the hearing on its calendar for this month," which "remains to be decided." Myer added that Rauh had reported that government lawyers "set forth some new aspects of their position," indicating that Kutcher's appeals from the original adverse Philadelphia loyalty board hearing "may well have been illegally decided because they were limited to the sole question" of SWP membership, while maintaining that "the original suspension and discharge was made on other and additional grounds" and that "on that account they would be willing to offer new administrative appeals to Kutcher." Novack sarcastically commented that this offer was "exceedingly generous on their part, seeing that the whole procedure is rigged." Novack concluded, "We do not want the case to be dragged out indefinitely but would like to get it up to the highest court within the next year or so if possible."

Myer responded to Novack in a June 13 letter, which concluded that the "sum total" of the *Bailey* and *McGrath* rulings left the law concerning loyalty programs "on a fulcrum and that the Kutcher case may be the vehicle to tip it in a favorable direction." Myer informed Levy the same day that the "latest developments" left "little possibility of a trial this month," that Rauh was about to formally file for summary judgment, and that the government would also request summary judgment, as a result of which there is "more likelihood that the court will grant one of the two motions, thus disposing of the case in the trial court and making it possible for the loser to proceed with an appeal." Rauh sent Myer a copy of his motion for summary judgment on June 13, indicating that he planned to file the next day and that he believed the government would also then file a motion for summary judgment. He added that the pretrial conference set for June 14 "will be indefinitely postponed" and that he expected that the judge would instead set a date for oral argument on the contending motions for summary judgment. On June 16, Rauh informed Myer that he had filed his motion on June 14 and that Judge Curran had set June 26 for oral arguments on the competing motions, but that Justice Department official Kovner had reported that the government's motion had been delayed "because of stenographic difficulties," although he planned to "rely on the argument that we [i.e., Kutcher's lawyers] did not have a Hatch Act case at all, so we are going ahead with writing our brief [in support of Kutcher's motion for summary judgment] on that supposition." Rauh indicated that Curran wanted very short oral arguments, absolutely limited to no more than 30 minutes per side. He added, "I suppose we will have to use most of the short time available to make the argument that it is unconstitutional" to fire a federal employee "because he belongs to an organization without at any stage having a hearing on that organization and to rebut the government's argument" that "this point is not actually involved" because the "initial board's action was not based on SWP membership." During the period between the April 1949 adverse LRB ruling and the filing of Kutcher's federal court appeal in February 1950, Myer billed the KCRC for slightly over $1,303, compared to a total of $800 between October 25, 1948, and March 31, 1949 ($600 of the earlier billing was in connection with his preparation for and attendance at the March 31, 1949, LRB hearing). Myer's bills were one of the leading expenses of the KCRC, and one that the committee generally had difficulty in paying, leading Myer to write Novack on May 17, 1949, that he "would appreciate some payment on my bills." Novack responded on May 23 that "at the present moment we are in the tightest financial situation we have been in for a number of months," because they had just reimbursed Kutcher $500 for his travel expenses and because contributions had "fallen off quite a bit during the past month." Novack promised Myer a payment of "at least $100 as soon as we have it," although his first subsequent check, sent in July 1949, was for only $75. Upon dispatching a subsequent check for $153.68 on March 15, 1950, Novack expressed "chagrin" at being unable to pay more but related that the KCRC only had enough "money in the treasury right now to keep us afloat for the next month or so." (Novack sent an additional $250 in December 1949 and another $200 in May 1950.)

Kutcher's brief for summary judgment, cosigned by Rauh and Myer, was filed on June 14, supplemented by an eight-page double-spaced typed "points and authorities" in support of their request and a separate eighteen-page legal brief. Kutcher's filing maintained that summary judgment in his favor was required because there was "no issue as to any material fact in this case" and because his firing violated the facial terms of Truman's loyalty order and Fifth Amendment due process guarantees by denying him an opportunity to "demonstrate that he was personally loyal, that his [SWP] membership" provided "no basis for a conclusion that he was disloyal and the party did not advocate the overthrow" of the government. Their central contention was that Kutcher's dismissal was fundamentally flawed because there was "no possible question" that it was based solely on his SWP membership coupled with the group's AGLOSO categorization, which the government maintained made his firing "mandatory" under the Hatch Act and the loyalty program. They declared that the government conceded designating the SWP without notices, charges, or hearings while rejecting a specific SWP request for a hearing, and therefore Kutcher's firing was clearly "not based on any showing that he was "[personally] disloyal or subversive or believed in use of unconstitutional methods" to overthrow the government, especially as the government had presented no charges or testimony alleging "any wrong doing on his part on or off his government job." Indeed, Kutcher's lawyers argued, both VA administrator Gray and the LRB had openly "failed to consider" Kutcher's personal "loyalty and relied solely on Hatch Act grounds" in firing him.

However, they argued, such a firing was illegal because the loyalty boards had been "foreclosed from considering anything other" than his admitted SWP membership, which LRB chairman Richardson had "determined should [alone] be a basis for mandatory discharge," thus rendering his hearings an "empty formality" in violation of the Truman loyalty order guarantees of an "administrative hearing" with the rights to "present evidence on his own behalf" and a determination based on "all the evidence." But even absent the Truman requirements, they added, Kutcher was denied his constitutional rights because *McGrath* had determined that "minimum" Fifth Amendment due process "demands" required a "notice and hearing" concerning the SWP's AGLOSO listing. Kutcher's case was thus not one "in which an inadequate hearing was held" but rather one "in which no hearing was held," since he was denied a hearing "on the very issue [of the SWP's classification] on which he was discharged." Moreover, they argued, this determination had "never been the subject of a hearing at any time," so that neither Kutcher nor the SWP had ever been afforded "any opportunity to know the nature of the evidence against the Party or to present evidence in its behalf," and "no hearing was afforded on the issue of plaintiff's disloyalty" but focused solely on the SWP, "which has been designated, without a hearing, as a ground for discharge." This "complete absence of consideration of any evidence" on the "crucial question in his case" differentiated Kutcher's situation case from *Bailey*, they argued, especially as his firing flew "in the very teeth" of Truman's order by violating its "plain on its face" requirement that AGLOSO membership did not "make dismissal mandatory."

To support this argument, Kutcher's lawyer quoted statements by President Truman and Attorney General Clark, as well as a 1949 Justice Department Supreme Court *McGrath* brief, which declared that AGLOSO membership was "simply one piece of evidence which may or may not be helpful" in reaching loyalty determinations in "particular" instances. They especially stressed Clark's widely publicized November 24, 1947, letter to the LRB declaring that it was "entirely possible" that individuals with AGLOSO affiliations were "loyal to the United States," that "guilt by association" was not a principle of "American jurisprudence," and that dismissals under the program required establishing "reasonable grounds" for "concluding that an individual is disloyal." They also cited a recent appeals court ruling in post-*McGrath* litigation that termed AGLOSO designations solely a means of "information and advice" for loyalty boards, and argued that Richardson had given the SWP listing a "conclusive determination which the court of appeals said it did not have" by holding that "no matter how wrong the Attorney General might be, no matter how his determination might conflict with plaintiff's experience" with the SWP, Kutcher "must bow to the designation and either give up a lawful activity or give up a needed job." Such a dilemma, they concluded, was "shocking to our sense of fairness, doubly so since the Supreme Court has held that the Attorney General issued the list without prior notice or hearing, in violation of the due process clause."

Although the government's motion in response to Kutcher's arguments, which asked for summary dismissal of the case, does not survive in existing records, Rauh reported in a June 21 letter to Myer that a Justice Department official had summarized their position to one of Rauh's subordinates as arguing that no hearing on the SWP designation was required and that even if this was the case, "Kutcher was not suspended" due to his SWP membership "but was properly found disloyal on general grounds" under Truman's executive order and "therefore he was properly suspended." Therefore, Rauh related, "it seems clear that we will have to devote the entire half hour [of oral argument before Judge Curran scheduled for June 26] to demonstrating that a hearing is required and that Kutcher was not removed on a general loyalty basis but rather on his membership in the 'unheard' organization." In his autobiography, Kutcher quotes the government brief as "falsely" stating that the Philadelphia VA loyalty hearing indicated that he favored the violent overthrow of the government by means of quotations that were "twisted" and "torn out of context from his testimony."

As the June 26 federal court hearing date approached, the KCRC engaged in a flurry of fundraising and publicity activities. Thus, in a June 23 letter to its supporters, the KCRC labeled the "case of the legless veteran" the "only loyalty case before the higher courts" and one that presented "the basic issues involved in the clearest and most dramatic form." Therefore, the committee declared the case "may turn out to be the decisive one," which could "go far toward determining the constitutionality and status of the entire loyalty program."

According to Kutcher's autobiography, during the June 26 hearing, government attorneys argued that he was not entitled to any additional hearing and denied that SWP membership was the only basis for his discharge, because Gray and the LRB had ultimately simply upheld the Philadelphia VA branch loyalty finding, which had been based on "all of the evidence." Kutcher adds that his attorneys retorted that he was only suspended, not dismissed, until Gray's actions and the LRB finding, and that those decisions were clearly based solely on his SWP membership and the LRB's Memorandum 32, and thus deprived him of the hearing that he had been entitled to because they did not consider "all the evidence." According to Kutcher, Judge Curran sided "completely" with the government, ruling that VA administrator Gray and the LRB had "only affirmed" the actions of the Philadelphia VA board and that although it was true that these "appellate tribunals, so to speak," stated that Kutcher was removed due to his SWP membership, he was originally dismissed by the Philadelphia board and "the important thing is, was that action correct? It has been affirmed [by Gray and the LRB]. The grounds for the affirmation were immaterial."

Rauh reported in June 26, 1951, letters to Myer and Levy that, following oral arguments that morning, Judge Curran had ruled against Kutcher and granted the government's motion for summary dismissal (Curran's finding was formally registered on July 2). Rauh told Levy in his letter that Curran had held "against us as I had assumed he would do" in an "asinine" and "ludicrous" ruling that reflected his "obvious eagerness to avoid" Kutcher's "basic point." Rauh maintained that neither Curran nor the Justice Department had been able to "answer our basic contention that the Party never got a hearing, so the Judge relied" on the original Philadelphia VA loyalty board finding and, "in effect, affirmed that" ruling without "regard to the action of the appellate boards," which had "ruled against Kutcher on the basis" of his SWP membership. Rauh similarly told Myer that the judge had ruled for the government "on the ground that the initial board had acted properly under the executive order and therefore it did not matter what the two appellate boards did" and that it was "clear from the outset that his mind was running that way and I did everything humanly possible to shake him on this point, but it was hopeless." Rauh told Myer that "we should aim at argument in the Court of Appeals in October and in the Supreme Court by late winter or early spring" and that he would begin working on an appeal brief "as soon I have had a chance to let the matter turn over in my mind for a couple of weeks." The KCRC immediately announced the launching of a new fundraising campaign to defray the costs of appealing Curran's ruling; it declared that "the law regulating conditions of public employment under the loyalty program now hangs in the balance and the Kutcher case may provide decisive in clarifying the situation."

Between Judge Curran's June 26, 1951, ruling and Kutcher's appeal filed on October 23, 1951, with the U.S. Court of Appeals for the District of Columbia, the major issue that concerned the KCRC was whether to seek to raise an estimated $1,000 to cover the costs of printing materials for submission to the appeals court and, presumably, eventually to the Supreme Court, or to seek to appeal "in forma pauperis" (without having to pay the costs due to inability to do so). Rauh reported to Novack in a September 8 letter that he had "perfected" his appeal brief and had been able to reduce the estimated printing costs substantially by getting the Justice Department to agree to print "necessary parts of the record as an appendix to its brief; thus saving us the cost of printing this material as an appendix to our brief"; he added that the government had also agreed to "waive the filing of the bond for costs so that we will not have to bear this expense either." Rauh also noted that in another highly publicized federal loyalty case reported in the press on August 23, federal appeals court judge Thomas Swan had written a "wonderful paragraph" denouncing AGLOSO as lacking any "competency to prove the subversive nature of the listed associations" as it was "a pure hearsay declaration by the Attorney General." Novack responded on September 10 that he hoped that Rauh could use the reference to "good effect in your argument in Kutcher's case" while also noting that former attorney general Biddle had attacked AGLOSO in the August 4 issue of the *Nation* magazine. Novack expressed the hope that while Biddle's view might not carry the "legal weight" of Judge Swan, "it may have some moral influence with more liberal justices." Kutcher told reporters shortly before his appeals court brief was filed that he had "persevered in my case because I believe it is a test case for democracy, which cannot survive long if citizens are deprived of their jobs merely because of their ideas and associations." He also expressed confidence that the "present witch hunt hysteria will yet be overcome and the Bill of Rights preserved for all."

Kutcher's federal appeals court brief, filed on October 23 by Rauh and Myer, largely repeated their previous arguments but considerably contrasted in format with their earlier legal submissions: it was printed (rather than typewritten), much longer (at 40 printed pages, plus cross-references to the 150-page joint appendix of relevant documents included with the Justice Department's response), and thoroughly interlaced with citations to a variety of prior court rulings (whereas their earlier filings were almost entirely bereft of such legal references). While their basic position was unchanged, Rauh and Myer, unsurprisingly, especially highlighted their disagreement with Judge Curran's adverse ruling and concluded that it should be reversed and Curran should be directed to grant Kutcher a favorable summary judgment, "including a declaration that his dismissal was illegal" and that he was "entitled to reinstatement with back pay." Although the Justice Department's reply brief does not survive in available records, according to news accounts the department argued that lawful procedures had been followed in connection with Kutcher's case and that he had been properly dismissed.

While Rauh and Myer's brief was structured around what they characterized as six key "questions presented" by the case, they treated first, and at greater length than any other point, the issue of whether Curran had acted properly in upholding Kutcher's dismissal based upon his conclusion that the findings of the VA Philadelphia loyalty board "had warrant in the record," although VA administrator Gray had later upheld the firing "for different reasons." They maintained that Curran had "erred" in so ruling, because Truman's order characterized the role of agency loyalty boards as "making recommendations" subject to the right of appeal to agency heads, who were empowered in the case of appeals to "make the [final] determination." Since Gray was "bound" to consider Kutcher's loyalty "according to the standards dictated by the President and to reach his conclusions uninfluenced by extraneous considerations" but "did not do so," Rauh and Myer argued, "the discharge was invalid" and Curran had made a "palpable error" by holding that Gray's grounds affirming the Philadelphia board recommendation were "immaterial" since "there was ample evidence to sustain" it. They argued that since Gray was empowered to make the final determination and had not done so on "valid grounds" under Truman's order, it was irrelevant that the Philadelphia "board might have acted correctly" or Gray "could have made a valid discharge had he acted other than he did." In summary, they maintained that Curran had exceeded his authority by seeking to "substitute" his "judgment for that of the Administration and purport to affirm" the Philadelphia board because Kutcher "was entitled to have his personal loyalty determined" by Gray, and Curran had thus erred, in violation of legal precedents, by "reaching back into the administrative process and reviewing the action of the 'recommending' agency rather than that of the 'deciding' agency."

Kutcher's lawyers stated that the second key question involved in his case was whether Gray was entitled to make a dismissal finding "without considering any evidence except membership in a particular organization," based on the LRB's regulation mandating such action, although Truman's loyalty order had established as the standard for removal the conclusion that based "on all the evidence, reasonable grounds exist for belief that the person involved is disloyal to the Government of the United States." Their conclusion that such a firing was "illegal," as not based on an evaluation of Kutcher's "personal loyalty," and that the LRB directive was "inconsistent with the executive order," an inconsistency that was "patent and potent and renders the regulation invalid," essentially repeated their earlier argument. Concerning what they analyzed as the four other basic questions raised by the case, Rauh and Myer argued that: (1) the attorney general's determination that the SWP was "subversive" had "no competency" and could not justify a Hatch Act dismissal from federal employment absent a hearing concerning the group's nature, a point bolstered by federal appeals court Judge Swan's recent dismissal of AGLOSO as pure "hearsay"; (2) application of the Hatch Act to justify Kutcher's dismissal based solely on the SWP's "star chamber" AGLOSO listing was "manifestly unconstitutional," a "matter put to rest" by *McGrath*, by depriving Kutcher of "his rights without fair play"; (3) the Hatch Act was unconstitutional because it amounted to a "meat cleaver" hacking away at Kutcher's "fundamental rights of speech and assembly," without demonstrating the "likelihood of any evil, grave or otherwise" that he posed, as he held a "completely non-sensitive position," thus illegally resulting "in greater restriction of rights" than "necessary for removal of any public danger"; and (4) *Bailey* was inapplicable because there the issue was "an inadequate hearing," while Gray granted Kutcher "no hearing" whatsoever concerning his personal loyalty, but instead simply ruled on the basis of Kutcher's admitted SWP membership, even though the SWP had requested and been denied a hearing "on the nature of its activities." The Rauh-Myer brief was supported by an ACLU "friend of the court" brief that stressed that Kutcher's firing allegedly violated fundamental due process protections of the Constitution.

Oral argument was held before a three-judge federal appeals court panel on April 10, 1952, with Rauh and ACLU attorney Levy (with Myer's approval) appearing on Kutcher's behalf and Justice Department attorneys Edward Hickey, Joseph Kovner, and Charles Ireland representing the government. According to press accounts, Rauh told the judges that Kutcher and the SWP posed no threat to the country because they were strongly anti-Stalinist and, given "their infinitesimal number, their doctrinaire belief in no way constitutes" the "clear and present danger" to the country's security that could justify his dismissal. Daniel Pollitt, an assistant to Rauh, wrote Kutcher on March 31, declaring that "your cause is just" and "our brief is sound and I certainly hope that justice triumphs and that your discharge will be set aside."

On October 16, 1952, the federal appeals panel, in a unanimous opinion written by Judge James M. Proctor, gave Kutcher his first victory more than four years after the original filing of charges against him in August 1948, holding that Gray's dismissal decision had been illegally based solely on Kutcher's SWP affiliation and that he was therefore entitled to further administrative hearings to determine his loyalty based on "all" the relevant evidence. The panel held that while the original recommendation of the Philadelphia VA board had adhered to Truman's executive order requirement that federal loyalty determinations be based "on all the evidence," VA administrator Gray, who had the power to make a "final decision," had not ruled based on this required standard but instead, following the LRB's "dictum," had held Kutcher's dismissal was "mandatory" solely on the basis of his admitted SWP membership. The judges held that Gray's determination violated the clear terms of the loyalty order, especially in light of President Truman's and Attorney General Clark's statements that organizational membership was "simply one piece of evidence" to be considered in making loyalty determinations, and that therefore the LRB's directive concerning mandatory Hatch Act dismissals was "without validity or force and should be disregarded." They said that they were not suggesting that "membership in and activities connected with a designated organization" might "not, in the circumstances of a case, justify disbelief in the loyalty of an employee," adding (in seeming contradiction to *McGrath*) that Clark's AGLOSO designations were "competent evidence" to be considered against Kutcher because the loyalty program was "administrative in character, in no sense criminal" and therefore did not "require the constitutional and traditional safeguards of a judicial trial."

However, the judges declared that neither the Hatch Act nor Truman's order proscribed SWP membership by federal employees and that "neither Congress nor the President has seen fit to make membership in any organization designated by the Attorney General cause for removal from Governmental employment." Therefore, it concluded, a "final and controlling determination" concerning Kutcher's loyalty "still awaits the Administrator's decision" due to the deficiencies in Gray's ruling, and it ordered that Judge Curran reverse his holding granting the government summary judgment and set aside Kutcher's dismissal "without prejudice to the order suspending Kutcher and [further] consideration and determination" by Gray "as to whether on all the evidence reasonable grounds exists for belief that Kutcher is disloyal."

In response to the ruling, Kutcher reported in his autobiography, he was "so dazed I almost dropped the phone" when a reporter called to get his reaction. News accounts, which described Kutcher as a "short, bald smiling man," add that he told reporters that it was "a great victory, not only for myself, but for the civil liberties of all Americans," one that "convinces me more than ever that it pays to resist any and all encroachments on our democratic liberties." He also expressed his hope that "this decision means I will be able to get back my job with the VA on the same basis as before," and that it would lead to the abolition of the "unconstitutional" AGLOSO listings that had "arbitrarily designated" groups without providing them "a hearing or the right to know the specific nature of the charges against them" and would "encourage others to join together in militant defense of the right of all Americans to speak, write and associate freely." Kutcher added that he expected the government to appeal to the Supreme Court and noted that the ruling had not "answered the basic question" whether the SWP "belongs on the subversive list or whether a subversive list is unconstitutional."

In an October 22 letter to supporters, the KCRC assessed the ruling in a considerably more tepid, but also more accurate, manner than Kutcher's immediate reaction that it was a "great victory." Instead, the committee termed the holding a "partial victory," which did not "abolish the practice of 'guilt by association' but limits its application," and maintained that Kutcher's suspension from the VA pending further administrative decisions seemed to sanction the fundamental legitimacy of AGLOSO and, by upholding nonjudicial standards for administrative loyalty hearings, left Kutcher "subject to star-chamber procedures, where the accused is not considered innocent until proven guilty."

In response to a query from a KCRC representative as to what the "next step" in the case would be, Rauh responded on October

17, 1952, that the government could decide to either appeal the court ruling to the Supreme Court or "have the Veterans Administrator reconsider his action in the light" of the judicial holding. Rauh expressed the hope that an appeal would be taken to the Supreme Court "because I believe we would get an even broader decision in our favor than the one we obtained from the Court of Appeals," but "my guess" is that the government would "let the [legal] matter lie" and send the case back to the VA for reconsideration on "all the evidence," in which event Kutcher would presumably request a new hearing. According to LRB memos from late October and early November 1952, in response to an October 21 request from the Justice Department for a recommendation on the advisability of appealing Judge Proctor's ruling, the board voted against recommending such an appeal "under the circumstance" of the Kutcher case and also acted to "bring the LRB regulations in line" with the judicial holding. On January 10, 1953, Rauh wrote Kutcher to tell him that he had been "informed yesterday that the Government does not plan to take your case to the Supreme Court" and that he intended to request the district court to "enter its new order next week and, armed with that," would soon ask the VA "to see what action they intend to take." Myer wrote Rauh on January 14 that while little could be done until Judge Curran formally issued the mandated order, "when that is done, I believe the real job will be to see whether the Veterans Administration can be prevailed upon to reinstate Kutcher instead of proceeding with another hearing, or perhaps simply re-examining the present record."

During the three-and-a-half year period between the LRB's April 1949 ruling upholding the VA's dismissal of Kutcher and Kutcher's October 1952 federal appeals court decision overturning his firing and returning the issue to the VA for further consideration, the Kutcher affair continued to garner considerable news coverage, primarily in connection with court decisions and with Kutcher's speaking appearances. By far the greatest burst of news stories during this period (and, up until then, during the entire Kutcher controversy) followed the 1952 appeals court ruling, which was massively covered in the national press, including editorials and front-page articles in both the *New York Times* and the *Washington Post*, among other leading newspapers and periodicals. Such stories, as well as earlier news accounts during the 1949–1952 period, used the term "legless" in their headlines less often than did earlier accounts, although the term was still frequently used early in their texts: thus the *Post* account, headlined "Court Voids Firing Based on Federal 'Subversive' List," referred in its second paragraph to "James Kutcher, 39, legless veteran fired by the Veterans Administration." According to the *Post* article and several other accounts, the ruling was "the first legal setback the Government has received in an individual loyalty case since the loyalty program began in 1948" and was especially significant as it demonstrated that "the courts will place some limits on the administration of the loyalty program." The article also quoted LRB chairman Hiram Bingham (who had replaced Seth Richardson) as declaring that the Kutcher case was the only instance in which a disloyalty finding had been based solely on AGLOSO membership and that the LRB would soon withdraw its directive making such membership a sufficient basis for dismissals where the groups had been placed in the Hatch Act category.

The *Chicago Tribune* account added that Kutcher's case was the first heard before a VA loyalty board. In editorials, the *New York Times* welcomed the court ruling as placing the emphasis on individual "guilt" rather than "guilt by association or by decree" and as "strengthen[ing] the bulwark of American civil liberties," while the *Washington Post* demanded that AGLOSO groups be granted hearings on their designations "if not in the name of due process, then in the name of common sense." The *Nation* called for AGLOSO's complete abolition, declaring that until then, in the light of *McGrath* and the Kutcher ruling, the government will "be in the untenable position of maintaining an illegal official 'blacklist,'" which would severely "undermine freedom of political association" and thus "continue to work grave injustice on a great many citizens," most of whom had never even worked for the federal government.

Aside from the massive national press coverage of the October 1952 federal appeals court ruling, media accounts about Kutcher during the prior three-and-a-half years included smaller, but still substantial, bursts of national coverage when he filed his federal district court suit in February 1950; when sixty Harvard University professors criticized his firing in March 1950 (a story given front-page treatment in the *Boston Globe*); when Judge Curran ruled against him in June 1951; and scattered local stories throughout the period that primarily focused on Kutcher's 1949 speaking tour. The *Newark Evening News* of October 30, 1949, reported that when Kutcher returned from his six-month speaking tour he claimed the support of about 1,000 different organizations with a combined membership of 5 million. He was quoted as saying about his supporters, "Virtually none hold my political ideas but all agree that my discharge was an example of thought control that menaces the democratic fights of all Americans," adding that the only organization against him was the CP, as the SWP was "on the blacklist of Stalin as well as Truman." According to a February 28, 1950, KCRC statement, Kutcher's backers then included "226 CIO bodies, 101 AFL bodies, and 98 other organizations."

Probably the most sympathetic "mainstream" media coverage of the Kutcher case was an interview with Kutcher and accompanying commentary by then Los Angeles newsman (and later national NBC nightly news anchor) Chet Huntley, which was televised by station KNX on August 31, 1949. Some by-then routine responses by Kutcher to Huntley's queries as to his political views were sandwiched between introductory remarks and concluding commentary by Huntley that were intensely critical of the Red Scare climate in general and, by clear implication, of the treatment of Kutcher in particular. Thus, Huntley, who introduced Kutcher as a veteran "whose legs were left on an Italian battlefield," stated after the interview concluded, "It is apparent that there is fear in the minds of people, fear of being seen with the wrong people, fear of being caught working at the side of the wrong person, fear of signing your name, fear of supporting the wrong candidate, and fear has no place in the minds of Americans." Directly addressing Kutcher, he added, "This reporter will be called perhaps a Communist and subversive for putting you on the air today" and "believe me, I thought about it" and "hesitated because it isn't pleasant to be called a Communist." However, he concluded, "But then it occurred to me that we must get over this fear and stop this business of branding a man guilty on the basis of association. . . . We shall perhaps one day look back upon this period with considerable uneasiness and, I think, deep humiliation." (The FBI included a full transcript of Huntley's remarks in its files.)

By 1950, Novack declared, the KCRC had made "the case of the legless veteran" "nationally recognized as one of the crucial test cases of the loyalty purge procedures" and had "imparted courage and stiffened the backbone of many people alarmed by the invasions upon democratic rights." Despite Kutcher's administrative defeats, he maintained, "from the standpoints of organizing an effective defense committee and nation-wide protest movement we have done well, and even better in certain respects" than originally anticipated, especially given "the intimidation generated by the witch-hunt atmosphere."

In fact, between 1948 and 1952 the civil liberties atmosphere steadily worsened, due partly to actions of the Truman administration, partly to Congressional and judicial actions, and partly to external developments that greatly heightened the Cold War atmosphere. In 1948, the Truman administration brought a Smith Act conspiracy case against top CP members, who were all convicted in a sensational 1949 trial that also led to contempt of court findings against all of their lawyers. Also in 1948 Truman and his top aides repeatedly red-baited the new, leftish Progressive Party headed by former secretary of agriculture and former vice president Henry A. Wallace (under FDR, 1940–1944), with the result that most non-Communists quit the party, leaving it significantly in CP hands, and largely destroying voter support. Meanwhile, also in 1948, the Justice Department began a major program of seeking to denaturalize or deport or both CP members, with Progressive Party supporters and leaders of left-wing unions especially targeted; 100 CP members were arrested for such purposes between February and May 1948 alone.

In Congress, HUAC and other committees continued widely publicized investigations into alleged Communist infiltration in the federal government, labor, and elsewhere, leading to the particularly sensational 1948 espionage charges by CP defector Whittaker Chambers against Alger Hiss, a former high-ranking State Department official who by then was head of the widely respected Carnegie Endowment for International Peace. In 1948, Congress passed (over President Truman's veto) the Taft-Hartley act, which, among numerous restrictions imposed upon organized labor, effectively banned Communists from holding union leadership positions, which they had gained, in democratic elections, in about one-third of all CIO unions. In 1949–1950, the CIO expelled unions believed to be under CP leadership, reflecting general Cold War pressures and especially the impact of the Taft-Hartley Act and numerous congressional investigations. Americans' fears of Communism were greatly heightened in 1949 when Russia exploded its first atomic bomb (aided by Soviet espionage at Los Alamos) and civil war in China ended in a Communist triumph.

The civil liberties climate worsened yet further in 1950–1952. In 1950 Congress passed (over Truman's veto) the Internal Security (McCarran) Act, which established a new sort of AGLOSO, but one that provided hearings and cross-examination for groups accused of being a CP "action" or "front organization," with groups so found and their members subject to numerous penalties. The 1950 law also provided for the summary arrest and detention without charges or hearings of persons deemed likely to commit "espionage or sabotage" during a presidentially declared "national emergency." Also in 1950, the outbreak of the Korean War and the emergence of Senator Joseph McCarthy on the national stage, with his repeated wild allegations of massive Communist infiltration of the government (especially the State Department), greatly furthered a deterioration of the civil liberties climate, as did the espionage arrests of Julius and Ethel Rosenberg. They were accused of giving the Soviets atomic bomb secrets and eventually executed on that charge in 1953, touching off a massive controversy over their guilt that has continued until the present. (Most scholars today believe Julius was guilty but have serious doubts concerning Ethel, and most agree that compared to information about the bomb provided by other Soviet spies, the information provided by Julius was relatively insignificant.) Meanwhile, the judiciary also considerably fostered the Red Scare, with the Supreme Court upholding the 1949 Smith Act convictions of the top CP leaders in *U.S. v. Dennis* (1951) as well as most other anticommunist laws and administrative acts, including the 1948 Taft-Hartley provision effectively banning CP leadership of unions and, as previously related, in *Bailey v. Richardson*, the denial of the right of cross-examination in government loyalty proceedings. The *Dennis* ruling led to a new wave of Smith Act prosecutions against lower-level CP leaders by both the Truman and Eisenhower administrations.

As the Kutcher case gained increasing national attention in the early 1950s, the FBI stepped up its surveillance and reporting on Kutcher, with repeated indications that the Bureau was especially concerned about past and potential adverse publicity concerning the federal loyalty program, AGLOSO, and the Bureau's own role in tracking the case. Thus, an October 17, 1952, internal FBI memo to Assistant Director Alan Belmont not only reported the federal appeals court ruling reversing "previous findings" concerning the dismissal of Kutcher on loyalty charges on the grounds that a federal employee "may not be fired solely" due to "membership in a subversive organization," but that the matter had "received considerable newspaper publicity in the past as Kutcher lost both legs due to enemy action in World War II." The memo included a copy of an October 17 newspaper account of the appeals court ruling and noted that it indicated that Kutcher would remain in "suspended status" pending VA administrator Gray's determination "of whether all evidence in the case justifies the conclusion that Kutcher is disloyal to the government" and that, due to the ruling, the LRB had announced an imminent meeting to "modify its regulations requiring dismissal of Federal employees" due to AGLOSO membership. FBI director Hoover was apparently highly concerned that its interest in the Kutcher case not be publicly disclosed: thus, his October 23 memo to the FBI Washington, D.C., field office requested that a copy of the decision be "promptly and discreetly" obtained so that "the information therein will be available to the Bureau."

Despite the Bureau's massive resources, obtaining such a copy of a public record federal court ruling at least temporarily apparently posed a difficult problem. On October 29, the Washington field office informed Hoover that "discreet inquiries" to obtain a copy from the appeals court had failed, as the court clerk had advised that "they have no additional copies and have only a file copy at present" and "do not contemplate printing any other copies." The report added that although the clerk had reported that the "United States Attorney and the Department of Justice had each been given approximately fifteen copies each," further "discreet efforts" to obtain a copy from the U.S. attorney had "failed because all the copies are presently in use by those attorneys represented in the case." The report closed by suggesting that the FBI borrow a copy from the Justice Department's Law Library (without explaining why the Bureau, itself part of the Justice Department, could not simply request a copy from high-ranking department officials). A December 24 memo to Belmont reported the Bureau had since "obtained a copy of the opinion through the Department," although such copies apparently remained generally difficult to find: the memo reported that the FBI New York field office had telephoned at 11:45 AM that day to inquire about getting a copy in response to a query from the prominent federal circuit court judge Learned Hand, who had informed the office that "he had made several attempts to obtain the complete opinion but had only been successful in obtaining a digest of same." Apparently reflecting a decision to withhold from Hand any indication that the FBI was following the case, an addendum to the December 24 memo reported that at 2:30 PM that day the New York office was instructed to advise Hand that it "did not have a copy" of the ruling and to "tactfully" suggest that he "might wish to obtain a copy of the decision through the Department."

Subsequent internal FBI memos included a January 15, 1953, report to Hoover from the FBI's Washington, D.C., field office that noted a January 12 *Washington Post* report that the government had decided not to appeal the appeals court ruling ordering Kutcher's case back to the VA for reconsideration and an "urgent" February 14, 1953, teletype to Hoover from the Newark office reporting that a local newspaper had reported Kutcher's appeal to President Eisenhower for reinstatement with back pay and seniority in his Newark VA position. In the meantime, a January 28 request from Hoover to the FBI's Newark office requested a "supplementary report setting forth" Kutcher's SWP activities "and other information concerning his loyalty," and noting that it would be "necessary to submit additional loyalty reporting" until a "determination is received concerning his status with the Government," so that the FBI could disseminate such information "to fulfill our obligations under the Loyalty Program."

In response, the FBI Newark field office reported on February

11, 1953, to Hoover, with copies to nine FBI field offices, that it had uncovered more than two dozen reports in its files about Kutcher, apparently concerning his travels and speeches and the activities of local Kutcher support committees, from FBI offices in Boston, Cleveland, Detroit, Los Angeles, New York, Pittsburgh, Philadelphia, St. Louis, and Seattle, for various dates between December 1947 and August 1952. The Newark memo does not make clear whether all of these reports had been forwarded to FBI headquarters or not, but requested that each of the named local offices "search indices and report any info pertinent concerning Kutcher," with copies "designated for Newark as Kutcher" was the subject of investigation there and that it was "necessary for Newark to have copies made for exhibits and obtain handwriting specimen." It added the Newark FBI files reflected that Kutcher had signed a 1946 SWP nominating petition for a candidate for governor in New Jersey. On February 19, the Newark office reported in a memo to Hoover that as an "active member" of the SWP Kutcher attended meetings "almost weekly" and requested guidance as to "what specified intervals it wishes additional supplementary reports submitted." On March 11, Hoover responded with the direction that further "supplemental reports" should be submitted "every 60 days until you are advised of the findings of the Civil Service Commission concerning the disposition" of Kutcher's case.

The requests by Hoover and Newark for additional information on Kutcher spurred a series of reports from Newark and other local FBI field offices beginning in February 1953. Thus, on February 19 the Newark office provided FBI headquarters with a twenty-seven-page double-spaced typed memo (plus attachments) on Kutcher, beginning with the news of his August 25, 1948, press conference to announce that he intended to fight VA loyalty dismissal proceedings, tracing subsequent legal developments, including efforts to evict his family from their Newark public housing under the Gwinn Act (discussed below), and, especially, Kutcher's speaking tours and activities by the KCRC on his behalf. The memo was based on numerous newspaper articles, above all repeated and extensive references to reports about the Kutcher case published in the SWP newspaper the *Militant*, as well as on reports from FBI informants in Newark,

New York City, and Pittsburgh; reports from multiple Newark FBI informants including accounts of numerous SWP meetings, such as statements about Kutcher's participation and strategic discussions of his case. The memo reported extensively on Kutcher's speeches and on the activities of the KCRC and its local chapters, including the statement that its New York City informant had related that national KCRC was "controlled" by National Secretary George Novack (whose name is redacted at some points in the memo released under the Freedom of Information Act, but not others) and that Novack was a member of the SWP's national committee. Thus, the memo reported that according to the December 26, 1949, *Militant*, Kutcher had addressed a public meeting in New York City ten days earlier on the topic, "My Rights Are More Precious Than My Legs," that he had stated that he had discovered during his speaking tours that "there was a rising resistance to witch-hunts and thought-control and purges throughout the country," and that people were alarmed and "discouraged and demoralized by the trends in Washington and the advances that have been made towards transforming this country into a police state." Kutcher was quoted in an August 28, 1950, *Militant* article as terming disabled veterans the victims of capitalist wars that they had never wanted, which had maimed and sacrificed them on the "altars of big business greed," and that the "ruling class" and the "vampires of Capitalism" now sought to exploit disabled veterans by inflaming them with "jingoism," poisoning their minds with "police state" propaganda, and mobilizing them for the front lines of the "lynch campaign against democratic rights."

The Newark memo reported that Kutcher "when not away on speaking tours, regularly attended" Newark SWP meetings, that he had been observed selling and passing out SWP literature in Newark, and that he had signed four SWP nominating petitions for party candidates for office since 1940. It added that "Newark informants" had advised that the SWP considered the Kutcher case the party's "civil rights case" and was "building the reputation of the Party through this case." The memo included reproductions of the four SWP nominating petitions, which showed the names and addresses of Kutcher and numerous other signers, including, in three cases, that of Kutcher's father, Hyman, as well as a handwritten note (apparently written at FBI headquarters) declaring that the FBI laboratory had concluded that "James Kutcher signatures" appearing on the petitions "were written by the employee." A subsequent February 26 report from Hoover to the Newark office provided details about the laboratory test, which it recounted was based on a study of reproductions of the four SWP nominating petitions along with "fourteen negatives and fourteen photographs of the known signatures of James Kutcher," all taken from various VA documents that Kutcher had signed, including his 1944 application for disability benefits. The report failed to explain how, given Kutcher's admitted SWP membership and the entirely democratic nature of running candidates for elective office, the evidence concerning Kutcher's signing of nominating petitions could contribute to allegations of "disloyalty" against him, although providing evidence for this allegation was the basis given for the laboratory analysis.

The FBI Boston office, in a February 19 report on the activities of the local Kutcher committee there, related that its "informant" had reported the committee felt that Kutcher's January 22, 1952, speech in Boston had "successfully accomplished" its goals, namely to "stimulate local interest in his legal case and to raise funds" and to introduce the SWP "propaganda line first to the Harvard College faculty and student body" as well as others who might be "induced" to serve SWP purposes "in the future either as members or sympathizers." According to the Boston report, in his speech Kutcher did not deny SWP membership, related that the group "is a political organization," and followed the SWP "line of bitter denunciation of Stalinist tactics of historical compromise with capitalist countries, and opportunism, and the 'sellout' of the world working class in order to serve their own bureaucratic interests." A February 20 report from the FBI's St. Louis office indicated that an informant there witnessed Kutcher's attendance at SWP national conventions in 1950 and 1952, but that no official report could be submitted without jeopardizing the informant's identity, as apparently the informant was the "sole St. Louis delegate" to the conventions referenced.

In a ten-page single-spaced typed memo, the Seattle FBI office reported on February 20, 1953, about planning by the local SWP branch for a speech by Kutcher there as well as 1949 distribution of literature about his case by the local KCRC and by the SWP. The report, largely based on reports by multiple FBI informants and agents, included information about Kutcher's June 1949 Seattle visit and associated speeches and other activities, as well as about the background of "prominent" and "extremely active" local SWP members who helped to organize Kutcher's visit. Similar, although shorter, reports, also based on accounts of informants and FBI agents, with extensive accounts of Kutcher's local speeches and other activities, were filed by the FBI's Cleveland office on February 20, 1953, by Detroit on February 24, by Philadelphia and Pittsburgh on February 25, by Los Angeles on March 3, and by New York City on March 24. Thus, the Pittsburgh memo stated that "reliable informants" had reported that the Kutcher case "was being used to develop the SWP and effect removal of SWP" from AGLOSO.

Most of Kutcher's activities reported in these memos dated from the late 1940s, but the Philadelphia memo reported that Kutcher had been observed by an FBI informant in 1952 outside Philadelphia SWP headquarters "obtaining signatures believed to be" SWP electoral nominating petitions. While the various FBI memos often quoted Kutcher as advocating radical political views (termed "disloyal" in the Pittsburgh memo) none of them reported any apparently illegal activities. The Pittsburgh account stated that an informant reported that at a 1949 meeting there Kutcher had declared, while being "at least partially intoxicated," "To hell with this god damned government. I'm a red. I don't want any part of this government." It also quoted an informant as having seen and heard Kutcher demand that an American flag be torn up at the 1948 New York City national SWP convention, and additionally having heard Kutcher declare, at a New Jersey camp in 1950 or 1951, that the SWP could not obtain power through the ballot and therefore the only alternative was to "Kill them. Overthrow them. Get a new government." The report added that "such statements were commonly made by persons in attendance at the summer camp," and that, like virtually all of the informants, this informant was "unwilling to furnish a signed statement or to testify before the Loyalty Hearing Board."

Some of the FBI accounts were considerably less sensational, such as the March 3 Los Angeles report that at the conclusion of an "open" SWP meeting held there on August 21, 1949, at which Kutcher termed AGLOSO a "Capitalistic device to wage war upon civil liberties," a film entitled *From Czar to Lenin* was shown, which "stressed that the United States, Great Britain and France were opposed" to the 1917 revolution that brought the Communist Party to power in the Soviet Union. The Los Angeles memo was accompanied by a dozen attachments of flyers and other literature related to the Kutcher case. The New York City memo reported the less-than-shocking information that the *Militant*, the SWP's long-standing and openly acknowledged official newspaper, was a weekly "staffed and operated" by SWP members according to a confidential FBI informant "of known reliability," as well as an informant's sighting of Kutcher "at the annual spring dance" of the SWP at "Carvan Hall, New York City, on April 8, 1949." The New York City memo was accompanied by photostats of eight letters identified as "related to Kutcher's activities" and emanating from the New York City SWP local, which are described as "obtained" at the SWP Brooklyn branch headquarters. According to the New York City memo, an informant had advised that "in practically all instances the core" of the KCRC consisted of SWP members who "at every opportunity" associate the party with the Kutcher case "and in this manner gain publicity and new members" for the SWP. (Copies of the same FBI memos located in the National Archives and furnished by the FBI in response to a Freedom of Information Act request often have material unredacted in the former version but redacted in the latter: thus the Archives version of the March 3, 1953, Los Angeles memo identifies its author as "Special Agent William G. Carpenter," refers to various informants by designations such as "Los Angeles T-1," and identifies SWP members other than Kutcher by name, while the FBI version deletes Carpenter's name, names of other SWP members, and the coded informant designations, with the result that although the redacted memos indicate that informants furnished information they disguise that at least four separate informants provided material reported by Los Angeles.)

On April 24, FBI director Hoover forwarded "by special messenger" to the CSC copies of the nine field office reports on Kutcher, without any evaluation or summary of the material other than to state that they reflected the "results of a supplemental investigation" bringing the Kutcher "matter up to date" since the Bureau's July 31, 1948, submission to the CSC. On May 8 Hoover also forwarded to the CSC, again by "special messenger," copies of an April 21 report from the Bureau's Newark field office, which related, based on accounts from two informants, that Kutcher continued to be active in SWP activities, such as attending the "Friday night forums of the Newark Branch of the SWP held at the Newark Branch headquarters, 52 Market St., Newark, N.J." The new Newark Bureau report advised that its sources of information were being disguised to "conceal" that both the SWP's national headquarters in New York City and the SWP Newark branch were "under surveillance" by FBI agents.

The FBI memos to the CSC were in turn forwarded on May 5 and May 21, 1953, to the VA loyalty board reconsidering Kutcher's situation in "personal and confidential" documents transmitted "by special messenger." On July 3, 1953, the FBI Washington field office, responding to a June 22 inquiry from Newark, reported that Kutcher had been formally "removed" from the VA's employment rolls on June 18, in the aftermath of the VA Loyalty Board of Appeals April 20 action against him following his 1952 appeals court victory (discussed below). On July 9, the LRB sent FBI director Hoover a form letter "in accordance with your request" for information on the disposition of loyalty cases, that Kutcher had been found "ineligible and dismissed [from government employment] on loyalty [grounds]." FBI reports on Kutcher thereafter diminished markedly until late 1955 (when an intense media spotlight focused on Kutcher's plight for the first time in over two years), although a January 15, 1954, Newark field office memo reported that since June 1953 Kutcher, who was characterized as "unemployed," continued to engage in various SWP-related activities, including attending an October 17, 1953, celebration of the publication of his autobiography, entitled *The Case of the Legless Veteran*.

Kutcher's autobiography was published in Britain with an American price of $1 after Kutcher was unable to find an American publisher. Given the enormous publicity that had surrounded the case, Kutcher was almost certainly correct in concluding in the 1973 update to his autobiography (published in the United States by Monad Press and distributed by the SWP's Pathfinder Press) that American publishers were simply "afraid to publish my book" due to the severe deterioration in the civil liberties climate by the time he began seeking an outlet in mid-1952, and thus he eventually gave up "hope of getting the book accepted by any commercial publisher in the land of the free and the home of the brave." He reported sending the book to more than thirty-five American publishers, including all of the major houses, along with a cover letter explaining why he thought the case was of "great importance," pointing out that 800 national and local organizations had "actively concerned themselves" with his case" and offering to work with editors to modify the book so long as "none of the basic facts were omitted or distorted."

Although virtually all of the written rejections indicated that the publishers felt there was an insufficient market for the book, Kutcher reported that in follow-up personal interviews, two of the publishers indicated they were afraid of being labeled a "radical" imprint if they adopted it. Kutcher quoted one (anonymous) publisher as stating that "two, three years ago, we might have been willing to take a chance" on the book, but with the outbreak of the Korean War in 1950 and the 1952 election of Eisenhower, "I wouldn't take the chance even if your book was five times as good as it is and even if it meant a decent profit," since "sooner or later Sen. Joseph McCarthy or other congressmen are going to start in on the publishing business" and "no publisher today wants to be put on the spot and smeared for publishing any book that can be labeled as radical. You can call it cowardly if you want to, but I call it cautious and common sense."

In a November 16, 1953, letter, D. Conway, an employee of Pioneer Publishers, which was distributing the book in the United States, wrote to thank Carey McWilliams, editor of the American magazine the *Nation*, for planning to review the book, news Conway termed "especially gratifying" because of the "extreme difficulty we face in getting any publicity at all." According to Conway, the "metropolitan newspapers and book review sections" "not only" had refused to review Kutcher's book but wouldn't "even give it a listing [an announcement of its publication]—on the grounds that it is not an American publication" although the book was "by an American, on an issue of vital concern to Americans and even published in England only because no American publisher had the courage to bring it out." In a December 15, 1953, letter to its local branches, the SWP national office urged strong efforts to sell the book to "party members, sympathizers and contacts, present and former readers and subscribers to our press" while reporting that Kutcher's legal expenses had thus far cost over $13,000 and that Kutcher had announced that he would donate all book royalties to the KCRC. In a separate December 15 letter to SWP locals, SWP national secretary Farrell Dobbs termed the book a "powerful attack on the witch hunt" and a "coordinate part of the general campaign against McCarthyism."

In a January 25, 1955, letter to Kutcher, Pioneer Publishers representative Conway reported that the book had almost exhausted the first print run of 3,000 copies (having sold 2,758) and that "we hope it may be possible to publish another edition at a later date." Conway enclosed a royalty check of $137.90, based on 5 percent of the retail sales price of $1. The clearly respectable sales of Kutcher's book no doubt reflected the efforts of the KCRC and the SWP to promote it, as well as the fact that at least a scattering of publications printed favorable notices about it. Thus, according to the KCRC files, one San Francisco labor outlet praised the book as written in a "simple and interesting fashion" and "very informative," while another said the Kutcher case was an "almost perfect example of bureaucratic bungling in how not to handle a doubtful Loyalty case."

One of the few extensive accounts of Kutcher's plight to appear in the general press between the October 1952 federal appeals court ruling in his favor and a similar ruling three years later (in between Kutcher's case was considered and rejected again, as discussed below, by the VA) was Kutcher's own account that appeared in the February 28, 1953, issue of the *Nation*. Under the title "I'm Still Waiting: Four-Year Loyalty Case," Kutcher lamented that despite his appeals court victory he was "still barred from my job, and it make take another four years of litigation and appeal to obtain a final legal settlement." He added that thus far $5,000 had been raised to support his legal expenses and that his statement four years earlier that he feared that the loyalty "purge," unless "militantly opposed, would spread far beyond the confines of government employment" had been "confirmed by the growing effort to impose thought control on the American people."

During most of 1954, while Kutcher awaited the federal district court's response to a late 1953 filing appealing a renewed administrative finding of "disloyalty" (discussed below), he and the KCRC devoted most of their attention to promoting his book and raising funds to support his legal defense efforts. Kutcher embarked on a six-month speaking tour, beginning in mid-May 1954, cosponsored by Pioneer Publishers and local KCRC (and in some cases SWP) chapters, that included stops in Buffalo, Toronto, Detroit, Chicago, Milwaukee, Minneapolis–St. Paul, Cleveland, Pittsburgh, Seattle, San Francisco, and Los Angeles. In each case, local chapters were encouraged by a May 7 KCRC letter to schedule press conferences as well as short talks before "labor, liberal, church, minority groups, etc., both those that have supported him in the past and those to whom his case is new," with the main goal to raise funds and sell books by "reaching the mass organizations by getting Kutcher to appear before them rather than on relying on meetings confined to our own smaller political circles." In publicizing his July 23 Seattle talk, local organizers wrote to their supporters that the Kutcher case "has become nationally recognized as a critical test of the restrictions on democratic rights involved in the current loyalty purge proceedings." Similarly, flyers issued in Los Angeles and San Francisco in connection with Kutcher's appearances there in August and September respectively termed his case "the harbinger of the unbridled witch hunt sweeping the country for the past six years and more and which has given rise to the fascist McCarthyite menace" and a fight "against every phase of the Witch Hunt" and "the whole subversive list that makes the exercise of political opinion a crime."

Several letters in the KCRC archives indicate that Kutcher's speaking plans were at least somewhat hampered by difficulties with the CIO, especially in Michigan with the United Auto Workers, which had been steadily distancing itself from left-wing politics since the late 1940s. Thus, Kutcher's close friend George Breitman reported in a May 20, 1954, letter that "Kutcher was being treated most unfairly" by the "national CIO" because "someone—he doesn't know who—is accusing him of something—he doesn't know exactly what, some time—he doesn't know when," and "on that basis the cooperation from the CIO which he has relied on so heavily and publicly praised the CIO for is being withheld or put in question. It sounds like something out of a loyalty case. The least Kutcher has the right to know is exactly what he is accused of, so that he can answer the charge or charges. Especially since the fate of his whole national tour may depend on this." In a June 20, 1954, letter to Breitman, Kutcher indicated that UAW hostility had led to the cancellation of several planned talks in the Detroit area, including one instance where "the incoming and outgoing [UAW local] presidents wouldn't let me in. One said stay out and the other said we don't want to buy any Trotskyist literature here."

The difficulties with the CIO are clearly reflected in a July 28, 1954, letter in the KCRC files from CIO assistant executive vice president O. L. Garrison to a Seattle CIO official, which states that Garrison had been "advised that there has been previous difficulty in connection with James Kutcher" and maintained that Kutcher had engaged in a "misrepresentation" to suggest that the CIO was sponsoring his "present efforts to raise funds," as it was "in no way approved by the CIO." An August 7, 1954, letter to the national KCRC from San Francisco KCRC local official Lillian Kiezel reported that the CIO's West Coast Regional Office in Los Angeles had received a similar letter from Garrison and had informed her that "this letter had probably been sent to all the locals in the country." She lamented that "as a result of this letter we have been blocked from getting Kutcher a speaking date before many unions, including that of the Contra Costa, California CIO council." KCRC files also include a August 5, 1954, letter from national CIO assistant director of councils C. A. McPeak sent to all CIO regional directors, which declared with regard to Kutcher that although "some years ago when this man's discharge occurred, some CIO organizations, including [regional and state] councils, came to his defense in protesting against the method of, and the reasons given for his discharge," those promoting Kutcher's "current campaign" were incorrectly "using literature that implies that the CIO is a present sponsor" and that this was a "misrepresentation" that might persuade some CIO councils to "lend their names and facilities to the promotion." McPeak added that "any attempt to indicate that the present financing effort" had the backing of the "National CIO, or any of its committees or departments, would be misrepresentation," as no "endorsement, approval or sponsorship has been given, promised or authorized."

Kutcher responded to this letter, which was forward to him (in response to an earlier inquiry from him) by national CIO executive vice president John Riffe, in a lengthy September 27 letter to Riffe that included a long list of CIO unions and state and regional councils that had exhibited "moral and/or financial help to me in one form or another." Kutcher termed this support "generous and vital," adding that "without it I doubt that I ever would have been able to get my case into the courts, where it is still being litigated." Kutcher complained that McPeak had not consulted him or the KCRC about any alleged "misrepresentation" of CIO endorsement, which Kutcher said plainly was "based entirely" on the fact that KCRC letterhead listed as a sponsor the "National CIO Committee to Abolish Discrimination," a group that Riffe had indicated no longer existed; Kutcher said he was unaware of this "until after I started my current tour" and that as the "no longer existent committee" had in fact endorsed his fight, "there was no element of misrepresentation" or "motive of deception involved." Adding that he had urged the KCRC to delete the "name of the no longer existent committee from the letterhead" and "I am sure that this will be done without delay," Kutcher said that his current tour was sponsored by his publishers and by local KCRC branches and that "no effort was ever made anywhere, anytime, by anyone, to imply that this tour" had CIO backing. He concluded, "I hope that my relations with the CIO as a whole will be as friendly, as principled and as honorable in the future as they have been in the past, since 1948." McPeak responded to Kutcher's letter to Riffe on October 28 by telling Kutcher that actions taken by CIA officials "in this matter" were "in no way intended to pass judgment upon the merit of your case" and that his August 5 letter to CIA regional directors was simply intended to make clear that the "current" KCRC campaign "has not been specifically endorsed by any agency of the National CIO."

In an August 11 letter to Breitman, Kutcher declared that he was "running into the same difficulties" in Los Angeles "as I encountered in Michigan," with "ugly rumors going around" due to "letters going around to various CIO organizations" that "must have been sent out all over the country." In a July 28 letter from Seattle to Breitman, Kutcher also reported difficulty with the local ADA chapter, which had "backed away from me here" and "sent out a release saying that they had nothing to do with my meeting." An October 3, 1954, letter to Breitman from Cleveland KCRC supporter Jean Tussey reported that the national ACLU was "apparently weaseling on Kutcher support like the CIO," as, in response to a request for guidance from the Cleveland branch ACLU, the national office had reported that (in Tussey's words) it was against policy "to sponsor meetings for individuals" even in "cases they support" because "if they set a precedent in that regard, they would be unable to refuse similar requests from others, such as Communist or fascist groups" and that "they have to be careful not to have the political views of the defendants reflect on them; and that at such public meetings the speakers might express their political views." Tussey added that the Cleveland ACLU chairman expressed a wish to proceed with sponsoring a meeting for Kutcher, however, since "they already made the commitments" before hearing from the national office. These developments were reflected in an October 8, 1954, letter from Cleveland ACLU chairman Ralph Rudd inviting Kutcher to speak there on October 14, which stated that Tussey had given assurances that "your private political views will not be injected into the meeting except to the extent necessary for your personal identification and explanation of the experiences which you have had under the federal loyalty and security programs. I do not wish to seem over-squeamish in this matter, but we do feel it is important to avoid confusion in the public mind" between the purposes of the ACLU "and those of the persons whose rights it seeks to protect."

Similarly, a July 10 letter written by George Novack's wife, Evelyn, related to a supporter that Kutcher had reported that "some individuals and some organizations that were very helpful to him four years ago on a previous tour are now a little more cautious or timid," a development Kutcher "attributes to the general deterioration in the political situation during that time." In an August 14 letter, Breitman told Kutcher that any feelings of "gloom or despair about the CIO runaround or stab-in-the-back" were "not warranted" and that the "tour is making out better than could be expected, once we knew what their attitude was in Detroit." Breitman wrote to a correspondent on August 19 that a decision had been made not to respond publicly to the CIO allegations because such action would probably "succeed in closing all the CIO doors (and maybe even other union doors)," especially since "wherever the local CIO people wanted to fight for civil liberties" in connection with Kutcher's tour they "did not look for pretexts but gave aid forthwith." In an August 22 letter to Breitman, Kutcher indicated support for this approach because "people who might want to let me in to speak might not if we attacked the CIO publicly at this time."

Other difficulties with the tour were reported, involving people being out of town for summer vacations, alleged FBI harassment, a weakening of KCRC locals over time, pressure on Kutcher from female activists to address women's issues, and even Kutcher's mother's wish that Kutcher would write more regularly. Thus, a May 27, 1954, letter from Breitman to Kutcher indicated that Kutcher's mother was "worried about not hearing from you." Breitman told "Jimmy" that "there is only one way to deal with this, and that is for you to write her regularly." He specifically suggested that Kutcher "promise to write her at least once a week and then do it. Ok?" In a July 11 letter to Kutcher, Breitman wrote, "I assume you're not only sending checks to your mother but writing her regularly; or anyhow I hope so."

In a June 25 letter to Breitman, Kutcher reported from Chicago that the "chief difficulty here is that it's summer and so there are not many meetings going on" and "most everyone we wanted to get to speak at a meeting is not in town or is going to be out of town." A June 16, 1954, letter from prominent SWP activist Vincent Dunne in Minneapolis to Breitman reported problems resulting from the growing influence of conservative AFL unions, which had "barred" many "doors," and the fact that "the local KCRC Committee is something less than a skeleton," that "most of the local KCRC Committees have, between Jim's tours [referring to his 1949 speaking tour] changed for the worse or are paper organizations," and that "we claim no distinction here on that account." Breitman's June 21 response to Dunne reported that "what you say about the KCRC applies not only to Minn. [Minnesota] but to all the places I know of. In the places where we want a KCRC meeting, it has to be rebuilt (as in Buffalo). In other places it isn't necessary to have any more than a secretary's name and address" as "experience is that most of the former KCRC members aren't worth too much bother."

In an August 11, 1954, letter to Breitman from Los Angeles, Kutcher indicated that he had reluctantly, under pressure from local women activists, added a paragraph to his remarks calling for "full economic and social equality in America" for women. Reflecting a somewhat less than progressive view on this subject, as well as a strange inability to identify with others who faced discrimination, Kutcher said he "didn't know anything about the woman question," that "the only question that has ever occurred to me when I meet a woman is whether or not I can make love to her," and that "after that I don't really care," although "I certainly wouldn't stand in the way of anything the woman wanted to do. Things being the way they are I don't see why I should get excited over this question."

In a May 31 letter to Breitman, Kutcher reported he was not staying with his previous host in Buffalo anymore because "we learned that the FBI had been snooping around" and "put pressure" on his host's parents, who co-owned and shared the house involved. A letter to Breitman from a Buffalo KCRC official seemingly corroborated Kutcher's letter, reporting that while the "FBI and local authorities" had "been long exerting severe pressure on our organization here, with a view to disrupting our activities," Kutcher's visit had led them to intensify "their pressure to an almost unprecedented degree," including the presence of "no less than four FBI agents outside the headquarters" at a recent branch meeting and an FBI visit to Kutcher's host's parents, creating "such a reign of terror" that the "mother became hysterical" and a situation was created "which made it necessary to move Jimmy to other quarters."

Despite such reported problems, Kutcher's letters to Breitman and other accounts from local KCRC officials frequently related an encouraging response to his speaking tour, with multiple book sales and numerous appearances reported from many venues. Thus, a June 5 telegram from Buffalo reported that more than 150 people had attended Kutcher's "excellent presentation," with many book sales, providing a "big lift for branch and particularly for all friends of civil liberties who were delighted at such large turnout despite intimidation." According to a June 13 follow-up letter, although FBI agents were "stationed outside the hotel room, and around the [hotel] lobby" where Kutcher spoke in Buffalo in early June, their attempted "harassment" failed to "cut much ice" and altogether Kutcher "reached thousands and thousands of people in the Buffalo area" during his visit of several weeks there. A June 28 letter from Sheavy Goldman in Chicago informed Breitman that Kutcher's stay had been "very profitable" and that "all in all, considering the time of year, everyone here is of the opinion that the tour has been a success," although "practically all organizations and unions have been disbanded for the summer" and it quickly became apparent that "it would be impossible to hold a public meeting during the summer." Nevertheless, Goldman reported, Kutcher had spoken to numerous small groups, and 167 copies of his book had been sold thus far.

A June 30 letter from Detroit reported that Kutcher had spoken to nine unions there, with an estimated total attendance of 860 and 136 book sales; the letter added that Kutcher had held a press conference in Detroit but that "none of the papers carried any stories." In an August 10 letter to Breitman, Kutcher reported from Los Angeles that he had just had "the most successful meeting since Buffalo," with about 150 attendees, and in letters about his stops in Los Angeles and San Francisco, Kutcher reported having sold about 350 books. In an August 11 letter to Kutcher, Breitman wrote that "whatever we get out of the tour is gravy, and over-all reaction in the letters I get is satisfaction rather than disappointment" and that "when you look at the tour objectively" it had "done quite well, better than I would have predicted if we had all the facts [about CIO opposition] at the beginning." Breitman added in an August 27 letter to Kutcher that "financially the tour seems to be paying for itself despite the obstacles" and that he had feared that "we would end up in the red, and that was even before learned about the CIO; so I think there's an additional reason for feeling that things are turning out OK."

Kutcher's 1954 speaking tour attracted very little publicity. Thus, a June 30 letter to the national KCRC from Detroit reported Kutcher had held a press conference there but "none of the papers carried any stories," and in an August 29 letter to Breitman from San Francisco, Kutcher lamented having "made the rounds of all the newspapers" in the area but "no publicity" had resulted. KCRC files contain only about a dozen news clippings regarding Kutcher's 1954 tour. Almost all accounts about his speeches were from Los Angeles and Buffalo papers about his talks in those cities, while three clippings focused on disavowals of any sponsorship of the tour by CIO and ADA spokesmen.

CHAPTER FOUR

Kutcher's Troubles Mount as the Government Seeks to Evict Him from His Home and He Struggles on to Keep His Job (1952–1954)

Kutcher noted in his autobiography that while the October 1952 federal appeals court had ruled he could not be fired solely for his SWP membership, the case had simply been returned to the VA for further consideration; he had not been restored to his job, the court had not ruled on the constitutionality of the loyalty program, and it had specifically indicated that membership in AGLOSO groups could be considered as one basis for "disbelief in the loyalty of an employee." Thus, he noted, the VA could still fire him so long as his SWP membership was considered along with "all the evidence," and, in effect, the court had only rolled back "my fight for reinstatement to the position it was in four years before."

While waiting for the Justice Department to decide whether to appeal the case to the Supreme Court or return it to the VA, Kutcher learned about a new development that, he wrote in his autobiography, the "the witch hunters" had stirred up to "give me something else to think about for a while." This "something" was the Gwinn Act, passed by Congress in mid-1952, which banned any members of organizations listed as "subversive" by the attorney general from living in federally subsidized public housing. As Kutcher and his parents, both then 73, had been living in the Seth Boyden federal low-rent housing project in Newark since his army discharge, shortly before Christmas 1952, his father, Hyman, was asked to sign a statement from the Newark Housing Authority (NHA) indicating that no members of his household were AGLOSO members and was given three days to do so as a condition of continued residence.

According to Kutcher's autobiography, while their apartment was not luxurious, it was comfortable, and his parents, who had made friends among the neighbors, anticipated living there permanently. His father felt "terrible" upon hearing the news and at first blamed Kutcher, declaring, "There—I hope you're satisfied now. I've told you a hundred times to leave your party. Now we will have to move because you're so stubborn. And where will we go?" Since the apparent price to pay to keep his parents in the apartment would be for him to leave, Kutcher offered to move out, but his mother began to cry because she felt he wouldn't be able to properly care for himself. However, he recounted deciding that although the last thing he wanted "was to go into court with a new case," this was a better alternative, especially given his recent federal court victory concerning his job and especially since the loyalty program at least offered a limited hearing to individuals affected, while the Gwinn Act offered none.

According to Kutcher, he was able to convince his father that "his rights were worth defending too," and his father wrote to the NHA declaring his loyalty to the United States and his love for both "my country and my home." In the letter, Hyman related that he had wanted to "comply with all requirements for remaining in my home" but that his son had refused to leave the SWP, "saying that it is not subversive and he is not subversive. . . . What should I do? I want to sign the certificate, I do not want to move. I do not want to break up my family because my son needs help to take care of him. Please help me, please tell me what to do, so that I can keep my home."

James Kutcher said that no answer to the letter was received, but that he was able to obtain the support of the ACLU in bringing a test case of the oath along with another disabled veteran living in the Seth Boyden project, Harry Lawrence. A suit on behalf of Lawrence and the two Kutchers was then filed in the New Jersey Superior Court on February 2, 1953, asking that the Gwinn Act be declared unconstitutional and that the NHA be restrained from pursuing eviction procedures for failure to sign its oath. ACLU president Patrick Murphy Malin termed the case the beginning of an ACLU effort to overturn "this unwise and unconstitutional oath," which threatened "cherished traditions of American democracy, free speech and due process of law." Six weeks later New Jersey Superior Court judge Walter Freund issued a temporary restraining order directing the NHA to take no action against families that had not signed the Gwinn Act oath, pending a ruling on its constitutionality.

On January 31, 1953, Rauh wrote VA administrator Carl Gray requesting an interview with himself and Kutcher so that they could "present what we consider proper action" with regard to Kutcher's VA status, which he declared "required" a new administrative loyalty hearing before the Philadelphia VA loyalty branch board, thus "reopening the proceedings and starting anew." Rauh said only such a procedure could resolve the "conjectural question" as to whether the 1948 Philadelphia board had based its decision on "all" the evidence concerning Kutcher or instead, as Rauh maintained was "apparent from the charges, from the evidence introduced by the government and from the remarks of government counsel, had ruled against Kutcher solely due to his SWP membership," a grounds struck down by the recent federal appeals court decision. Rauh maintained that a new hearing was required because the earlier Philadelphia board ruling was four years old and therefore "stale and would not reflect the current conditions," since world events had "taken many twists and turns" and Kutcher might have changed his views or some of them might be "treated differently in light of today's conditions." He argued that the Philadelphia board was the appropriate venue for a new hearing rather than the VA Loyalty Board of Appeals because the latter's function was to "review the findings, the evidence and the suggestions made by the Branch Board to ensure regularity" and since the Philadelphia ruling was "stale," the "Branch Board rather than the Appeal Board is the proper body to investigate Kutcher's present reputation for loyalty among his neighbors, co-workers and hear witnesses presented by Kutcher and the Government."

Rauh also called for Kutcher's reinstatement with back pay pending a final determination because VA regulations called for suspensions pending loyalty determinations only if their "active duty" retention threatened damage to government property or would be otherwise "detrimental" to governmental interests or "injurious to the employee, his fellow workers, or the general public," possibilities that he maintained did not apply to Kutcher give the completely "non-sensitive" nature of his VA position, his positive job evaluations, and the "undisputed" evidence that he had never discussed politics with his fellow workers. In fact, Rauh maintained, reinstating Kutcher would actually "improve the morale" of other VA employees as it would "demonstrate that if for some reason they were wrongfully discharged, the situation would be remedied." Rauh also appealed for Kutcher's reemployment as a matter of fairness since he provided needed financial support for his parents and he had found it "next to impossible" to find another job while also contesting his discharge; reinstating him would allow him to "pay off some of the debts incurred during his long period of enforced unemployment."

In a January 24 letter to Kutcher, Rauh advised the former of his plans while informing Kutcher that he didn't "hold too high hopes" that the VA would reinstate him, which would entitle Kutcher to back pay "for the entire period since the suspension order," and predicted that "more likely" the VA would "refuse to do anything for you except to keep you on suspension and give you another appeal hearing." In that case, Rauh advised Kutcher to write directly to President Eisenhower with the information that years of even "successful litigation" had failed to gain his rights. "All I want to do," Rauh concluded, "is make a real fight inside the Veterans Administration before you go to the President."

As Rauh had predicted, in a February 6 letter Gray rejected Rauh's request that Kutcher's suspension be lifted, that he be returned to active duty, and that "proceedings be instituted anew under Executive Orders covering loyalty proceedings." The enormous sensitivity of the Kutcher case was clearly reflected by Gray's decision to separately write the Eisenhower's administration's new attorney general, Herbert Brownell, also on February 6, to inform Brownell about developments and advise him that the VA would take no action on the case until hearing from the Justice Department. Gray summarized his letter to Rauh, noted that the department had informed him on January 13 that the government would not seek review of the appeals court decision before the Supreme Court, and added that "informal contacts with your department" had led him to conclude that "we are not to proceed further administratively in the case until such time as your Department refers the matter to us." Gray suggested that it would be "well if we confer closely with respect to procedure and we will await your further advices."

In response to Gray's February 6 letter, Kutcher wrote a three-page double-spaced typed letter to the newly inaugurated President Dwight Eisenhower on February 11, 1953, with a plea "for an act of justice that has been denied me by the preceding Administration" by a World War II veteran "who served under your command" in the North African and Italian campaigns. Kutcher said that despite satisfactory work for the VA, he had suddenly been fired and "subjected to a stigma on my good name and honor" in 1948 "simply because I believed the same thoughts I believed five years earlier at San Pietro"; this was due to Truman's loyalty order and the AGLOSO compilation, which he maintained involved "some of the most arbitrary violations of traditional democratic procedure in the history of the Republic." Referring to Gray's recent letter, Kutcher complained that the VA administrator had "refused me even the courtesy of a meeting to discuss this matter" and asked that Eisenhower "not tolerate in your Administration such bureaucratic callousness to the needs of the individual citizen." Kutcher also referred to his threatened eviction from Newark public housing "solely because of my membership" in an AGLOSO organization" and concluded by asking Eisenhower to "advise" the VA to reinstate him "without further delay to my job, with back pay and seniority," to direct Brownell to "withdraw" the AGLOSO list, "which was prepared without notice or hearing," and to "dissociate" the Justice Department "completely from the arbitrary procedures connected" with it. There is no evidence that Eisenhower ever responded to Kutcher's letter, but on February 17, in response to receiving from the Justice Department a copy of Judge Curran's January 30, 1953, mandate enforcing the October 1952 appeals court ruling, VA administrator Gray informed his subordinates that "the order removing James Kutcher from employment is vacated and he will be returned to the employment rolls of this Administration in suspended status, such suspension to continued pending final decision on Mr. Kutcher's appeal from the decision of the VA Loyalty Board." He added that suspended status "does not make the employee eligible for pay covering any period of time from the beginning of his suspension on loyalty charges." Gray's directive was transmitted to the Newark VA office by "priority telegram" on February 19, and recorded in a VA "notification of personnel action" form filed on March 2.

On February 20, VA Loyalty Board of Appeals chairman George Lynch informed Rauh of VA action returning Kutcher to suspended status and also told Rauh that a panel of his board would hold a hearing in the case in Washington on March 9, thus rejecting Rauh's request for a rehearing before the Philadelphia branch board. A typed February 16 "memorandum for file" by Lynch makes clear that this decision was, at the least, concurred in at high Justice Department levels, recording that he had spoken by telephone that morning with Justice Department attorney Hickey, and that, in response to his query, Hickey had told him that there was nothing "so far as the Justice Department is concerned" to bar the VA from implementing the order or granting Kutcher a hearing. The memo also indicates that the Justice Department had decided to essentially ignore *McGrath* in supervising the loyalty program, as Hickey had reported "his understanding that Agency heads still proceeded" to utilize AGLOSO "as they did previously" to the ruling. Lynch wrote that at Hickey's suggestion he had checked with the LRB secretary, who had "confirmed the references made by Mr. Hickey and advised me that so far as the Loyalty Review Board was concerned the way was clear to go ahead and consider the Kutcher case," although, in response to his query, Hickey had "advised" that the VA Loyalty Board of Appeals "would have to entertain [hearing] evidence, if the same were presented," concerning the SWP's "nature and character," despite its AGLOSO designation.

Lynch concluded his memo by stating that he had informed both Hickey and LRB secretary Norris that he would "proceed forthwith" to set a hearing date for Kutcher and that they had "both agreed with me that the Board, on all the evidence, should make a conclusion respecting loyalty" based on the criteria in both Truman's 1947 loyalty order and a subsequent 1951 revision that lowered the standards needed to fire employees on loyalty grounds. Apparently acting with extreme caution given the explosive possibilities inherent in the Kutcher case, Lynch added a handwritten note dated February 17 to his memo stating that he had asked "Mr. Minor, Department of

Justice, who is in charge of new security-loyalty program to be" if there was "anything in the way of proceeding at this time to considering the appeal and granting Kutcher a hearing," and Minor had responded that "the way was clear and to go ahead." Deputy Attorney General William Rogers further confirmed this in a February 27 letter to Gray in which he reported that "members of my staff" had "informally" discussed the Kutcher matter with Lynch and that he understood that the "problems raised by your letter . . . have been met for the present" by the decision to handle Kutcher at the VA's "appellate stage."

The transcript of Kutcher's March 9 Washington VA loyalty board's three-man panel hearing, which filled seventy printed pages, clearly reflect the VA's decision, in light of the appeals court ruling, to hear Kutcher out on his political views, including his explanation about the views and character of the SWP, but it largely covered ground well plowed in the earlier administrative hearings. At the start of the hearing, which lasted for four and a half hours, including a luncheon break, Lynch termed it an "appeal from the decision" of the 1948 Philadelphia VA board, in light of the federal appeals court ruling that had vacated Gray's earlier disposition of the case solely on the basis of Kutcher's SWP membership and ordered a determination based on whether "on all the evidence reasonable grounds exist" for believing that Kutcher was "disloyal" to the American government. Rauh immediately requested that Kutcher be "reinstated without prejudice" to his position rather than placed in suspended status and that his case be referred back to the Philadelphia board since "there is no reason to assume that the facts today are the same" as over four years earlier, and thus "it could only be a fair hearing if we went back to the locality."

However, his motion was quickly denied by Lynch, who declared that the appeals court remand had specifically directed that Kutcher be maintained in suspended status with the VA pending a final determination and maintained that the Philadelphia board had not ruled "entirely" on the basis of Kutcher's SWP ties but rather "considered the case on the merits," while adding that if "the facts are different now" Rauh was "at liberty" to "tell us what the present facts are" (later in the hearing Lynch maintained, in what Rauh riposted was only "your view of it," that the court ruling "made no reference to remanding the case back to the original [Philadelphia] Board but indicated very clearly that it contemplated consideration by the Administrator on appeal"). Lynch added in response to Rauh's opening motion that the board would not consider matters "alone of the present record" but also would probe into Kutcher's loyalty on the basis of "all means available to us, and we are willing and ready to hear any further evidence you have," including witnesses "at the place of Mr. Kutcher's residence [i.e., Newark]."

Rauh then asked the board for any "charges which would state what in addition" to SWP membership the VA "considers Mr. Kutcher has thought, said or done which he can respond to and thereby show his loyalty," as what the 1948 Philadelphia board had considered "come[s] down to the simple proposition that he was a member and that is all." Lynch denied Rauh's motion on the grounds that while the 1948 charges "well could have been drafted more explicitly, there is no doubt about that," nonetheless they "were charging [Kutcher] with reasonable grounds for the belief that he is disloyal" in compliance with Truman's executive order. He added that even if the charges were based "at least to a large extent" on the finding that an SWP member "and one who has association and activity with persons, associations or groups" that were AGLOSO designated "may be a person who is disloyal to the government," the "essence of the consideration by the Board below and by this Board at the present time under" Gray's directive to comply with the federal court mandate was "the loyalty" of Kutcher. Thus, he maintained that SWP membership alone had "no conclusive element of disloyalty," although the Philadelphia charges, which all referred to SWP affiliations, "are in a sense factors in relation to the charge of disloyalty." As Rauh expressed puzzlement when Lynch added that "we are not relying alone" upon either Kutcher's SWP membership "or his activity within the Party," Lynch responded that the board would discuss "further" with Kutcher, when he testified, information that Kutcher had stated "certain things which we may believe are in further derogation of his loyalty."

When Kutcher took the stand, Rauh first led him through a series of affidavits attesting to his good character and loyalty, which were submitted by individuals identified as New Jersey CIO president Carl Holderman; Joel Jacobson, executive secretary of the Newark mayor's Commission on Human Relations; Kutcher's Newark chiropodist, Dr. Ben Markowitz; George Pfaus, Newark head of the ADA, which, Kutcher, in response to a friendly query from Rauh, declared "excludes communists and socialists from membership"; and Charles Allen, former president of the Newark Teachers Union, AFL. Each of these affidavits had a similar tenor: thus, Jacobsen stated that while he disagreed with "the political views of either Mr. Kutcher" or the SWP, he had never known Kutcher to have advocated the violent overthrow of the government or to have "ever committed any overt act of treason or disloyalty to this country" and that "unlike the professional patriots who merely shout about their loyalty," Kutcher had "demonstrated, in rather tangible form, his support of his country" at San Pietro, "where he lost both of his legs in combat against an enemy." Following submission of the affidavits, board chairman Lynch referred to Kutcher's positive VA efficiency ratings and "very frankly" conceded that "there is nothing" in his VA personnel record "which is derogatory to his loyalty" or to his "ability to carry on his job" in "relation to the character of his work."

Rauh thereupon led Kutcher through a friendly series of questions, the thrust of which was to establish that Kutcher had never sought to proselytize concerning his political views either in the army or at the VA post, that instead he limited his political activities to interacting with "people who come to" SWP meetings, that the SWP openly ran candidates for electoral office, and that neither he nor the SWP advocated violent or unconstitutional change in the form of the American government but only sought and expected to attain power and to bring about a socialist state dominated by workers via democratic means. Thus, Kutcher said that he felt that "the majority of the workers will begin to learn by their own experience that the ideas we advocate are correct ones, and they will turn to us in larger and larger numbers," but "in no respect would we ever try to force our opinions by force or violence." He specifically cited the example of the British Labor Party, which had just won the 1945 election after many years in the minority, a development similar to what Kutcher said he foresaw occurring in the United States "perhaps not in 4 or 5 years, but less than say 25 and 30," following a period during which the SWP's views would become "the views of [an American] Labor Party and, therefore, of the majority party without the use of force and violence."

When Rauh declared that he was prepared to produce evidence that the SWP had been improperly placed on AGLOSO via testimony from the "top officials of the organization," Lynch responded that the board would not "in any sense undertake" to "try out the case of the character and nature" of the SWP "as such," but would "determine this case one way or the other on the basis of what we find to be reasonable grounds for the belief with respect to Mr. Kutcher's loyalty." However, he added, "inasmuch as Mr. Kutcher's" SWP affiliations were "part of the charges here," the board "wanted to make it clear that we are not precluding you from making a presentation with respect to the nature of the Party if you so desire." Toward the end of the hearing, Lynch agreed to Rauh's request that he inform the panel within a few days if he wished to subsequently present the testimony of top SWP officials.

After Rauh concluded his questioning of Kutcher, which filled twenty printed pages of the hearing transcript, Lynch and other members of the loyalty panel took Kutcher through about another thirty printed pages of questions, which focused on Kutcher's political beliefs and activities, including his support for various SWP positions and publications, and especially on his views toward the use of force to bring about economic and political change in the United States. In response to board members' questions, Kutcher said he agreed with the views of the SWP's paper, the *Militant*, "more than" was the case "in any other newspapers," that he felt the achievement of a socialist government "say in the United States and other countries would give the Soviet people that assurance they need and they would then do away with Stalin," and that he had read a variety of left-wing publications, including the *Communist Manifesto* by Karl Marx and Friedrich Engels.

However, while agreeing that he wanted to "see our capitalistic system supplanted by some other system," Kutcher denied that either he or Marx favored the use of violent means to attain such ends. On several occasions Lynch referred, without further elaboration, to "information" that he said the board had concerning various SWP activities and policies, which since-released FBI documents establish were based on Bureau reports: Kutcher readily conceded the accuracy of "information" indicating that due to his close "association with the [Newark SWP] branch" that he "knew practically all" of its members, and he affirmed that he had delivered the May Day 1949 speech, which had been reprinted in its entirety in the *Militant* and which the FBI had repeatedly reported on. When Lynch expressed puzzlement as to what Kutcher had referred to by complaining in the speech about government "intimidation" designed to thwart the SWP's efforts, Kutcher riposted, "How many people do you think there are, especially today, that would go to attend a meeting of an organization that they know is blacklisted by the Government?"

Noting that before the Philadelphia board Kutcher had defended the use of violence against a minority capitalist regime that sought to maintain itself in power in defiance of majority wishes, Lynch tried to get him to agree that this accurately described the existing situation, but Kutcher refused to take the bait, conceding that "for the present the majority supports the system of capitalism," although he lamented that they were "not very wise" in doing so. As Kutcher repeatedly affirmed that "we would never use force and violence" to attain political power, Lynch declared that "your testimony may be a bit different that it was before the [Philadelphia] Board." In response to Lynch's question if he would respond to an SWP call for "militarization" of party members, Kutcher said he would not, because "I am against force and violence. I was in the war, I saw force and violence practiced in the war and I am sick of it. I just think there should be a better way for people to live." Rauh then intervened to concede that Kutcher's Philadelphia testimony concerning the use of force was "not the clearest testimony I have ever read," because Kutcher was "not a skilled technician either in questions and answers or in this very complicated problem you have," but maintained that Kutcher had earlier advocated violence only in resistance to a minority "coup d'etat against a properly elected government of his choosing." Lynch then reiterated that "I see some conflict in his answers," while adding "just what the effect of that will be, I am, of course, loath to say at this time without study of the whole record."

In response to further questions along similar lines from Rauh and panel member A. S. Mason, Kutcher reiterated that he would advocate force only "when the minority first took up force" to seek to block majority rule and added that "we don't advocate going out and saying you got to store arms, you got to hide guns and bombs and etc. in cellars and such to be ready" for such an eventuality, although "we would tell the workers that possibly this minority might try to use force and if they do that they are forewarned." In response to a question from panel member R. Y. Martin asking if he would "voluntarily go" to the FBI if he had "positive knowledge" that a "friend of yours was a communist, a member of the Communist Party of the United States," Kutcher said that he would not. Shortly after this exchange, Kutcher conceded, under prompting from Rauh, that, for fear of implicating others, he had falsely testified earlier during the hearing that he did not remember hearing speeches at SWP meetings by several other individuals named by Chairman Lynch on the basis of his otherwise unspecified "information." Kutcher said that "they spoke all right" but that he was "just afraid that those people would get into trouble if I testified in such a manner about them." When Mason then asked if his answer had indicated that "you would lie to keep them out of trouble," Kutcher responded, "I am afraid I did, sir."

Following the questioning of Kutcher by the panel members, Rauh presented a closing statement, in which he began by declaring that "a great deal" would be required to "overcome" Kutcher's war record and VA job efficiency ratings, especially given Kutcher's testimony disavowing any attempt to seek to promulgate his political views either in the army or during his VA employment. He conceded that it was hardly possible to "espouse any more radical views with respect to the economic system than Mr. Kutcher has espoused," but maintained that they were irrelevant to a "loyalty" determination, which could rest only on a finding that Kutcher sought to "couple" such views with undemocratic efforts to "accomplish this end of doing away with private property," especially since "some doing away with private property" through democratic processes had been involved in "practically every social advancement of the last 150 years," ranging from the abolition of slavery to various forms of governmental regulation of industry. Rauh argued that "if it ever gets in this country" to "saying it is disloyal to completely believe in a system of production for use you reach the stage where every change in the private property system will be related to your minds in a question of loyalty, and I don't think we want to get into anything like that in this country."

While Rauh termed Kutcher's belief that an American labor party would "in a couple of decades" persuade a majority to support his economic views a "fanciful" and "little bit unrealistic" goal to be obtained in a manner "a little bit fanciful," nonetheless, he maintained, "the nub of the question" was that Kutcher wished to "become the majority at this future period by education and the elections." Moreover, Rauh added—apparently suggesting that his arguments would be invalid were Kutcher a CP member and that the board could reasonably consider public opinion in making its determination—it was highly relevant that the loyalty program sought to "get rid of employees who might be loyal" to Russia and that "certain actions have been taken in Government agencies because of pressure from people like Joe McCarthy" and the "quite understandable feeling of the danger of public criticism if particular people were cleared" on the "thought that the employee really somewhat favored Russia," but it "just isn't true in [Kutcher's] case." Indeed, he declared, Kutcher's reinstatement "would be well received even" by McCarthy and others "who have been the most vociferous in their statements that the program required a more stringent enforcement."

Rauh closed his argument by declaring that the VA had no "more important function" than creating a climate favorable toward disabled veterans and that "if this Board feels that this is a case where reasonable men could differ they must come to the conclusion on the side of the veteran." However, he added, "I happen to feel that this is not a case in which reasonable men could differ," because "a man who has demonstrated his loyalty in action should not be punished" and face the end of his employment prospects "for expressing his views and trying to propagate his views however radical. . . . I cannot feel that a Board which is responsible for the future of veterans can find that radical views should override loyal action." Rauh repeated this formulation in a March 11 letter to Lynch in which he reported that Kutcher did not wish to call any additional witnesses (concerning the nature of the SWP, as the panel had agreed to hear), since "we are confident, on the record as it now stands, that Mr. Kutcher has demonstrated his loyalty to our country by his deeds and that this demonstration is not in any vitiated by the radical views which he holds."

On April 20, 1953, the VA Loyalty Board of Appeals forwarded to VA administrator Gray two separate documents that conveyed its unanimous finding that (quoting the standards established in Truman's 1947 and 1951 loyalty orders) "reasonable grounds exists for the belief" that Kutcher was "disloyal" to the American government and that "reasonable doubt exists respecting [Kutcher's] loyalty based on a careful review of the entire evidence." The board also reported that it found that Kutcher's case fell "within the purview" of the Hatch Act. While this public document was limited to these bare-bones findings, the other, private, communication filled over fifteen printed pages with the board's rationale, which ultimately amounted to a finding that Kutcher was an active, informed member of the SWP and that the SWP advocated the violent overthrow of the government. In reaching its conclusions, the board disregarded the great bulk of Kutcher's testimony, in which he had repeatedly disavowed advocating or supporting the use of force to overthrow the government, instead relying on his confusing testimony on this point at the 1948 Philadelphia VA branch board hearing and on two documents that had never been mentioned at any of his hearings: a letter from Deputy Attorney General Rogers sent to the board at its request on April 1, 1953, concerning the nature of the SWP, and, above all, the 1943 federal appeals court ruling upholding the 1941 Smith Act conviction of eighteen SWP members for conspiracy to advocate the forceful overthrow of the government and insubordination in the military. The thrust of the Rogers letter, as summarized by the panel, was that the SWP advocated the "transformation of the existing social order"; that the Smith Act trial ended with the conviction of eighteen SWP members for conspiracy to advocate and teach the violent overthrow of the government; that the SWP sought to "generally" accomplish its goal by "infiltrating labor unions, left-wing groups and so-called liberal movements" and by teaching Marxist doctrines "as interpreted by Leon Trotsky" at "classes and schools in several cities"; and that the SWP was AGLOSO-categorized as seeking "to alter the form of government of the United States by unconstitutional means."

The panel cited the September 20, 1943, federal appeals court ruling affirming the conviction of the eighteen SWP members for violating the Smith Act at great length, declaring that it "threw searching light" on the group's "character, nature, aims and purposes." Thus the VA board quoted the court's finding that the "drastic, complete change" in the American form of government advocated by the SWP was clearly sought to be accomplished violently and noted that the court had characterized the 1938 SWP founding "Declaration of Principles" as setting forth to "overthrow the existing government by force" and had quoted the "Declaration" as rejecting as an "illusion" the belief that "we live in a free, democratic society in which fundamental economic change can be effected by persuasion, by education, by legal and purely parliamentary methods" since the "existing institutions of the governmental apparatus" represented the "interests only of the capitalistic minority." The VA panel additionally quoted the court ruling as holding that the record of the SWP's own publications and public and private statements left "no doubt that force was the ultimate means to be used by the Party in the overthrow of the government" and characterized the SWP's formal 1940 withdrawal of the "Declaration" as a legal maneuver that "was not intended to have" the "slightest effect upon" SWP "doctrines and methods."

The VA board effectively conceded that, unlike Kutcher, most of the Smith Act defendants had been high-level SWP officials and that due to the October 1952 Kutcher federal appeals court ruling, SWP "membership alone" could not justify finding him disloyal "if it were shown that he was innocent of the [SWP's] subversive purposes and aims." However, the panel members concluded that Kutcher was an active and informed member of the SWP and that, while he had told them that "he would not advocate force" to achieve the party's goals, it was "inclined to the view" that his "original answers" before the 1948 Philadelphia board "more nearly reflect" his "true intent and understanding," and that they were "reasonably susceptible of interpretation that he then, in substance, admitted the Party's intended use of force, if necessary, as a means to the end sought." The board declared that Kutcher's original admittedly false testimony about not remembering hearing the speeches of other named persons at SWP meetings brought his "integrity" into "serious question." It added that his refusal to report to the FBI the names of persons whom he might know to be members of the Communist Party "in full knowledge of the present war between the United Nations (principally U.S.A.) and the Korean and Chinese Communists with avowed backing of the Soviets" demonstrated that his "pretended loyalty to this Government is overcome by his admitted loyalty to those who seek to destroy it." However, it added that it had given "full consideration" to Kutcher's military record and admitted there were "no acts of disloyalty shown" in connection with his VA employment and that Kutcher's "efficiency in his job has not been questioned."

In conclusion, the panel conceded that the specific allegations against Kutcher "all centered in his [SWP] membership in and activity," but concluded that as the SWP unquestionably advocated the "destruction of our present form of constitutional government by force, if necessary" to attain "its Communistic aims and purposes," and as the loyalty standard required "merely a question of the existence on all the evidence of 'reasonable grounds for the belief of disloyalty,'" there was clearly "reasonable doubt" as to Kutcher's loyalty, given that he had "knowingly" and "actively" participated in furthering the SWP's goals "over a period of years." Without any additional comment, VA administrator Gray marked the panel's recommendation as "approved" on April 23, three days after their submission to him. Gray's decision was transmitted the same day to Kutcher and to VA Newark regional office manager Joseph O'Hearn by VA assistant administrator for personnel F. R. Kerr. Kerr informed Kutcher that he was entitled to appeal the VA decision to the LRB within twenty days, in which case his current status of suspension without pay would be continued until the LRB "renders a decision," but otherwise his name would be "removed from the rolls of the Veterans Administration" within twenty days. O'Hearn telegrammed Kutcher on April 24 to request that he appear at the Newark VA office on April 27 (a Monday) concerning "a matter of importance to you," and Kutcher signed then to register his receipt of the notification, as O'Hearn notified Kerr by a "personal and confidential" letter of the same date. Meanwhile, the VA notified the LRB of its decision on "Standard form 98," captioned "Agency report on closed loyalty case." Kutcher wrote to the LRB on May 5 to report his wish to appeal the VA ruling, leading the LRB to request the following day that the VA transfer its files on Kutcher. In response, VA loyalty board executive secretary Frank Bentley sent Kutcher's file to the LRB on May 11, with a cover letter noting that he was enclosing "nine reports (each in triplicate) of supplemental investigation conducted" by the FBI, which had been received on May 6, along with an FBI cover letter, from the Civil Service Commission.

On May 21, the LRB notified Rauh and Kutcher that it was scheduling Kutcher's appeal hearing for June 4 in Washington; Rauh informed Novack in a May 26 letter that he had tried to get a later date for the hearing, but could not "because the Board is going out of business shortly." In the meantime, SWP national secretary Farrell Dobbs wrote Attorney General Brownell on June 4 to request a hearing under the new Justice Department AGLOSO administrative appeal regulations (adopted in 1953 in response to *McGrath*). However, Assistant Attorney General Warren Olney rejected the request on June 15 on the grounds that it did not comply with the new rules; in a subsequent exchange, Olney indicated that the department would not accept the request because it was signed only by Dobbs, and the regulations required that AGLOSO appeals be signed by the "executive officers" of an organization. "Information available to this Department establishes that [Dobbs] is not in fact the only [SWP] officer" and thus the "purported protest signed only by you as National Secretary is therefore not valid."

The June 4 LRB hearing, before a three-man panel, was extremely short, with the only testimony a brief (sixteen-page double-spaced typed) statement presented by Rauh's associate Daniel Pollitt (in Rauh's absence), which argued that Kutcher had: (1) been denied due process in the wake of the federal appeals court ruling by the VA's refusal to grant him a branch loyalty board hearing and by refusing to specify its charges against him; and (2) been denied a fair ruling on the grounds that the "evidence does not support the finding reached." Rauh's first argument was that under Truman's executive order, Kutcher was entitled to have loyalty proceedings commence "anew" with a "fact-finding type of hearing at the local level where evidence can be received and sifted" and that Gray's refusal to allow this had deprived Kutcher of his rights and was "illegal, arbitrary and contrary to the express provisions" of the order. This was especially so, he maintained, because Kutcher had "changed his views in a very important respect" since the 1948 Philadelphia hearing, as he then believed that "the majority would be justified in using force" to meet that exercised by "a minority group of capitalists and militarists" who would violently seek to thwart the SWP after it "had democratically reached a position of power," but he "no longer believed that the minority group would resort to force to prevent the majority socialist group from exercising governmental powers, if and when" the SWP "was able to convince the majority to its way of thinking."

Rauh also argued that Kutcher had been denied due process because he was refused information before his hearing about any specific "circumstances" that "justified disbelief in his loyalty" despite requesting such information from the VA Board of Loyalty Appeals. Quoting the requirement of Truman's order that an employee be provided with information about the charges against him "in sufficient detail so that he will be enabled to prepare this defense" and that such "charges shall be stated as specifically and completely as, in the discretion of the employing department or agency, security considerations permit," Rauh argued that information that surfaced during Kutcher's VA appeal hearing about his May Day speech, his hearing speeches by other SWP members, and similar matters were not provided to Kutcher "until the hearing was well under way," and he was thus deprived of the opportunity to "prepare a satisfactory explanation" of the incidents, in violation of Truman's order. Moreover, Rauh argued, if security considerations were involved, the VA administrator had "greatly abused" his authority, because Kutcher's May Day speech, Trotsky's writing, and possibly other matters raised at the hearings were items "of public record." In any case, Rauh concluded, supporting his argument with extensive quotations from the transcript of the 1948 Philadelphia hearing, the evidence did not support concluding that Kutcher was disloyal to the United States, especially as he had made it "repeatedly" clear at the recent hearing that he "does not advocate the use of force and violence" to "alter the present scheme of things," and therefore Gray should be directed to restore Kutcher to his "non-sensitive" VA position "where he has performed his job well and faithfully."

The LRB considered and rejected Kutcher's appeal on the same day as the hearing, informing acting LRB Chairman Harry Blair in a June 4 letter that after reviewing Kutcher's "entire file," it had unanimously affirmed "on the basis of all of the evidence" the findings of the VA appeals board, as approved by VA administrator Gray, that "there are reasonable grounds to believe" that Kutcher was "disloyal" to the American government, that there was "reasonable doubt" as to his loyalty, and that his case "falls within the purview" of the Hatch Act. The LRB ruling, officially an "advisory" opinion to VA administrator Gray to "forthwith" remove Kutcher from VA employment, was communicated in June 5 letters from the LRB to VA, Rauh, and Kutcher. Gray directed F. R. Kerr, his assistant administrator for personnel, to effect Kutcher's removal on June 15, and Kerr informed Kutcher of the removal in a June 16 letter. Newark VA manager O'Hearn also notified Kutcher that he had been removed from his job in a June 18 letter (signed for by Kutcher on June 19) accompanied by a copy of standard form 50, "notification of personnel action," which listed "removal" in the spaced marked "nature of action." The form listed Kutcher's (suspended) salary as $2,910.

In the meantime, Rauh associate Daniel Pollitt, who had cosigned the 1953 brief submitted to the LRB, lamented to Kutcher in a June 9 letter that the LRB had clearly not given his case "any consideration" and that "the idea of writing a letter on the 5th denying an appeal hearing on the 4th is rather shocking to me." He added, referring to Kutcher's book manuscript, that he felt Kutcher would be "much more successful at the bar of public opinion." Pollitt termed the book "wonderful—very simply and clearly written, but tremendously powerful." Rauh wrote Kutcher on June 10 to report feeling "awful" about the LRB decision, which he termed a "brutal result," but added that "I suppose you are becoming numb to these things and will go on trying."

KCRC national secretary Novack wrote Rauh on June 12 to inquire what steps should be taken next, adding, "We should very much like to keep the case going, if that is realistic and feasible." Novack specifically inquired about the possibility of an "appeal to the courts," how "much money and time" such an appeal would involve, and whether Kutcher's case could be appealed only on "technicalities, or could the subversive list be challenged?" In response, Rauh told Novack in a June 15 letter that "the more I think about this case, the sorer I get" and that he was "particularly burned up" that the LRB had held against Kutcher "in a way very deliberately calculated to make our re-appeal to the courts most difficult. Without going into detail at this stage, I must state that the chances of success in the courts, in view of the Board's decision, are certainly less than an even break." Rauh added, however, that he had never felt that "the decision whether to fight on in a case like this should be predicated on any mathematical quotation of odds," since the "real question is whether one is right— and on this I am firmly convinced—except for one point," which he described as "of course" referring to Kutcher's denial before the VA appeals board "of having heard certain persons speak at SWP meetings and his later admission" of being "untruthful" on this subject. This point was troublesome, Rauh continued, because "it seems to me that the Government does have a right to bar persons from employment who do not answer questions truthfully at duly constituted hearings," but, as his associate Pollitt had reported that this issue had not arisen at the LRB hearing, he would be "prepared to argue, if the Government raised this point in the court, that they had no right to dismiss Jim on any such unmentioned ground." Rauh estimated that legal costs up until then ("two courts and the two subsequent administrative hearings") amounted to slightly over $1,000 and that "if you could raise an equivalent amount, you would cover the expenses of any new fight for a considerable time, if not the whole way."

After the new VA administrator, Harvey Higley, rejected on August 28, 1953, Kutcher's August 14 request that he be reinstated with back pay and all other benefits that would have accrued absent his loyalty discharge, KCRC national secretary Novack gave Rauh the green light to proceed with the filing of a new federal court suit. Rauh informed Novack in a September 30, 1953, letter than he had completed drafting a complaint and "was perfectly willing to make the try," although "I think we are going to get licked." Rauh and his associate Pollitt filed a seventeen-page printed complaint in the U.S. District Court for the District of Columbia on October 16; it named Higley and the CSC as defendants and asked that they be ordered to reinstate Kutcher to his position and that his firing be held "void and invalid" as illegal under the First Amendment, the Truman loyalty order, and the Veterans Preference Act of 1944. They also asked that Truman's order be declared "unconstitutional and of no effect as applied" to Kutcher as in violation of his First Amendment rights.

Rauh and Pollitt lamented in the complaint that due to his firing, Kutcher had found himself "far more unemployable" than "by reason of the loss of both his legs in the wartime service of his country." They added that it was "clear" that Kutcher's "second discharge is again solely based" on his SWP membership, in violation of the federal appeals court ruling and of constitutional due process guarantees, because the government had refused either Kutcher or the SWP a hearing to rebut the SWP's AGLOSO and Hatch Act classifications and because, even if the SWP in fact advocated the forceful overthrow of the government, Kutcher's admitted membership would not necessarily "indicate his personal advocacy of force and violence or that he knows the Socialist Workers Party so advocates." Especially since "there is no evidence in the record to support a finding" of Kutcher's "personal disloyalty," they added, and the government had never presented any evidence against him beyond his admitted SWP membership, they concluded that "it can only be assumed" that Higley's endorsement of Gray's earlier ruling "was based solely on that membership and that his statement that it was based 'on all the evidence' is merely pro forma and without any substance."

Rauh and Pollitt also argued that Kutcher's discharge was unlawful because even "if there were circumstances and activities" connected with Kutcher's SWP membership "sufficient to justify disbelief in his loyalty, the second discharge is nonetheless invalid because the notice of charges failed to specify these circumstances and activities despite repeated requests for such charges." Noting that Truman's loyalty order had required that charges be presented "in sufficient detail, so that [an employee] will be enabled to prepare his defense" and be "stated as specifically and completely, as in the discretion of the employing department agency or agency security considerations permit" and that the Veterans Preference Act of 1944 required that "any and all reasons, specifically and in detail" be presented to justify proposed firings, Kutcher's lawyers proclaimed that, especially since no "security considerations" were ever "mentioned as justification for lack" of specifications, Kutcher's rights had been violated by the "repeated refusal" of the VA and LRB boards to provide such information and by Higley's refusal to reinstate Kutcher, which effectively "reaffirmed the discharge based on inadequate notification of charges." Finally, they maintained that, because Kutcher had occupied an entirely "non-sensitive" position that "could not threaten or affect the 'security' of the nation," his job ratings had been positive, and he had never sought to discuss his political views with fellow employees, his firing was simply an "act of vengeance against one whose political beliefs are unpopular" and therefore an unjustifiable violation of his First Amendment rights, the Truman order, and the Veterans Preference Act, including the latter's provision that discharges could be made only "for such cause as will promote the efficiency of the service." This was because, they argued, any "valid restraint" of First Amendment rights had to be "reasonable and justifiable," while in Kutcher's case there was "no reasonable relationship" between his views and the "internal security" of the country and therefore "as a practical matter" he had been "denied the right to express himself concerning his political beliefs although such expression in no way and at no time can affect the security of the United States government."

U.S. attorney Leo Rover and three assistant U.S. attorneys filed a ten-page typed double-spaced motion with the district court on February 4, 1954, calling for dismissal of the complaint on the grounds that it had failed "to state a cause of action" because "no rights of the plaintiff, constitutional, statutory, or judicially-defined" had been "invaded," as the government had "carefully complied" with the earlier federal appeals court ruling. Rejecting the argument that Kutcher's First Amendment and due process rights had been violated, Rover maintained that legal precedents had made it "clear that insofar as retention of government employment is concerned, no one has any constitutional rights, procedural or substantive," and thus all allegations "which charge invasion of constitutional rights fail to state a cause of action."

The government's motion backed this position by quoting from the federal appeals court in *Bailey*, upheld by the Supreme Court's 4–4 ruling in 1951, which had found that there was no constitutional bar to the "dismissal of government employees because of their political beliefs, activities or affiliations" and that the "due process clause does not apply to the holding of government office." The government also quoted from the Kutcher appeals court ruling ordering the VA to reconsider Kutcher's firing, which, in seeming disregard of *McGrath*, had found the SWP listing "competent evidence in the administrative proceeding against Kutcher." Rover and his fellow U.S. attorneys also rejected the charge that Kutcher's "second discharge" had violated the terms of the federal appeals court ruling on the grounds that Gray's 1953 dismissal was based on a finding of "disloyalty" following "further hearings" and "additional testimony." They maintained that the appeals court "was not ruling upon the question of what might support a finding of disloyalty" and that existing legal precedents established that in fact "the courts will not inquire into the basis for dismissal," and therefore that "all allegations" that "defendants have acted contrary to the Court of Appeals decision do not state a cause of action."

The government also rejected Kutcher's allegations concerning a lack of specificity in the charges against him by noting that he had not questioned the "sufficiency of the notice of charges in the first [1948 Philadelphia VA branch loyalty board] proceedings" and by maintaining that the appeals court had made "no suggestion" that new charges were "required." It maintained that "the original charges carried over with equal applicability to the second proceeding which had as its sole purpose" a determination of Kutcher's "personal loyalty" and that the *Bailey* appeals court had found that specification of charges was "wholly discretionary" in the executive branch, as indicated by Truman's order. Concerning the argument that Kutcher's firing violated the Veterans Preference Act ban on dismissals which did not "promote the efficiency of the service," the government cited a phrase in the Kutcher appeals court ruling declaring that "the efficiency of public service as a whole, rather than efficiency of performance by a single employee," was at issue, and therefore it could "not be argued that removal of a disloyal employee is not promotive of the 'efficiency of the service.'"

A remarkable August 18, 1954, letter from Rauh associate Daniel Pollitt to KCRC national secretary George Novack reported that, after Kutcher's lawyers filed a memorandum in opposition to the government's motion to dismiss, the government withdrew its motion. According to Pollitt, a new government lawyer assigned to the case, whom he characterized as a "close friend of mine" (later identified as Joseph Ryan), "started to read the record" and then submitted on August 11 a "motion for summary judgment [for the government] instead of some other motion at least partly because I asked him to do so." Pollitt added that Ryan had appended to his motion "all the papers in the case since the [August 1952] Court of Appeals decision," which he termed "very interesting, as they included [the] lengthy [April 20, 1953] memorandum giving the rationale" for the VA Loyalty Board of Appeals decision, previously withheld from the defense. Pollitt declared that this new development put the defense "in a pretty good position," because although the district court "will undoubtedly grant the Government's motion" in light of a recent federal appeals court affirming a separate loyalty dismissal "on the basis of *Bailey*," with "the whole [Kutcher] record" now before the court there would be "no need for a trial" and "we can go all the way up to the Supreme Court and get a decision on the merits." Pollitt added that the district court had asked for a defense response to the motion for summary judgment within a month and that oral argument (although not a full-fledged trial with witness testimony) in the case would then be scheduled.

Oral argument before federal district court judge Alexander Holtzoff was held on October 13, 1954, followed by a ruling on November 3, which to the great surprise of the defense (and no doubt also to the government), granted Kutcher's request for summary judgment on what Rauh termed (in a June 9, 1955, letter to Novack) the "most peculiar ground" that VA administrator Higley, in upholding his predecessor Gray's dismissal of Kutcher without specifying any rationale, had "failed to make the definitive determination" of Kutcher's "disloyalty as required" by the 1952 federal appeals court ruling. In response to this ruling, Higley signed a "review decision" on February 3, 1955, which declared that he had adopted Gray's April 23 finding and that it was his determination that "on all the evidence there are reasonable grounds for doubt" as to Kutcher's loyalty and "reasonable grounds for belief" that Kutcher "is disloyal to the Government of the United States."

The government filed this declaration with the district court by on February 7, along with another motion asking for summary judgment, which entirely incorporated its earlier August 11, 1954, motion and all the attached exhibits. According to the filing, which was signed by U.S. attorney Rover along with three assistant U.S. attorneys (including Ryan), the court was required to grant the motion "since there is no dispute as to any material fact and defendants are entitled to judgment as a matter of law." Rauh and Pollitt then filed on May 9, 1955, a cross-motion asking for summary judgment on Kutcher's behalf on the identical grounds cited by the government. In oral argument before federal district court judge Burnita Matthews on May 10, Pollitt declared that Kutcher's job had "no more to do with the security of the country than a grocery clerk," and thus his firing violated his First Amendment rights, that Kutcher was never told why the government viewed the SWP as subversive, and that Kutcher had not been given details of the charges against him before his original 1948 VA loyalty board hearing. In response, U.S. attorney Ryan maintained that federal court precedents required Kutcher's dismissal.

Judge Matthews rejected Kutcher's position and granted the government request for summary judgment on June 2, 1955, without a written opinion, holding that there was no dispute over the facts and that the government was entitled to summary judgment under the law. Kutcher was thereupon given thirty days to file an appeal, along with a required $250 appeal bond. In a June 9, 1955, letter informing Novack of these developments, Rauh reported not "having heard from you or Jim Kutcher for a long time" and asked for a prompt reply as to "what your present thoughts are on the case," which Rauh termed "not as strong as it was the first time we went to court, particularly because the [VA Loyalty Board of Appeals] said it didn't believe Jim." Rauh added that "no case is hopeless" and that "if you want an appeal we are game to try it," but that, in addition to the refundable bond about $1,000 would be required for additional legal costs "largely for help in preparing the appeal brief" because "although I will continue to work without compensation," his office's schedule was "too crowded for anybody here to write the brief and we will have to get some additional help to write it under my supervision." Although KCRC records for this period are incomplete, apparently due to the onset of what was diagnosed as a case of "nervous exhaustion" in KCRC secretary Novack, the group apparently immediately decided to authorize Rauh to commence working on an appeal. In response to a letter from Rauh reporting that bond companies "don't want to get involved in cases involving political minority groups," KCRC treasurer George Weissman asked ACLU attorney Herbert Levy on June 9 if the ACLU could provide "critical" assistance by posting the appeal bond, since the KCRC "has only a small bank balance and it will strain its resources to raise the necessary $1000." According to Weissman's handwritten note in the KCRC files, the ACLU reported on June 30 that it was arranging for a bond company to post the $1,000.

In the meantime, on June 23, 1955, AGLOSO was dealt a sharp blow by a federal appeals court ruling that held that Max Shachtman, leader of the AGLOSO-designated Independent Socialist League (ISL), a split off the SWP, could not be denied a passport solely because he belonged to an AGLOSO organization. The court termed the government's action "arbitrary" because the ISL had been designated "without notice or hearing or presentation of evidence or opportunity to answer." Weissman informed Rauh in a July 12 letter that he was taking "charge" of the KCRC due to Novack's illness while also reporting that "everyone interested in civil liberties was delighted with the outcome of *Shachtman* and the disorderly rout of the passport officials that followed so quickly," especially since the 1952 Kutcher appeals court ruling had been cited in it. In answer to an August 2 plea from Rauh for him to "promptly" come up with money for the appeals costs, on August 5 Weissman sent a $300 "first installment" check, reporting that "our fund raising campaign is just getting under way" but that he would "of course, send you the next payment as promptly as possible" and would "not dally on raising the balance of the expense money." Weissman added that, aside from the *Shachtman* case, "we have all been watching the developments" with regard to the Justice Department's initiation of an AGLOSO-designation administrative appeal hearing granted to the ISL "with gratification and high hopes for the future." Referring to several other recent court rulings, he added that "from the succession of court victories in civil liberties cases and the political trend it represents, we are convinced the Kutcher case will come to have a greater civil liberties significance than ever." After the KCRC directed Rauh to proceed, Kutcher's lawyers gave notice of their intent to appeal to the federal appeals court for the District of Columbia on July 1, 1955 (with the ACLU providing money for the appeal bond).

Weissman's reference to *Shachtman* and other recent favorable court rulings, including a number of Gwinn Act cases discussed in the next chapter, reflected a clear improvement in the general civil liberties climate that was evident by mid-1955. In the 1954 congressional elections, Democrats won control of both houses for the first time since 1946, despite the use of the "soft on communism" issue against them by many Republicans, and in December 1954 Senator McCarthy was "censured" for misconduct by the Senate by a 67–22 vote, with all Democrats and half of the Republicans voting against him. Earlier in 1954 he had been considerably discredited by a now famous television program anchored by leading CBS newsman Edward R. Murrow as well as during the sensational, nationally televised so-called Army-McCarthy hearings, related to his charges that the army had sought to cover up alleged tolerance of Communists. In 1953, the death of Russian dictator Stalin and the end of the Korean War had helped to considerably ease Cold War tensions. By mid-1955, several congressional committees were holding hearings of alleged abuses in the federal loyalty program, including AGLOSO, and numerous press commentaries were taking note of an increasing backlash against perceived civil liberties abuses during the Red Scare.

CHAPTER FIVE

Kutcher Wins Three Victories within Four Months (1955–1956)

On October 17, 1955, Kutcher's lawyer Joseph Rauh filed a brief with the federal appeals court for the District of Columbia, appealing from Kutcher's June 2, 1955, loss in federal district court in his struggle to regain his job. Rauh reiterated what were by then well-established arguments, namely that Kutcher had been denied due process of law because the original 1948 charges against him were inadequately specified under both loyalty program and VA regulations; that while Kutcher had been fired "merely because" of his SWP "membership and activities," that organization had never been allowed to contest its AGLOSO listing; that both Kutcher and the SWP denied that the group was subversive; and that, since Kutcher admittedly had held a "non-sensitive" position at the VA and his "political views had no more to do with this country's security than do those of a clerk in a chain super market," his dismissal was a violation of his "constitutional free speech and substantive due process rights" under the First and Fifth Amendments.

Rauh also complained that Kutcher had first learned about the VA Loyalty Board of Appeals' lengthy secret April 23, 1953, justification for recommending his dismissal during the recent district court proceedings and that the board had relied in its statement upon "matters entirely beyond the notice of charges," including alleged acts and utterances by Kutcher and references to a memorandum from the attorney general and the circumstances of a 1943 appeals court ruling resulting from the 1941 Smith Act convictions of top SWP leaders. Rauh maintained that the board's reliance upon Kutcher's "associations and public utterances" in determining his knowledge of the SWP's purposes "constituted fatal departure from the stated charges" and that its heavy dependence upon the attorney general's memo and the 1943 appeals court ruling—information that "easily" could have been furnished Kutcher at his hearing but was withheld—created a situation in which Kutcher "could hardly have refuted such information without the benefit of clairvoyant powers."

In complaining about the government's failure to grant the SWP a hearing to challenge its AGLOSO listing, Rauh maintained that the 1951 Supreme Court *McGrath* ruling and the recent federal appeals court ruling in *Shachtman* suggested that such failure constituted a "patent violation of constitutional due process guarantees." Rauh concluded that Kutcher was the "victim of a 20th century inquisition into his social, economic and political beliefs" and that unless his dismissal were reversed it would cast a "broad censorship over minority and non-conformist political and economic views" held by both current federal employees and

> all those who have an eye to future Government employment. . . . In essence, the Government has sought to punish by discharge those of its millions of employees whom it could not reach through criminal proceedings because their only "crime" was membership in or association with unpopular organizations. . . . The resulting sacrifice of traditional liberties of association and speech in the name of "security" interests has produced only a profound insecurity among millions of loyal Federal employees.

While the federal appeals court considered Kutcher's arguments, important developments occurred in his case against the Newark Housing Authority in connection with the 1952 Gwinn Act, which had required the expulsion from federally subsidized housing of all families with any members who belonged to AGLOSO organizations. In response to the lawsuit that Kutcher and the ACLU had filed in February 1953, seeking to have the Gwinn Act declared unconstitutional and to enjoin the NHA from further pursuing eviction proceedings, Judge Walter Freund had stayed the eviction on March 19, 1953, pending a ruling. In October 1953, in final briefs filed in the case, the NHA argued that no constitutional rights were breached by excluding public housing tenants who refused to sign a non-AGLOSO oath in a case in which the "selfish few would prevent the court from protesting the rights and happiness of many." It added that nonsigners "should not be permitted to dictate under what rules they will accept bounties of Congress." After considering the case for eighteen months, on March 18, 1955, New Jersey Superior Court Judge G. Doxon Speakman enjoined the NHA from evicting non-signing families on the extremely narrow and technical grounds that while the Gwinn Act required federally subsidized tenants to disavow membership in organizations deemed "subversive" by the attorney general, the NHA oath required residents to swear they did not belong to *any* of the almost 300 AGLOSO groups, even though only a handful (including the SWP) had been specifically subcategorized as "subversive." Thus, the court avoided any constitutional ruling while still awarding a victory to Kutcher and the other plaintiffs.

The NHA appealed the ruling on October 10, 1955 (one week before Kutcher filed his appeals court brief in the job dismissal case), to the New Jersey Supreme Court, which unanimously upheld the lower court ruling on December 15, 1955, in a holding that was reported on the front page of the December 19 *Newark Evening News*, and the next day in many other papers, including the *New York Times* and the *Washington Post*. Writing for the court, Judge Harry Heher adopted the same approach as the lower court, holding additionally that even membership in a subversive group would not sustain an "administrative decision to evict a tenant from public housing absent proof that the individual had knowledge of the organization's 'character.'"

While the ruling provided a final victory for Kutcher at the state level in the Gwinn Act matter, New Jersey could still appeal to the federal courts. However, after the federal Public Housing Authority had lost numerous other Gwinn Act cases in a series of lawsuits around the country, the Justice Department announced on August 3, 1956, that it was abandoning further efforts to enforce the act, on the grounds that it was "temporary legislation" that had expired. Kutcher relates that the victory was "most welcome in our home," as his father, suffering from diabetes, had just had his right leg amputated.

In the meantime, the greatest controversy yet concerning Kutcher had erupted when the federal government initiated action shortly before Christmas 1955 to have Kutcher's World War II disability pension, his sole remaining source of income, cut off due to his political activities and affiliations. On December 12, 1955, the VA informed Kutcher by letter that it was considering canceling his World War II disability pension of $329 monthly under a 1943 congressional statute that declared such benefits void in cases where a veteran had been determined to be "guilty of mutiny, treason, sabotage, or rendering assistance to an enemy of the United States or of its allies."

The VA informed Kutcher that its basis for considering such action was his active SWP membership and his "numerous activities over the year" seeking to further "its aims and activities," given the SWP's classification by "duly authorized" American officials as seeking the unconstitutional alteration of the government. In addition, the VA said that "it appears" that Kutcher had provided "aid and assistance" to an enemy of the United States or its allies by "espousing and defending" the SWP, thus providing "aid and comfort to the enemy" by influencing others to undermine the "public interest and cooperation and confidence" in the American government's "administration of the [Korean] war effort and hampering and obstructing such effort." Furthermore, without indicating to Kutcher any sources (but clearly drawing upon, for example, the February 25, 1953, Pittsburgh FBI memo, based on reports from confidential informants), he was charged with stating at an SWP camp in 1950 or 1951 that he liked the "red" system of government, "which gave to workers all that they earned, while under the existing system half of workers' earnings went to the government"; that the American government was composed of "crooks and cheaters who oppress the working people"; that he had urged camp members to cause strikes and, along with the SWP, to gain key positions to control the American government; and that he had stated that the existing government should be overthrown and its members killed and replaced by a new government. The VA informed Kutcher that he was entitled to a formal hearing, with counsel, on its proposed action, but that the matter would be determined without his input if no response was received from him within thirty days.

After receiving notice of the December 12 VA letter from Kutcher, KCRC treasurer George Weissman wrote to inform Rauh about the new development on December 15, terming it a "most alarming attack since the pension is his only means of support—and his parents are poor and aged." Weissman reported that he had asked Kutcher not to publicize the matter or reply to the VA before he had received advice from Rauh and asked the latter for a "preliminary opinion," which "would serve to help Jimmy out of the despairing frame of mind he is now in." Before Rauh could respond, the VA contacted Kutcher again, on December 15, and without any further explanation, announced that it had suspended his disability pension "effective the date you were last paid by this Administration," pending a final determination by the VA's Central Committee on Waivers and Forfeitures.

In his autobiography, Kutcher noted that the rest of the country learned about the VA's decision "just before Christmas, a matter of timing that probably increased the public's indignation with which the news was greeted," but that "nobody's indignation was greater than mine," as although he had been relatively stoic about "the loss of my job and the threat to our house," this attack "struck me as a really foul blow," especially as the pension issue had never been raised during the prior seven years. It was "all the more shocking that the government not only raised it in 1955 but proposed to do something about it without delay," Kutcher wrote. Moreover, since the December 12 letter specifically referred to "all" VA benefits, he feared this would include "not only the pension, but the artificial limbs, free medical care, hospitalizations at the VA hospital, etc."

Upon receiving the news, Rauh wrote a bitter four-page single-spaced typed letter to the VA committee on December 22 terming the allegations against Kutcher "meaningless and unfounded," demanding that the VA "immediately dismiss the charges and revoke the suspension," and requesting a hearing "at the earliest possible moment" if this was not done. Rauh termed the suspension, which he said was based on charges that were either untrue or protected under the First Amendment, an instance of "punishment without trial" that would leave Kutcher "without any means of livelihood or support for himself or his aged parents." He added that while he had represented a variety of people before congressional committees and government loyalty boards, "we never thought we would be forced to defend a treason charge against a legless veteran before an agency set up to protect veterans' rights" and that not even Senator McCarthy would "stoop to make the allegations you have made against a penniless, crippled war hero" simply because he had "criticized our country."

Rauh declared that Kutcher had explicitly disavowed supporting "force or violence of any kind" in his loyalty board hearings, maintained that the SWP AGLOSO listing had been nullified by the Supreme Court's 1951 *McGrath* ruling, and argued that "even if your charges were true they couldn't possibly amount to aid to the enemy," which Rauh noted that the VA had alleged Kutcher "appears" to have engaged in. Rauh said that any schoolchild would "laugh at the thought" that Kutcher's actions constituted "treason," as this was the "only crime specifically defined in the Constitution" and required a criminal trial with "traditional safeguards," and could not be "determined without trial, by administrative officials acting on hearsay assertions by undisclosed informants," but "apparently any citizen who has been crippled in combat fighting for his country, may be found guilty of 'treason'" by VA officials "without any hearing of any type." Rauh also denied that Kutcher could have rendered assistance to the enemy even if the charges against him were true, since the United States was "not at war" (a reference to the fact that the country had never formally declared war during the Korean conflict).

Rauh declared that the VA appeared "unaware" that the First Amendment protected freedom of speech and was "laboring under a cultural lag because it doesn't know that McCarthyism was ended in 1954," an apparent reference to the very recent Senate censure, and denied that the charges in any way indicated that Kutcher had given "aid and comfort to any enemy," an allegation that he maintained could just as easily be leveled against Republican critics of President Truman's Korean War efforts, including President Eisenhower, who during his successful 1952 presidential campaign had declared the war had resulted from the "weak" foreign policies of the Truman administration. Rauh asked, "Are you going to find every major Republican leader in this country guilty of treason, as you propose to do in Mr. Kutcher's case, because during the 1952 campaign when we were at war they criticized their Government?" In fact, Rauh alleged the VA itself was "under your own standards" guilty of rendering "aid and comfort to the enemy" by "undermining public interest and confidence" in the government by its action against Kutcher "far more effectively than any of the conduct" alleged against him, and "certainly our communist enemy will be comforted in knowing that our crippled veterans may no longer criticize this government or its leaders without being branded as traitors and forced to look to charity to stay alive." SWP national secretary Farrell Dobbs, in a December 22 letter to local chapters, sarcastically termed the VA's new action a "Christmas present" for Kutcher, accompanied by "outrageous new witch-hunting charges" against him; in a follow-up January 6, 1956, letter, written after Kutcher's VA hearing on the proposed termination of his pension but before a decision had been announced, Dobbs urged that local KCRC committees "redouble" their efforts and reported that "record publicity" about the matter and the "generally sympathetic nature of the publicity should help promote a mass response to Kutcher's appeal for aid in his heroic defiance of the witch hunters."

No doubt in response to Rauh's letter or to intense and widespread press coverage and criticism of the VA's suspension of Kutcher's pension pending a hearing, VA chief benefits director Ralph Stone suddenly announced on December 23 (only six hours after the story was first reported in the *New York Post*), following a high-level meeting of VA officials, that the agency was reversing its position and restoring the pension until the matter was resolved "out of a sense of fair play and to prevent hardship" to Kutcher. Stone added that the original order had been countermanded because Kutcher's was an "unusual case," since suspensions had never been ordered prior to a formal determination in other cases except where veterans had been convicted under the 1940 Smith (sedition) Act, as with at least two Communist Party leaders.

Kutcher, who would turn 44 on December 26 and (as discussed above) had just won a major New Jersey lawsuit against attempts to evict his family from their federally subsidized public housing, told reporters upon receiving the news about the pension suspension reversal that he viewed the decision as a "reprieve, but not a victory" and that his lawyers would "insist on my right to confront my accusers" at the forthcoming hearing and "I think we will win." He denied making any of the "wild statements" attributed to him by the

VA, adding that the "only thing" he had "ever said is that I prefer a socialist" to a capitalist system of "government," a change to be "accomplished by constitutional means. There is certainly nothing illegal about that." Kutcher also told reporters that he was currently taking printing courses at a New York trade school and watching western "shoot-'em-up" movies during his spare time.

Kutcher's mother was quoted as telling KCRC treasurer George Weissman at the Kutchers' apartment that "all America has been calling here" since word of the suspension began to circulate, while a VA official reported that "my phone has never stopped ringing" with press inquiries about the matter. Weissman termed the reversal of the pension suspension a "sign that public opinion in this country is going to force the Government to give Jimmy Kutcher his due." Among such indications were an announcement of an investigation of the Kutcher matter by House Veterans Committee chairman Olin Teague, expressions of concern by several senators, and denunciation of the VA by the American Veterans Committee and even leaders of the New York City CP, which in general had been cool to Kutcher's plight in light of long-standing disagreements between the SWP and the CP, but now termed VA officials "heartless hacks."

After the VA informed Kutcher (apparently on December 27) that it was scheduling a hearing of its Central Committee on Waivers and Forfeitures to hear his appeal on December 30, Rauh immediately telegrammed VA administrator Higley, again denying that the VA had the authority to charge Kutcher with "treason" or hold a hearing on such an allegation, and demanding that that the hearing be open to the press since "no one should be tried under charges of treason in a star chamber proceeding and least of all someone who has given so much for his country—Kutcher has nothing to hide." Rauh's demand for an open meeting was publicly supported by Tennessee Democratic senator Estes Kefauver, who had gained national prominence as chairman of a committee investigating organized crime a few years earlier. Kefauver declared that not only as a "veteran with a gallant war record but as an American citizen" Kutcher was entitled to a "public hearing and a full opportunity to confront his accusers." Rauh also demanded that Kutcher be confronted with his accusers at the hearing, since "whoever says Kutcher has committed treason in rendering assistance to an enemy" should be willing to explain such allegations, especially since the Constitution declared that no one could be convicted of treason without two witnesses charging such in open court. Although Rauh conceded that Kutcher's "punishment" by the VA would not be imprisonment, he declared that loss of his pension would be "equally serious" and that to "convict Kutcher on charges of treason in a secret hearing without witnesses and without proof of any overt act" would be a "mockery of due process of law."

Apparently again in response to Rauh's appeal or to massive press coverage and criticism of the VA's action against Kutcher, the VA announced on December 28 that the December 30 hearing would be open to press (including television) coverage, with acting VA administrator John Patterson wiring Kutcher that "your wishes in this matter will be honored." All prior such hearings had been closed to the press, although a VA spokesman reported that media access had never been requested before and added that, based on past procedures, Kutcher would probably not be allowed to confront his accusers. According to press reports, the VA decision to allow media access was reached at a 3½-hour meeting of top VA officials, who also reportedly decided not to allow Kutcher to confront his accusers given the government's policy of not permitting such proceedings during loyalty-related hearings. Numerous reporters attended and provided massive coverage of the hearing, which convened at 1 PM on December 30, 1955, and lasted two hours and whose transcript filled seventy-five double-spaced typed pages.

Three members of the VA Committee on Waivers and Forfeitures, including acting chairman Peyton Moss, along with members John Cumberland and George Hunter, convened the hearing; Rauh and his associate John Silard appeared, along with Kutcher, on the latter's behalf. Kutcher, described in the press as a short, balding, stocky man, dramatically entered the hearing room walking on his artificial legs with the assistance of his two canes. Moss began the hearing by reading the text of the December 12 VA letter to Kutcher, after declaring that the hearing was "not a trial" but was solely intended to offer him an opportunity to rebut the "charges" against him, with the understanding that the pension of a "seriously disabled combat veteran" would be suspended only if the "evidence shows beyond a reasonable doubt that the veteran has committed one of the offenses" specified in the 1943 law. He then added, in response to Rauh's communications, that although the language of some of the allegations in the December 12 letter was similar to the constitutional definition of "treason," the VA's general counsel, in a January 15, 1954, opinion, had held that the 1943 statute described a "different offense from that of treason," and that while war had not been formally declared in the Korean conflict, "there can be no possible doubt that a war" had in fact existed since June 1950 and that North Korea and China were enemies of the United States. Moss also declared that under a May 17, 1954, presidential directive the "sources of the evidence" leading to the allegations against Kutcher "will not be disclosed."

Kutcher thereupon took the stand and swore to testify truthfully, after which an exchange immediately followed between Rauh and Moss that dominated the massive press accounts concerning the hearing. When Rauh asked for a "copy of the rules and regulations governing this hearing," Moss responded, "No, sir" and "we can't do that" because "there are too many rules and regulations" and "we couldn't give you that to cover any particular hearing." After Rauh asked, "Do I understand that there are no rules governing this hearing," Moss responded that there "certainly" were and that as acting chairman "I will, in a sense, determine what shall be done at the hearing." When Rauh persisted in requesting to be informed about the "rules we are going to go by," Moss responded that he "didn't see that has a pertinent bearing" and that the "request comes a little too late," and if Rauh "wanted all the rules you should have consulted us beforehand. We can't bring any of the regulations and rules and laws in here right now." Rauh thereupon suggested that "you don't have any rules for this hearing"; Moss said, "Certainly we have rules but you cannot get them." During subsequent exchanges, Rauh declared that this was "the first time in my life I have ever been to a hearing of an administrative tribunal in which there were no" rules, and VA acting general counsel Meyer Lipps conceded that "there are no written published rules for guidance" and that the committee was "guided by their own procedures of manner in conducting the hearing." When Rauh thereupon asked, "In other words there are no rules for conducting . . . this hearing?" Lipps conceded, "That is correct," and Moss declared, "Okay. I will make the rules as I go along then."

Rauh then repeated his complaint that even if all allegations made against Kutcher in the VA's December 12 letter were correct this would not justify withdrawing Kutcher's pension because they effectively charged Kutcher with treason, but such a finding required a jury trial "after all the fair play of a court room," because "this body has no authority to find Mr. Kutcher guilty of anything," and because the "sole forfeiture authority is in cases where the courts" had made findings of guilt. Moss then denied a request for dismissing the case on the grounds cited by Rauh, and Lipps declared that the VA "is authorized to make a finding of guilty of its own" with regard to denying benefits. Rauh maintained that the VA had never done so before without a court finding, but Moss responded that there were "numerous" such cases, especially with regard to American veterans in the Philippine Islands and Italy. In response to a query from Rauh, Moss conceded that he was unaware of any cases in the United States during the four years he had served on the VA committee in which a veteran had "lost his pension except after conviction in a court of law."

Rauh then argued as a second "ground for dismissal" of the case that even if the charges against Kutcher were all true, "no crime has been alleged," because the constitutional definition of treason required seeking to aid an American enemy and "there is no allegation of a particular act of helping the enemy, there is nothing in here except a censorship of Mr. Kutcher's public statements." He maintained that "nothing in the letter of charges could possibly have done as much to undermine the war efforts" as statements made by Republican critics of the Truman administration's Korean War effort during the 1952 election campaign, and "when you start censorship of what people have to say you can't stop." Rauh maintained that what the VA "is doing here is setting itself up as a right to censor what pensioners may say" by threatening to take away their benefits, and that, in any case, "I believe that the courts will bear us out if we have to go there, that there is no allegation" in the December 12 letter of "any crime within the meaning" of the 1943 statute. When Moss thereupon denied Rauh's "motion" to dismiss the charges on these grounds and Rauh asked if it would be "too much to ask for a reason for the denial," Moss responded, "Yes. I don't think that is customary" and "I don't think that is necessary."

Rauh thereupon declared that he had no alternative but to "go on with the case" but again argued that "so far as I am concerned this is a trial" of Kutcher for "rendering assistance" to an American enemy and "if it is the last thing I ever do, if this pension is taken away we will be in court if we have to be there for the same seven years we have been in court on Mr. Kutcher's loyalty case." He added that the "burden of proof" appeared to be on Kutcher as the VA has not "put in one iota of evidence" and "done nothing" to prove its case, leading Moss to respond that "we are affording Mr. Kutcher, and naturally his attorneys, an opportunity to answer the charges" and that the VA felt that it had a "prima facie" case against Kutcher under the 1943 law. When Rauh declared that the December 12 letter was "not evidence" but "charges," and "not a whit of evidence has been put in," Moss responded that "this is not a court trial."

Acting VA general counsel Lipps then suggested to Moss that it was "proper to emphasize" that the VA "is not, repeat, is not charging Mr. Kutcher with treason," to which Moss responded, "Certainly we are not charging him with treason." When Rauh asked what the difference was between the allegations against Kutcher and a charge of treason, Moss responded, "the charges have been set forth in the charge letter, and I don't think I'm called upon to define the crime" otherwise. Making clear that his strategy was aimed at gaining sympathetic press coverage, Rauh then declared that he would "leave it to the gentlemen of the press to decide whether this is a treason trial or not," leading Lipps to proclaim that the hearing was "not criminal, it is administrative," and although the charge of "rendering assistance" might have "substantially the same meaning" it was not "treason because the Congress [in the 1943 law] saw fit to add another offense not criminal."

After a prolonged exchange along these lines, Moss directed Rauh to "go ahead and answer the charges." When Rauh asked "the name of the country that Mr. Kutcher is supposed to have aided," Moss responded, "Communist China and North Korea," but when Rauh asked for specifics of how he had aided them Moss declared, "I can only repeat what we have already written to Mr. Kutcher. Mr. Rauh, I will just simply read this over again, since it appears that you don't understand it." This comment set off a series of bitter exchanges between Moss and Rauh, with Moss declaring, to Rauh's disbelief, that "a man who causes strikes during time of war," along with the "other things" that Kutcher "did and said," was "rendering assistance to the enemy." When Moss added that his understanding was that the SWP was "sympathetic with the North Koreans," Rauh offered to "take you out of your ignorance," which he amended to "out of your lack of knowledge" when Moss declared, "I object to your saying that." Rauh declared that the SWP opposed the governments of both North Korea and China and that "right now I don't know what" Kutcher was accused of as he was seemingly "being charged with rendering assistance" to governments that he opposed. Moss then retorted, "I can't help you in your ignorance," referring Rauh to Kutcher's "activity over the years as a member of the Party" as "outlined in the charge letter" when Rauh asked for specifics as to how Kutcher how aided the enemy.

Moss then began to question Kutcher without responding to further questions from Rauh about specific charges. When Rauh's associate Silard sought to "interject," Moss responded that Silard should "let me proceed" as "I am conducting this hearing." When Rauh then objected that Moss seemed to be "changing the rules in the middle," Moss declared, "I am making the rules now and I am going ahead with these questions. I have given you an opportunity which you haven't taken." Moss proceeded to ask Kutcher questions about his SWP activities, sometimes allowing Rauh to object, but at other times cutting Silard and Rauh short by declaring, "I am asking questions here and I don't propose to be interrupted every minute while I am doing it" and "if you will wait until I finish my question then you can make your objection." At one point during Rauh's subsequent questioning of Kutcher, Moss and Lipps both declared that Rauh's queries seemed to lack "any bearing on the hearing," although Moss told Rauh, "if you feel that they do" that he "may proceed."

In response to questions from Moss (and later from his own attorneys), Kutcher denied urging that an American flag be torn up during an SWP convention in New York City (as had been alleged in one FBI report) and he denied making what he termed supposed "wild statements" during an Ohio appearance (as another FBI report alleged) that the SWP would engage in forceful means to take over the government. When Moss said his latter denial was "inconsistent with the information we have," Rauh declared that it had come from a "secret informer that you won't produce face to face with us." During his question period, Rauh declared that Kutcher was the first person in American history to be charged with "treason or rendering assistance" to American enemies as a result of "belonging to a political party" that appeared on American ballots "or for criticizing the government of the United States here at home during war time." Kutcher told Rauh that he supported himself and his two parents, both of whom he reported were in their mid-seventies, with his $390 monthly disability pension, that the first indication that he might lose it was "just a few weeks ago," and that no one had doubted his loyalty when he had lost his legs during World War II, even though he had already joined the SWP by then. Kutcher denied to Rauh ever being guilty of treason or sabotage or "knowingly consciously" giving "assistance to an enemy of the United States or of its allies," "knowingly obstructing the war effort" in any way, or ever advocating "betrayal of this country, mutiny, desertion, sabotage, or any crime of any kind."

Kutcher also denied making all of the specific statements attributed to him in the December 12 VA letter, including the allegation that those currently in the American government "should be overthrown and killed and then [the country] should get a new Government," terming them "nothing but an unmitigated lie." In response to Rauh's questions, Kutcher reiterated his past statements supporting the introduction of a "socialist society" in the United States by peaceful means, which he declared had been his "views over the last 18 years" as "an ordinary" SWP member, as well as those of the party itself. He specifically denied that he or the SWP advocated the violent overthrow of the government, repeating an earlier statement that the "only time in my life" he had practiced "force and violence" was "when I was in the Army of the United States." Kutcher also declared that the SWP and the Communist Party had been "bitter opponents" throughout his SWP membership and that he had consistently viewed the Soviet Union as a "degenerated workers' state" and a "dictatorship." Kutcher agreed with Rauh's characterization that "you and your party" view the North Korean and Chinese Communist regimes as "dictatorships" and "are opposed to them," while adding that "people there should be left alone to work out their problems without any outside interference" and that "if I or any member of my party were to go to the Soviet Union or to Communist China or North Korea, we would be dead." Kutcher added that, whatever the outcome of the hearing, he would remain an SWP member.

After concluding his questions, Rauh closed by declaring that the statements that Kutcher was accused of making "largely" dated from before the 1950 outbreak of the Korean War and thus he could not have "rendered assistance to an enemy" because "there wasn't any enemy prior to 1950." He added that to find Kutcher guilty "you have got to produce" instead of "presuming guilt," but by failing to produce any witnesses or "one fact against Mr. Kutcher" the VA had "nothing" and provided not "one iota of evidence" that Kutcher had rendered assistance to the enemy "whether you call it treason or rendering assistance." Since Kutcher had denied all specific allegations and the VA had produced "no evidence against him whatever," Rauh declared that "when you clear him" the committee would be doing both Kutcher and the American people a favor as "there is enough feeling in this country about this case that if you take away his pension, a lot of people will give their nickels and dimes to support him" and "keep him and his parents from starving to death."

Rauh added that the "American people" would be "ashamed" were the VA to take away "the pension of a man who gave his health for his country on the basis of what has happened here today," which he characterized as a hearing with "no evidence against us" and "without rules and regulations," "without adequate charges," and based on allegations that "should have been tried in a court room." Rauh concluded by declaring that the American people wanted a "favorable decision" to Kutcher "and they want it quickly," and there was no reason why the committee could not make such a ruling "this afternoon and terminate this business," as there was "still time—it is only three o'clock." Both Moss and Lipps declared during Rauh's questioning that the VA did not view SWP membership alone as constituting "aid to an enemy of the United States," but Moss made no additional substantive remarks in concluding the hearing, stating only that while no decision could be made that day, a transcript would be made and carefully studied "before we do render our decision."

On January 8, 1956, less than three weeks after his New Jersey Gwinn Act victory, Kutcher was handed another enormous moral victory when the VA announced (in a letter to Kutcher dated January 6) that it had decided to continue Kutcher's pension, based on what the agency's Central Committee on Waivers and Forfeitures said was a lack of sufficient evidence to establish "beyond a reasonable doubt" that Kutcher had "knowingly and intentionally" rendered "assistance to an enemy of the United States." The committee reported that Kutcher's case was "a very difficult one" and that it believed that if some of his reported statements could be proved they would disqualify him from continuing to receive his pension, but that it had determined after "very careful review" that "the available evidence does not measure up" to the "quantum of proof" required to meet the "beyond a reasonable doubt" standard. The committee also stated that while it had the authority to take away Kutcher's pension, it was "pertinent" that its records "do not reveal" any instance in which an American veteran had been deprived of benefits unless they had been previously "convicted of charges involving subversive activities." It added that while SWP leaders had been convicted in 1941, that conviction was not based on "mere membership" but on "active participation in a conspiracy" to violently overthrow the government, and that Kutcher "while admitting membership in said party, has denied" having "purposes and intent" to seek the government's overturn.

Kutcher responded to the news by declaring that he had been "vindicated" and was "filled with elation and relief" and that the VA had been forced to "retreat from their position" due to the massive publicity given to the pension issue. Kutcher added, "I think now the court ought to rule favorably on my plea to get my job back and the government ought to stop trying to evict me and parents from our home." He declared that obtaining the VA job in 1946 made him feel "of use to somebody for the first time since my legs were amputated," although "the fear of eviction is my parents' primary worry now." A January 9, 1956, KCRC press release termed the VA ruling an "important" civil liberties victory that had resulted from a "wave of public indignation," while urging continued support for Kutcher in connection with his still-pending attempt to regain his job and a possible appeal by Newark public housing authorities in their attempt to evict Kutcher from his public housing there (which, in fact, never eventuated). In a January 11 letter to local SWP branches, national secretary Farrell Dobbs termed the VA's ruling a "big victory" that had given "new impetus" to the "whole fight against the witch hunt," in which individuals faced "star chamber hearings" in which they were "slandered by faceless informers and victimized through the brutal concept of guilt by association."

The VA's mid-December 1955 decision to suspend Kutcher's disability pension and its December 30 hearing on this topic attracted by far the greatest wave of media attention to Kutcher's case since his original firing and hearings in 1948–1949. This wave of press attention was actively fostered by the KCRC and Kutcher's lawyers and carried a strong tone of disapproval of the VA's conduct, both explicitly in editorial comments and implicitly in that carrying prominent news stories about the issue inevitably implied that the VA was acting in a peculiar way.

The December 15 VA decision to suspend Kutcher's $329 monthly disability pension was massively reported in the American press and was even the subject of a short Reuters news agency article in the December 24 *Manchester Guardian* of England. The VA's December 23 restoration of Kutcher's pension pending a hearing and its December 28 accession to Rauh's demand for an open hearing on December 30 also attracted widespread press attention, with front-page coverage of the former story in the *Washington Post*, *New York Times*, and Allentown, Pennsylvania, *Morning Call* of December 24. The proposed suspension was also the subject of several extremely hostile editorials, including a December 24 *Washington Post* declaration that "few Americans" could read about the Kutcher affair "and not weep for their country." The *Post* asked, "What has the majesty of the United States descended to when a crippled veteran can be so hounded and harassed in the name of national security? Perhaps the only words fit for this folly are words peculiarly appropriate for this season: 'Forgive them Father; for they know not what they do.'"

Editorials in the December 23 and December 28 *New York Post* termed the VA officials who sought to deprive Kutcher of his pension "witless or heartless" officials who were engaged in "madness" and a "national disgrace" that was provoking "millions of Americans" to feel "shame and apprehension" and creating the "degrading" spectacle in which Kutcher was "literally being forced to his knees in quest of a pension." At the "very least," the newspaper suggested, the government "would seem obliged to return [Kutcher's] legs before cutting off the $70-a-week bounty he has received in token recognition of his loss," a result of nothing more than "unorthodox or inflammatory ideas" that Kutcher expressed in support of the SWP, a group so insignificant that the claim that "he and his associates constitute anything resembling a clear and present danger to the republic is a palpable absurdity." The December 29 *New York Times* declared that the country could "in no way benefit from the long campaign of harassment against Mr. Kutcher," which simply amounted to "retaliation for extremist political views," but failed to change the fact that he seemed "clearly entitled to compensation for his wartime injuries" and "isn't the kind of action that sits well in a free democracy."

The December 27 *St. Louis Post-Dispatch* said that "loss of a pension earned on the battlefield is punishment and punishment is certainly not more just because it is occasioned by an administrative list [AGLOSO] rather than by a fair trial." Referring to the attorney general, the *Post-Dispatch* said that Kutcher's ordeal therefore raised the "larger question" as to the wisdom of "giving one government official such broad if indirect power to punish political association." The December 30 *Pittsburgh Post-Gazette* declared that the VA was "wrong to cut off Mr. Kutcher's pension so arbitrarily" and that any law authorizing depriving Kutcher of his disability benefits was "wrong" if he was only guilty of SWP membership, since Kutcher "did lose two legs in the service of his country" and "surely for that his private political opinions may be indulged, however 'screwball' the rest of us regard them."

The December 30 VA hearing and the VA's January announcement that it was restoring Kutcher's pension were the subject of coverage in newspapers across the country, including front-page stories in the December 31 *Pittsburgh Post-Gazette*, *Toledo Times*, *Philadelphia*

Inquirer, *Washington Star*, and *Washington Post*, with accounts of the hearing and, especially, editorials frequently stressing the apparent lack of "due process" accorded to Kutcher by the VA. The *New York Post*'s December 30 story was headlined "VA Pension Hearing Board Refuses to Let Kutcher Face His Accusers," while the *Washington Post*'s story termed the hearing "a type of proceeding unlike anything that has come into public view before" due to the lack of procedures, witnesses against Kutcher, or "any facts to back up the charges against him except the charges themselves."

New York World Telegram columnist Inez Robb lamented on January 3, 1956, that Kutcher had not been "allowed to face his accusers as he did the enemy in Italy 13 years ago," while an editorial in the next day's *Washington Post* termed Kutcher's hearing's "rigmarole" that marked, "let us hope, the nadir of the loyalty-security program," and denounced the lack of rules, witnesses, source of charges, or evidence provided Kutcher, concluding that it "is hard to believe that such a 'hearing' could take place in the United States." Editorials in the January 6 editions of both the *Christian Science Monitor* and the *Milwaukee Journal* similarly attacked the nature of the proceedings, with the former declaring that Kutcher had been given a "star chamber" hearing that deprived him of the right to confront, refute, or even "know his accusers," and the latter terming Kutcher's case an "egregious" example of the gradual "erosion" of America's "hard-won freedoms," in violation of the presumption of innocence and marked by accusations by "nameless, faceless persons whose veracity" Kutcher was not allowed to challenge.

A *Washington Post* editorial cartoon by Herblock, reprinted in the January 8 *New York Post*, depicted the hearing as part of a chapter from Alice in Wonderland, with Moss depicted in the guise of the mad Queen of Hearts and quoted as declaring, "I'll make up the rules as we go along." A January 1, 1956, story in the *New York Post* quoted Rauh as terming the hearing "the worst" he had ever attended and saying that even Senator McCarthy "never ran a hearing as outrageous as this. No rules. No statement of charges. No witnesses. No evidence." Pictures of Kutcher walking with his canes accompanied coverage of the general pension issue, and especially the December 30 hearing, in many newspapers, including the December 24 *New*

York Times and the December 31 *New York Daily News*, *Philadelphia Inquirer*, *Milwaukee Journal*, *New York Times*, *Washington Star*, *Los Angeles Times*, *Toledo Times*, *Pittsburgh Post-Gazette*, *Cleveland Plain Dealer*, and *St. Paul Pioneer Press*.

The VA's January 8, 1956, ruling to allow Kutcher to continue to receive his pension received front-page coverage in the next day's *New York Times* and *Washington Post* and was widely reported in other papers throughout the country (the *Minneapolis Morning Tribune's* January 9 story ran under the headline, "Veterans Pension Is Restored to Legless Trotskyite"). The ruling was hailed in a number of editorials, including the January 11 *Washington Post*, which declared that the VA had corrected a "blunder," but attacked the VA committee for failing to issue a "retraction" of the "generous sort the situation demanded" and charged that "its whole basis for threatening" Kutcher's pension was "invalid" because while it had suggested that if Kutcher's alleged statements had been proved his discharge would have been warranted, in fact "reckless talk, agitation for strikes, unfair and extravagant criticism of the Government do not constitute mutiny, treason, sabotage or assistance to an enemy." The January 12 *Christian Science Monitor* similarly declared that while the VA had "now done the decent thing," the procedures that allowed it "to rule without due process or a court trial" ran "counter to the traditions of justice which have been part of the fabric of the 'American way.'" In a January 12 letter to the editor of the *New York Post*, which first broke the story of the VA's decision to consider terminating Kutcher's pension, Kutcher reported that after the *Post* had printed his address he had received a "great number of letters and phone calls from Post readers" and expressed thanks "for their expressions of support and sympathy." The conservative journal *National Review* lent a dissenting voice to the generally favorable news coverage of Kutcher's plight in a January 25, 1956, editorial, declaring that while "we reserve comment" on the Kutcher pension issue, the entire Kutcher affair, including his affiliation with the "anti-Moscow" SWP, lent itself "perfectly to demagogic exploitation by civil libertines" like Rauh who sought to use such a "heaven-sent opportunity" to "smash the government's entire security system."

Kutcher's victory in the VA pension case and the massive wave of favorable publicity that accompanied it spurred the KCRC, the SWP, and Kutcher to renewed activity in early 1956 in connection with his continuing legal fight to regain his VA post. Thus, on January 26, 1956, Kutcher again wrote to President Eisenhower, appealing for restoration of his job in light of the VA ruling, which he termed a "personal vindication against the lies of the faceless informers as well as a refutation of the monstrous charge that holding Socialist beliefs is treason." However, he received in response only a February 28 letter from special White House counsel Gerald Morgan informing him that "national security" personnel decisions were specifically vested in department and agency heads and thus Kutcher's case was within the VA's "exclusive jurisdiction." Meanwhile, the KCRC and the SWP issued numerous appeals to supporters to contribute to Kutcher's struggle financially and with other means. In a February 8 letter to Wayne County, Michigan, CIO Council secretary-treasurer Al Barbour, KCRC treasurer George Weissman lamented that since Kutcher's October 1952 federal appeals court victory, the KCRC had not engaged in "much activity" and that it was "so strapped for money that it had to borrow the expenses incurred by Kutcher" to attend the December 30, 1955, Washington, D.C., pension hearing, although recent developments had resulted in a "little money" coming in and the "revival of some of the local Kutcher committees." Kutcher himself addressed public meetings in Chicago on February 10, 1956 (which generated a net profit of almost $300 to support his legal costs) and in New York City on February 17 to support his job fight. VA officials turned down an invitation to participate in the February 10 meeting on the grounds that Kutcher's job suit was pending in the courts, and it "would obviously be improper for anyone from this agency to discuss the case while it is so pending."

In challenging the VA to send a representative to the Chicago rally, Kutcher declared that he was convinced that if its actions were "discussed in the open, before the American people, this erosion of our liberties will be stopped," and that if the VA had "nothing to hide, if it is not ashamed of what it has done, it will send a speaker to this meeting." Kutcher also spoke in Detroit on March 15 and in Newark on March 9. During the Detroit meeting, Kutcher, clearly referring to the VA decision to continue his disability pension, which he termed "an ungracious ruling in my favor," declared that "an aroused court of public opinion" was aiding his fight to keep his job and that the press and public had forced a retreat by "those would turn administrative hearings into courtroom trials."

In the aftermath of Kutcher's VA pension victory, two significant national magazines carried prominent stories about Kutcher. The January 27, 1956, issue of *Commonweal* noted that Kutcher's plight had "aroused considerable public interest in recent weeks" and that he had run "afoul" of "national security regulations" in three different arenas with the loss of his job, the threat to his pension, and the attempt to oust his family from Newark public housing. *Commonweal* said (somewhat incorrectly) that "no one paid much attention" when Kutcher lost his job, but that the threat to his pension had forced the VA to abandon, "under the spotlight of publicity," its original plans for a secret hearing on the issue. While reporting that the VA had decided to continue Kutcher's pension on the grounds that alleged statements made by him "had not been proved beyond a reasonable doubt," the article maintained that the VA's real "error" was in seeking to take away the pension in the first place since the "whole idea that remarks made in conversation, however extreme politically, constitute 'rendering assistance' to the enemy so as to merit forfeiture of a disability pension seems to us nonsense." If Kutcher's political views were not "enough to bar him from the draft" and to prevent the army from "sending him to the war in which he lost his legs," *Commonweal* argued, "they should not now be used to deny him his pension," and to argue otherwise "seems to us a gross violation of ordinary common sense and of elemental national decency." The magazine also denounced the attempt to evict Kutcher and his parents from public housing as lacking in "rhyme or reason," since the concept of security "applies properly to national defense" but "extending it arbitrarily to areas like public housing projects which in no way involve the national safely makes the whole concept ridiculous." However, *Commonweal* maintained that the government was "well within its rights in denying re-employment" to Kutcher, as federal employment was "legitimately in the area of national security" and it was unnecessary to take AGLOSO "completely at face value to presume that in this instance responsible public officials have decided that Mr. Kutcher's loyalty is to a genuinely revolutionary party." It concluded that those who would "indiscriminately deny Mr. Kutcher pension, housing and government job, as if they were all in the same category, and those who would equally indiscriminately fight for all three are guilty of the kind of distortion which makes a rational approach to the problem of security increasingly difficult."

A lengthy story in the March 1956 *Commentary* also touched on all three of Kutcher's struggles, which it termed "in some ways the most outrageous example of its kind which has so far come to light," especially since "no other person seems to have been exposed to the multiple forms of jeopardy which the government has visited on him." Adding that while the "infliction of a single injustice is bad enough," a "triple injustice is certainly worse," the article, by Maurice Goldbloom, declared that Kutcher's case had a "special pathos because of his personal circumstances: a persecution which would in any case be wrong becomes a supreme example of bureaucratic callousness." The article termed Kutcher a "shy and almost timid man," who gave no impression of familiarity with "or even interest in the fine shadings of doctrine which distinguish Trotskyites from all other men, and the Socialist Workers Party" from "all other Trotskyites" in either his book or his hearing boards testimony, and who, at least until his 1949 firing, had primarily utilized his SWP membership to supply him "with a social life of sorts," including the joining of some picket lines, the distribution of "a good many leaflets," and the filling of "many of his leisure hours with the addressing of envelopes." Goldbloom declared that Kutcher's case had never "even remotely" involved issues of "security, or even suitability," but was simply "intended to punish him for his beliefs and affiliations, and it seems neither to have had nor pretended to have any other purpose," and thus amounted to an instance of "pointless cruelty."

Goldbloom focused especially on the pension issue, which he declared was "what many regarded as the most outrageous attack of all" of those made by the government against Kutcher and which he said had resulted in "an immediate outcry throughout the nation, from conservatives as well as liberals. Indeed, it would be hard to find a voice which defended the proposed revocation." He suggested that the attempt to take away Kutcher's pension had ultimately been dropped by the VA because its Committee on Waivers and Forfeitures had "apparently realized that the Kutcher case was a very hot potato."

On February 10, 1956, the same day as Kutcher's Chicago rally, oral argument in Kutcher's job lawsuit was conducted before a three-judge panel of the federal appeals court in Washington, D.C. Representing Kutcher, Rauh argued that no hearing had been granted the SWP before it was AGLOSO-designated and that Kutcher was asking "not for pity but for due process of law." Rauh added that Kutcher "proudly affirms" his SWP membership "as he sits here today" and that if his 1948 dismissal from his then $42 a week VA clerkship was upheld then "no one is safe," because if the attorney general "wanted to list the Democrats as subversive, this situation could apply." In response, federal attorney Benjamin Forman declared that all legal procedures had been followed before Kutcher had been fired and that Kutcher had been allowed to testify about his view of the SWP's goals.

On April 20, 1956, Kutcher won his third major victory in four months (following his December 1955 win in the Newark public housing eviction case and the January 1956 VA ruling to continue his World War II disability pension), when the federal appeals court, overturning the June 1955 ruling by federal district judge Burnita Matthews, ruled that Kutcher had been illegally fired by the VA. In a narrow 2–1 ruling penned by Judge E. Barrett Prettyman, the court essentially held that when the VA decided in April 1955 to uphold its original 1948 firing of Kutcher, it had improperly based its decision on different grounds than had first been brought against Kutcher and on information about which he was not aware. Prettyman noted that although the VA had reconsidered the Kutcher case in 1955 due to the 1952 federal appeals court ruling that Kutcher had been illegally dismissed in 1948 solely for his SWP membership, no additional charges were lodged against him aside from those originally made in 1948, which essentially amounted to the allegation that Kutcher was "a member of, employed by and made a contribution to [the SWP] an organization listed by the Attorney General." However the Court held that the VA Loyalty Board of Appeals, in its lengthy April 1955 memorandum justifying its recommendation to uphold Kutcher's original dismissal, had relied upon a "substantially" different finding, namely that the SWP "was found to advocate the overthrow of the Government by unconstitutional means, and Kutcher was found to be aware of that aim and to support it consciously and actively" (although the VA board had conceded to discovering no disloyal acts by Kutcher and no problems with his job performance).

The court noted that the board had defined the issue as to whether Kutcher was "innocent of the subversive purposes and aims" of the SWP, in which "he continues his membership and activity," and had concluded that Kutcher had "knowingly participated" in activities "which would destroy, if necessary by unconstitutional means, our system of government." However, the court declared that the loyalty board's memorandum, which it said "made extensive findings and conclusions in support of its final recommendation" to dismiss Kutcher and "stands as the statement of the reasons for Kutcher's discharge," had been withheld from Kutcher until he had filed a challenge to his dismissal in federal court. The court added that the loyalty board's memorandum relied upon a 1943 federal court finding that the SWP had sought to advocate the forceful overthrow of the government, FBI reports, and a summary of Justice Department findings that had led to the SWP's AGLOSO designation, documents that had led to the VA board's conclusion that the SWP "advocates the destruction of our present form of government" and that anyone who "knowingly participates in the furtherance of such an organization over a period of years" could not "stand without reasonable doubt as to his loyalty to our existing form of government." However, the court noted that "no change" had been made in the formal charges preferred against Kutcher since those provided in 1948, and that therefore "the reasons for Kutcher's discharge" as indicated in the memorandum were based on information Kutcher was unaware of and therefore could not have "fairly been anticipated from the [1948] charges preferred against him." Thus, the court held that the VA had, in violation of its own procedures, which required that its employees be informed of "any and all reasons, specifically and in detail," in connection with proposed firings, failed to adequately inform Kutcher of the basis on which he was being fired, reasons that differed "substantially from the charges made." Therefore, it ruled, Kutcher had not been given enough notice that would have enabled him "adequately to prepare and present his defense." The court added that it had specifically held in an earlier federal firing case that "only findings upon the charges, specifically identified, can be the 'reasons' required to be stated" in any "ultimate adverse ruling" and that "the employee must have a fair chance to defend himself upon the very grounds upon which he may be discharged."

The court also held that the 1948 charges lodged against Kutcher, which it had ruled could be the only basis for a dismissal, could not justify his firing. It noted that the 1952 federal appeals court had determined that SWP membership alone could not support a loyalty discharge, and that the other original 1948 allegations, that Kutcher was employed by the SWP, had made a financial contribution to it, and was associated with a subversive group, either had not been relied upon by the 1955 VA board, or, in the case of the last allegation, was "wholly vague" and a "broad and sweeping charge embracing numerous unspecified activities and associations." The court concluded, "Since only findings on charges, specifically identified, can constitute reasons for removal, a reading of the charges must demonstrate the reasons for removal, assuming all the charges are sustained. That is not so here." The court made no mention of any basic constitutional question raised by the case, such as the SWP's AGLOSO designation without a hearing, but ordered that Kutcher be restored to his VA position "or in the event such position no longer exists, to another position of like grade and seniority, with such rights and privileges as he may be entitled to under the law."

The April 20, 1956, federal court of appeals ruling ordering Kutcher reinstated to the VA post he had been fired from eight years earlier attracted substantial press attention, including front-page accounts in the *New York Times* and the *Newark Evening News* and prominent coverage in many other papers. In an April 27, 1956, editorial headlined "More Waymarks to Sanity," the *Christian Science Monitor* termed the appeals court ruling another example of a continuing march "back towards sanity and towards the American way of justice" in the loyalty-security controversy.

Kutcher told the press upon hearing the news that he had "great expectations" for returning to his VA post and that the ruling was an "important victory" for civil liberties. Noting that he had been fighting to regain his job since 1948, he declared, "Though I'm eight years older, I'm still ready, willing and able. All the VA has to do is phone me or send a letter." He added, "I liked the job very much. It was the first one I had after I lost my legs and in it I came to feel that despite my handicap I could be useful to myself and others. Besides vocational rehabilitation for veterans is important work and gave me personal satisfaction." Kutcher added that he had "tried a few other jobs" since his dismissal but "wasn't able to hold them down" and that "recently I've been going to school to learn a skill but if can go back to the VA I prefer that. You know job-hunting when you have no special skill and when you have two artificial legs is tough enough. Add to that a smear on your record as 'disloyal' and there's practically three strikes against you."

According to the *New York Post's* account, Kutcher got the news at a New York City printing company where he had been working once a week reading proofs for an SWP publication. In the immediate aftermath of the court ruling, VA officials and Justice Department officials were quoted as declaring that the department would have to study it to determine whether or not to appeal. Although some news accounts suggested that upon reinstatement to his VA post Kutcher would be entitled to collect $20,000 in back pay for the 1948–1956 period of dismissal, VA officials were additionally quoted as stating that the court ruling would have to be studied before a decision could be made on that subject (as is discussed below, Kutcher ultimately had to return to court to gain his back pay).

Although the federal government was entitled to appeal the court ruling to the Supreme Court, on May 21, 1956, district court judge Matthews carried out the mandate of the appeals court by ordering the Veterans Administration to reinstate Kutcher on the grounds that his firing had been "procedurally defective and therefore unauthorized." On June 5, according to an internal Justice Department memorandum, the decision was reached not to appeal the adverse court ruling to the Supreme Court. Upon forwarding a copy of Judge Matthews's order to Kutcher on May 22, Rauh warned that it was "impossible" for him to judge "if they will really restore you or just have you come in and then suspend you again" (some press accounts following the appeals court ruling suggested that the government might try to once again initiate loyalty dismissal proceedings against Kutcher as soon as he was reinstated). Rauh cautioned Kutcher that "whatever happens, don't make any public statements of any sort without consulting" him and pleaded that "if they do restore you to your job be careful not to discuss politics or your case or anything else. Just go in and do whatever they tell you and keep in touch with me." Concerning the question of regaining Kutcher's lost back pay, Rauh reported that he had "no idea what's going to happen" but "we will certainly make a fight for it. Be careful you don't sign any documents relating to back pay without discussing them with us."

On June 20, 1956, in accordance with a directive that day from VA administrator Higley, Newark Regional VA administrator Joseph O'Hearn sent Kutcher a telegram to his home reporting that "I have been instructed to restore to your former position or a comparable position." O'Hearn asked Kutcher to "kindly phone me" to arrange an interview at a convenient time. Internal VA files indicate that, in the meantime, Kutcher's personnel record had been reviewed and it had been determined that while Kutcher's annual pay had been $2,423 when he had been suspended in October 1948, he would be entitled upon reinstatement to $3,470 due to interim federal pay increases. The VA files also report that when Kutcher had been suspended in 1948 there were 1,655 employees in the regional office, which had since been reduced to about 760. Widely published press accounts reported Higley's June 20 decision, in which he was quoted as declaring that he had ordered Kutcher's immediate reinstatement with "full seniority." O'Hearn was quoted as stating that he would call Kutcher "as soon as we can find a position available, at the most within a week." O'Hearn added that while the VA staff was much smaller than when Kutcher had been fired, Kutcher could be reemployed without dismissing anyone else to make room for him.

According to a June 22 memorandum from Newark VA personnel officer Charles Miller, Kutcher would now be assigned to a "mail & file clerk position in the medical division" (he had formerly been attached to the Registration and Research Section of the Vocational Rehabilitation and Education Department). According to Miller, Kutcher's job would involve "screening incoming and outgoing file material and alphabetizing such material for insertion in the treatment folders" as well as "establishing and preparing replacement treatment folders." Miller added that Kutcher would not be required to "stand or walk" to carry out his new duties. Newark VA regional manager O'Hearn reported by telegram on June 25, 1956, to VA administrator Higley that, following instructions, he had met with Kutcher that day and that the latter would be "restored to duty effective opening of business tomorrow, Tuesday, June 26." He added that the interview and "position arrangement" were both "very satisfactory" to Kutcher. Kutcher's reappointment is officially noted on a VA standard form 50, "Notification of Personnel Action," signed by Miller and dated June 26, 1956, which stated that Kutcher's "entrance performance rating" was "satisfactory."

Although as these lines are written in late 2015 James Kutcher has become almost entirely forgotten, his case and the massive publicity that it received, largely due to his "legless" condition, made a substantial contribution to discrediting the post–World War II Red Scare, both legally and, especially, politically. Although the "Army-McCarthy hearings" of early 1954 and the Senate censure of McCarthy later that year were certainly the key turning points, both before and after those events the Kutcher case clearly had a significant impact in leading many people to conclude that the Red Scare in general, and the loyalty program and AGLOSO in particular, had reached outlandish levels. Thus, the 1952 federal appeals court ruling that AGLOSO affiliation by itself could not justify dismissal from federal employment and Kutcher's 1955 New Jersey victory in his challenge to the Gwinn Act ban on AGLOSO members living in federally-subsidized housing both placed important limits on AGLOSO's reach and drew considerable attention to its procedural deficiencies. After 1954, the federal government ceased adding new organizations to AGLOSO, and when several organizations challenged their listings thereafter the government "delisted" them rather than risk going to court and having AGLOSO declared unconstitutional in its entirety.

Furthermore, Kutcher's ultimate victory in his loyalty dismissal case, after eight years of highly publicized struggle, although based on technical grounds, highlighted the procedural lacks of the loyalty program and clearly bewildered many people who could not understand how a man who had lost both legs fighting for "Uncle Sam" could be considered disloyal to the nation, especially given the especially given the menial level of his Veterans Administration position. After his ultimate 1956 victory in his job dismissal case, the Supreme Court began to place limits on the loyalty program and it gradually lost significance (the Court also began striking many other aspects of Red Scare procedures, including, for all practical purposes, the 1940 Smith [sedition] Act, which had been used to prosecute the SWP in 1942 and the top CP leadership in 1951). Most of all, the tone-deaf attempt of the VA to take away Kutcher's World War II disability pension in late 1955 and what appeared to many as the kangaroo court nature of its proceedings against him not only led to a humiliating backdown by the VA, but to extraordinary publicity that by any measure hugely discredited the Red Scare. Although he could not recover his legs, in the end Kutcher kept his job, his apartment, his disability pension, and his rights. His "case" proved to be a huge blow against the excesses of the Red Scare.

CHAPTER SIX

The Ironies of Kutcher's Post-Triumphal Life (and Death), (1956–1989)

The period following Kutcher's victories in his fight for his job, his pension, and his home was filled with ironies. Although Kutcher had won his job back, the government refused to reimburse him for lost back pay. Yet in 1958, while Kutcher was still attempting to recover his back pay, the VA awarded him a ten-year service pin, even though he had been suspended during almost all of that period. Although the courts had failed to support the government's finding that Kutcher was "disloyal," the FBI continued to closely monitor his movements; shortly after his court victory on this score, it began a massive program designed to sabotage the SWP even though the SWP had been reduced already by Cold War repression to a tiny group of less than 500 people. In 1987, the SWP won a major lawsuit against the FBI for violating its constitutional rights, decided by a judge who found no evidence of any criminal conduct by the party. Although Kutcher had suffered enormously for his SWP loyalty, in 1983 he was expelled from the party as part of a purge of members who resisted a new turn in SWP policy. And although during his life Kutcher's story had repeatedly provided front-page copy to sell newspapers, when he died in 1986 not a single major newspaper carried a word about his death.

After Kutcher resumed his job in June 1956, the issue of back pay moved to the fore, with Newark VA manager O'Hearn asking VA administrator Higley in two separate June 25 telegrams to "kindly advise" him on this issue, noting that Kutcher's first new paycheck was, if authorized, due on July on 11 and that if Kutcher was entitled to back pay for the seven years he had been suspended that would make a considerable difference. In his autobiography, Kutcher says he wanted the money "both as a manner of principle and because I hoped with it to buy one of the special homes built for amputees." In a separate June 25 letter to the VA's chief benefits officer, O'Hearn reported that during his interview that day Kutcher had specifically asked if he was entitled to back pay and stated that he knew that the attorney general would issue a ruling on the question "within a week." Higley responded to O'Hearn's June inquiries with a telegram that same day, which reported that while Kutcher's payment "of current salary for services rendered and subsequent to June 26, 1956 is authorized," no action should be taken concerning "any retroactive period." Instead, Higley directed that if Kutcher filed a claim for back pay, it should be "processed to [the Washington] Central [VA] office for further handling."

Apparently at least partly in response to Higley's message, O'Hearn wrote to the VA chief benefits director on June 27 to report that questions had now "arisen" as to whether Kutcher was entitled to federal pay increases implemented since his 1948 suspension. O'Hearn reported that the federal appeals court order appeared to "dictate" that Kutcher be "restored to duty retroactively in which case credit would be granted for [interim pay] step increases," but that the answer to this question had a "bearing on the issue of back pay provisions" of federal law in the case of improper separations, and that issue "has not yet been decided." On July 2, O'Hearn was instructed by VA headquarters that Kutcher had been correctly restored, pursuant to Higley's June 20 directive, at a yearly salary of $3,470, the salary Kutcher "would have attained had he remained on the rolls continuously from the day of separation." While assuring O'Hearn that "this action on your part was correct," the instructions directed that he should still "take no action with respect to retroactive pay" but forward any such claim to the central VA office.

In the meantime, on June 29 Newark VA personnel office director Miller reported to O'Hearn that on June 27 Kutcher had been provided with "an application blank, a loyalty form, and an office form," and it was explained that the forms "were needed to complete his personnel records." Miller added that Kutcher had accepted the forms "with few comments" and had been granted permission to "take them home for further review." According to Miller, on June 28 Kutcher had reported that he was "sending the forms to his attorney for legal advice" and would "let us know the outcome of this referral." O'Hearn reported in a July 5 memorandum for the files that Kutcher had told him that day that his lawyer, Joseph Rauh, had instructed Kutcher to inquire about the back pay situation and had said he would sue "if the back pay was not forthcoming." O'Hearn added that he had told Kutcher that he was entitled to "make a written request, over his own signature, for back pay" and should present such a request to O'Hearn. Clearly reflecting that he perceived the matter as extremely sensitive, O'Hearn immediately forwarded a report about Kutcher's declared intentions to VA chief benefits director Ralph Stone, informing Stone that he considered the information "of such importance as to warrant its submission to you without delay." The VA's security office in Washington soon after requested that Kutcher's personnel file be forwarded from Newark by registered mail, a task accomplished by Miller on July 9. In the meantime, the VA requested the CSC on July 2 to undertake a "security investigation for a "nonsensitive position" on Kutcher.

On July 9, 1956, Rauh sent Kutcher a draft letter for him to present to Newark VA regional manager O'Hearn. Kutcher's letter, which he reported in a July 21 letter to Rauh that he had recently dropped off with O'Hearn's assistant after being unable to personally give it to O'Hearn, formally applied for "back pay for the period I was out of work." Quoting the recent federal district court order finding his original dismissal "unauthorized," Kutcher's letter, dated July 14, told O'Hearn that "under these circumstances, it seems clear that I am entitled to back pay" and that "in view of the many years of struggle" he had "been forced to undergo" to regain his position, "I hope I may receive the back pay due me promptly and without any requirement of further legal action." Kutcher concluded by thanking O'Hearn for the latter's "cooperation since my return to duty" and assuring him of "my continuing loyal devotion to the job to which I have been assigned." O'Hearn acknowledged Kutcher's request in a July 18 letter that reported that it would be sent to "our Central Office without delay for their determination and processing." While waiting for an answer to his back pay request, Kutcher responded to what, in an August 6 letter to a supporter, he termed "hundreds of letters from friends, supporters and well-wishers from all parts of the world." He noted that "current aspects of my case still remain unresolved and my current public activity is subject to counsel of my lawyer," but that, "as in the past, I intend to do all in my power to continue the fight for the democratic rights of all victims of the witch hunt" and those being "persecuted for holding and advocating views and opinions unpopular with the ruling powers."

VA chief benefits director Stone informed Newark regional manager O'Hearn on August 17 that Kutcher should be informed by letter that "preliminary to any consideration of his claim" Kutcher would have to submit an affidavit "setting forth specifically and in detail the amount of his net earnings" throughout the "entire period during which he was not" on the VA payroll, along with a total amount for his claim. Perhaps unaware of the VA's request to Kutcher for additional information (which O'Hearn forwarded to Kutcher on August 21), on August 24 Rauh wrote to KCRC treasurer George Weissman that he assumed Kutcher had heard nothing further since the July 18 acknowledgment of his claim and that "it seems to me that we must start moving on this point aggressively." Rauh suggested that Kutcher and Weissman visit O'Hearn "promptly and ask what has happened to Jim's claim for back pay," stressing the "great hardship which Jim has been through and his serious need for the funds." Rauh further advised Weissman to inform O'Hearn that Weissman intended to write President Eisenhower "if the money is not forthcoming promptly, and if that does not succeed, to take legal action in the courts." Rauh added that Weissman should "keep stressing" that "you do not want to do any of these things as Jim has had all the struggle one fellow should have to go through, but if it is necessary to do more to get his just rights, he will take the other actions." Rauh concluded, "The only way we've gotten anything in this case to date is by scrapping, and I suppose that is the only way we're going to get the back pay."

On September 6, Newark manager O'Hearn reported to VA chief benefits director Stone that Kutcher had not yet "officially responded" to his August 21 letter requesting that Kutcher submit additional information. Stone's September 6 message to Washington may have reflected that, on the same day, Newark VA personnel officer A. De Maio reported that Kutcher had called seeking verification of the "computations he had made in preparation" for his back pay submission, which included a total claim of $23,483.92, but that De Maio had told Kutcher that "it would be improper for me to the make the computation in his behalf since the responsibility for presenting the claim was his. [Kutcher] accepted my explanation with no objection."

The extraordinary sensitivity with which Kutcher's situation continued to be treated by the VA was clearly reflected in a four-page single-spaced typed letter concerning his job reinstatement and claim for back pay sent by VA administrator Higley directly to Attorney General Brownell on September 6, 1956. Respectfully soliciting "your assistance and advice concerning certain problems" that had arisen in connection with Kutcher's "restoration" to duty, Higley reported that, "as you are no doubt aware," Kutcher had been fired twice on loyalty grounds but had just been reinstated for the second time by a federal appeals court ruling. Kutcher's 1948 dismissal had been first set aside in 1952 on the grounds that he could not be fired solely for being an SWP member "without any finding in respect to Mr. Kutcher's loyalty" to the American government, Higley noted, while the "second removal action was held by the court to be improper because the charges were insufficient." Higley informed Brownell that Kutcher's request for back pay posed a "problem" because various congressional appropriation acts had barred the payment of federal funds to any employee who "advocates, or is a member of an organization that advocates" the violent overthrow of the government. While Higley noted that Kutcher denied that the SWP engaged in such advocacy, he maintained that the 1943 federal court of appeals ruling had determined that the SWP in fact sought the government's violent overthrow, and "it seems to be clearly shown" that Kutcher "now knows, and at all times during his" SWP membership and 1946–1948 VA employment "and subsequently, has known" the "line of action advocated by" the SWP, along with its "aims, purposes and objectives." Higley added that various congressional enactments also banned the federal employment of anyone who "knowingly" belonged to an organization that advocated the "overthrow of our constitutional form of government" and that when Kutcher was first fired it had been determined that Kutcher fell into this category.

Higley conceded that the VA's earlier findings with regard to Kutcher's ineligibility for federal employment and pay had to be "considered" in light of the two federal appeals court rulings holding that his removal had been "procedurally defective," and asked for Brownell's opinions on five interrelated (if not completely duplicative) questions raised by the Kutcher matter. First, noting that the federal government had placed the SWP on AGLOSO, Higley inquired if the organization was viewed as advocating the overthrow of the American government. Secondly, Higley asked if the 1943 federal appeals court findings concerning the SWP's aims and objectives could be "accepted as conclusive proof" in any administrative proceedings to determine whether Kutcher's removal from employment "would promote the efficiency of the service," or, if not, if the findings might be "accepted as prima facie proof of the present aims and objectives of the Party so as to shift to Mr. Kutcher the burden of producing contrary evidence." Thirdly, Higley inquired whether, if proceedings were begun to determine if "Mr. Kutcher should be removed from his position," whether it could be "tried and resolved" in such proceedings as to whether the SWP "is an organization advocating the overthrow of the government." Fourth, Higley asked, if it was determined that Kutcher was "not disqualified" from receiving "current and prior" federal appropriations, if the VA could "properly allow and pay back salary" to Kutcher for the period between his 1948 dismissal and his 1956 "restoration to duty." Finally, Higley asked if, in view of the specific congressional ban on federal employment of anyone who advocated or was a "knowing member" of an organization that advocated the overthrow of the government, "may the Veterans Administration legally pay Mr. Kutcher current salary for current services."

Higley added that he would "not presume" to suggest to Brownell "what approach should be adopted," but that it would be "helpful" to the VA if a "complete review of the files is made, particularly in reference to matters reflected in recent investigative [presumably FBI] reports which came in after the administrative record was made upon which the last judicial review was predicated." He also asked Brownell for guidance as to "what portion, if any, of the evidence referred to in the reports" might be made "available for use in an open hearing" should one be conducted. Higley concluded by urging Brownell to take "prompt action" to determine if Kutcher "should be continued" on the VA payroll and if he should receive his claimed back pay, and therefore asked his "early consideration and reply to the questions herein presented." Despite the sense of urgency that Higley sought to convey in his September 6 letter to Brownell, the Justice Department waited until September 21 before shuttling Higley's questions off to its Internal Security Division (ISD) "for disposition." ISD head and assistant attorney general William F. Tompkins did not respond to Higley until October 25, and then only reported that the matter had been referred to him and was "receiving our careful attention and you may expect a reply in the near future."

The questions raised by Higley's September 6 letter to Brownell were considered at a meeting between high-level Justice Department and VA personnel on the "Kutcher matter" on November 2, according to a November 8 memorandum written by Justice Department official Joseph Alderman, chief of the Subversive Organizations Section (in charge of AGLOSO listings among other matters) to Justice Department ISD executive assistant William Foley. Alderman reported to Foley that at the meeting department officials told the VA representatives that it would be a "tremendous job for us to review the 54 file sections" on the SWP and determine what information could be made available "for use in an open hearing," but that material in the file indicated that the SWP "does advocate forcible overthrow of the government and indicated that we assume such information is available to the VA" via the FBI. According to Alderman's letter, the other matters addressed by Higley raised questions that would have be resolved by other divisions within the Justice Department or were "more appropriately within the purview of the Civil Service Commission and/or the Comptroller General." Alderman's memo added that the VA representatives at the meeting were "not desirous of proceeding against Kutcher unless the law so required," but indicated concern about paying "an employee who belongs to an organization designated by this Department" as seeking the unconstitutional overthrow of the government and that therefore the department's advice about the SWP's character "incorporated in a reply letter might help their agency in making a determination about this matter."

Alderman suggested that the department therefore inform the VA in writing that its files contained information "which indicate that the SWP is an organization that advocates the overthrow of our government by force and violence and the overthrow of our constitutional form of government," but that whether this conclusion could be "substantiated by witnesses and documentary evidence at an open hearing without disclosure of classified information" could be answered only following a "careful review of the voluminous files on the SWP and subsequent contact with the FBI as to the current availability of its sources." According to the text suggested for submission to the VA by Alderman, such a review would "ordinarily take several months of careful preparation and inquiry," and past experience with public hearings had suggested that "it is particularly difficult to obtain the cooperation of the expert and fact witnesses to appear for the government due to the personal inconvenience, loss of income and resultant publicity which is usually involved."

Alderman also declared that it would be "desirable" that the proposed letter indicate that information gathered by the FBI about the SWP "is available" to the VA and therefore VA attorneys could "evaluate the investigative material and determine the sufficiency of the available evidence before deciding what action to take" with regard to Kutcher, but that if FBI material "is not available" to the VA that the FBI "might furnish a breakdown of all the evidence which could be used at a public hearing." In any event, Alderman continued, available and "non-available" evidence could be separated out, potential witnesses interviewed, and applicable literature "studied and an overall evaluation of the admissible evidence should be made before a decision is made." Alderman concluded that Justice Department officials were preparing a memorandum for the ISD with regard to the questions posed by the VA and stated that while the November 2 conference "did not resolve the questions raised by the VA, it indicated "some of the problems involved in proving the nature of an organization like the SWP and also served to indicate that an answer could not be expected to the VA's letter until we have further opportunity to look into the various complicated issues involved."

While, unknown to Kutcher, the VA and the Justice Department were puzzling over how to handle his case, Kutcher formally filed with the VA on September 22, 1956, an affidavit setting forth his claim for back wages, along with the request that the VA expedite the matter "in any way possible." According to Kutcher's affidavit, "had I not been fired" in October 1948, an action that the federal appeals court had since determined to be "illegal," the regular wages, including the periodic step increases and pay adjustments that he would otherwise have received before being "restored to my old job on June 26, 1956," amounted to $23,492.48. He reported that the only earnings he had received during the period of his dismissal had been a total of $60 from two companies in Newark, paid in October 1950, plus approximately $600 in unemployment compensation received in the late 1940s. Kutcher added that if the earnings and unemployment compensation "are to be deducted from the total of pay due me," he believed that he would then be entitled to $22,832.48 "plus interest if it is the government's practice to pay interest in such cases."

Kutcher's affidavit was forwarded from the VA Newark office to the VA's benefits office in Washington on September 27, along with additional VA pay records and documents. Apparently referring to the upcoming October 1956 presidential elections or to a perceived general easing of the civil liberties climate, Joseph Rauh, Kutcher's lawyer, urged KCRC treasurer George Weissman to suggest that Kutcher contact VA officials "right away" concerning "what the status is and begin indicating some impatience to take this matter to the public," because the VA was "probably more susceptible to public opinion now than they will be later on" and there thus "may be a better chance of getting Jim Kutcher's back money in the next couple of weeks than later on." After a November 13 follow-up letter from Rauh to Weissman inquiring about the "present status of the matter," Rauh wrote Weissman on January 23, 1957, that he had "pestered the Veterans' Administration about Jim Kutcher's back pay so much that I can't tell whether I am sicker of them than they are of me." Rauh reported that at first the "whole thing was over at the Justice Department" but "now they tell me they are putting the matter up to the Comptroller General in a letter that should go forward this week." Rauh added that the VA had promised to tell him when they sent the promised letter and that he would then "try and see what I can find out" from the comptroller general.

Kutcher's struggle for back pay attracted relatively little press attention. However, in a December 6, 1956, editorial entitled "How Long, Oh Lord?" the *New York Post*, which had repeatedly covered Kutcher's plight, denounced the government for failing to promptly repay Kutcher his lost wages, declaring that it had originally assumed that such action would be "routine," but the government had turned it into another demonstration of its "capacity for taking infinite and needless pains." The editorial termed Kutcher's case "the classic American saga of mindless bureaucracy," in which the government had inflicted "numerous petty acts of harassment," and declared that the prolonged delay in responding to Kutcher's application for reimbursement, which it declared was "kicking around somewhere between the VA and the Justice Department," suggested that "somewhere in the bureaucracy where a human heart should be there rests only an old bundle of frayed red tape." On May 9, 1957, the *New York Times* reported what Rauh had been informed of months earlier, namely that the issue had been referred to the U.S. controller general for a final determination.

While Kutcher continued to fight for his back pay, on January 16, 1957, the Newark VA office awarded him a ten-year service pin, although Kutcher had been on leave during almost the entire period involved. The rich irony of this latest VA decision yielded long articles in the *New York Post* and the *Washington Post*. The *New York Post* quoted Kutcher as declaring that he was "happy to get the award" because it recognized that "for almost eight years I was illegally deprived of my job and legally I have been an employee of the VA since 1946. I now hope that the government follows the logic of giving me the back wages coming to me. If it can decorate me for 10 years' service, it isn't too much to ask that it pay me for the same 10 years." He added that during the presentation ceremony he had been tempted to raise this question but "that would have marred the occasion for the others. Also, I know that the question is out of the hands of the regional VA officials." Kutcher said that in Washington "they are tossing it from one to the other like a hot potato." In the meantime, the newspaper reported, Kutcher was wearing his ten-year service pin, which featured the official VA shield, a crossed anchor and rifle surmounted by a screaming eagle.

VA officials continued to closely monitor Kutcher's case. Thus, Newark regional manager O'Hearn in a March 5 memo to his files noted that during a meeting in his office the previous day he had "reaffirmed the urgent necessity of being constantly alert to any and all situations which might affect" Kutcher's status, with "emphasis" placed on the "responsibility of each of the individuals involved to keep me informed of potential developments ahead of time in order that I may, in turn, alert Central Office in consonance with instructions received" from VA administrator Higley. In apparent response, on March 8, Newark regional VA medical administrative officer Oscar Wexler, who was Kutcher's supervisor in Kutcher's assigned position as file clerk in the medical division, reported that Kutcher had been restored to duty although he "could not perform all of the duties outlined in the position description" due to his physical limitations, so it had been "agreed to allow him to occupy a file clerk position with primary emphasis on the duties of alphabetizing and maintenance of files." Wexler added that Kutcher's performance had been "satisfactory," that he had been "conscientious in his duties," and that Kutcher has "talked or socialized very little with other employees and seems to mind his own business" under the "close supervision" of Wexler and the supervisor of the "files group." In a document dated April 19, 1957, O'Hearn reported that he had advised the VA's "central office" that he intended to rate Kutcher as "satisfactory" in performance and in response had been advised to follow the "usual method" in such cases. A formal written evaluation of Kutcher's performance as satisfactory was subsequently submitted by VA Newark files groups supervisor Charles Mellor on May 29, 1957.

On July 11, 1957, the U.S. controller general issued a finding denying Kutcher's back pay on the grounds that all congressional appropriation acts since 1947 contained provisions barring payment of salaries to members of organizations advocating the forceful overthrow of the government, that Kutcher had admitted membership in the SWP, and that the U.S. Court of Appeals in 1943 had found that the SWP sought the forcible overthrow of the government. Without explicitly saying so, the opinion made clear that court rulings holding that Kutcher's *firing* for SWP membership were irrelevant to the question of *back pay* because under the cited congressional provisions "this Office would not be authorized to expend appropriated funds" for such purpose "in the absence of a judicial determination of the merits of your [specific] claim [for back pay]," even "if you would otherwise be entitled to back pay." Adding further irony to Kutcher's situation, on August 8, 1957, Assistant Attorney General William Tompkins advised VA general counsel Guy Birdsall that following an "exhaustive review" it had been determined that Kutcher would not be subject to "criminal proceedings" based upon his denial of membership in "any organization" that sought the violent overthrow of the government, as the Justice Department's Internal Security Division had determined that "the evidence which would be available for use in a judicial proceeding is insufficient to warrant" such proceedings. He added, in response to the VA's "query," that no further "civil proceedings" against Kutcher were "contemplated at this time" and that the "basis for such inquiry is not clear." (Judging from a contemporaneous internal Justice Department memo, this statement was intended to convey that, despite the controller general's opinion, the department was not planning to seek recovery of any past government appropriations paid to Kutcher, which, following the logic of the denial of back pay, would presumably also be illegal.)

In the wake of the government's denial of Kutcher's claim to back pay, Kutcher and Rauh decided to appeal once again to President Eisenhower. Kutcher's August 23, 1957, letter to Eisenhower received at least a sprinkling of press coverage, as did his subsequent decision to file yet another lawsuit, now over the question of back pay. Rauh, who drafted Kutcher's letter to the president, declared in exasperation in a July 31, 1957, letter to KCRC treasurer George Weissman that "there seems to be no end to some of these cases." In his letter Kutcher appealed to the president to restore his back pay "to prevent an injustice by the Government in whose military service I lost both my legs."

After summarizing his World War II service and his legal victories after "innumerable hearings and courts," Kutcher declared that he thought he "had finally won and it was over" after the federal courts ordered his reinstatement in May 1956, since the appeals court had specifically ordered that he regain his seniority rights, which would "normally" include "back pay—in my case for the years when I was unemployed and practically unemployable more because of the stigma of [being fired for] disloyalty than because of the loss of my legs." He recounted that upon returning to his VA post he had had "visions of being able to lead as normal a life as a legless man can" and had planned to use his back pay to buy a "small home in which my ailing parents and I could spend our lives together." However, he added, the comptroller general's ruling that "he won't pay me because I belonged and belong to" the SWP created the "ridiculous" situation in which the government was currently paying him under the same appropriation acts that were being used to deny him his back pay. "Please don't make me use up my money in high-priced litigation in the Court of Claims to get my back pay," Kutcher pleaded with Eisenhower. "I know that if you told the Attorney General to look into this matter and to urge the Comptroller General to reconsider my case I will get these funds. If it is legal to pay me bi-weekly now, it is certainly equally legal to pay me what I would have earned had I not been illegally discharged. This is probably the only chance I will ever have to buy a home of my own. I do not think the back pay due me is too much to ask."

The only response Kutcher received to his letter from Eisenhower was a September 13, 1957, letter from VA administrator Higley reporting that Eisenhower had referred the request to him and that he was bound by the comptroller general's finding since the "order of the Court" reinstating Kutcher did not "pass upon the question of back pay." Higley added that in view of this determination by the comptroller general "and his responsibility, your letter is being sent to him for his consideration [!]" (the comptroller general reiterated his earlier finding in a November 26, 1957, letter to Kutcher). Faced with this stone wall, Kutcher released his letter to Eisenhower, to moderate press coverage, at a September 11 press conference and proceeded with Rauh to file a lawsuit for his back pay in the United States Court of Claims on December 5, 1957.

At the press conference, Kutcher, wearing his ten-year VA service pin, complained that it was "tiresome and discouraging" to have received the comptroller general's rejection and that "you feel as though you're being kicked around like a football. I just want to be left alone in peace, with all of my rights. I don't want to fight with anybody, but

I don't want to be pushed around either." In a September 15, 1957, editorial entitled "Split Personalities," the *New York Post* lamented that as a result of the comptroller general's decision, the VA "now employs a loyal American named James Kutcher and the Comptroller General continues to impose his punishment on a dangerous character named James Kutcher." The latter comment was more accurate, in terms of the government's evaluation of Kutcher, than the *Post* could possibly have known: according to a secret October 18, 1957, internal Justice Department memo from ISD chief William Tompkins to recently appointed Attorney General William Rogers, Kutcher was one of only nine government employees who were listed on the department's "Security Index," a list of people who were to be rounded up and detained outside of normal legal procedures in the case of a national security "emergency." Tompkins's memo also revealed that the comptroller general had consulted with the ISD before making his ruling.

On December 5, 1957 (as noted in a brief *New York Times* article the following day), Rauh filed on Kutcher's behalf a lawsuit in the United States Court of Claims, asking for "$23,000, more or less" in back pay. In informing KCRC treasurer George Weissman of his action in a December 5 letter, Rauh declared that in his view Kutcher's claim was "clearly right" and therefore he "will ultimately get the money," but he lamented that "it just seems a shame to have to work so hard to get what Jim is obviously entitled to." The filing argued that Kutcher was clearly entitled to his back pay due to the April 20, 1956, federal appeals court ruling that his original firing from the VA was illegal and largely consisted of a history of his case, including the full texts of Kutcher's August 23, 1957, letter to President Eisenhower and the comptroller general's July 11, 1957, letter denying his claim.

According to Rauh, the comptroller general's argument maintaining that Kutcher could not be rendered his back pay due to congressional appropriations provisions was invalid because, among other reasons, Congress had recently stopped including the relevant riders to its appropriations act and "there are no restrictions on presently appropriated funds to persons because of their membership in any organization or organizations"; in any case, such riders could not apply to SWP members because the federal appeals courts had twice determined in Kutcher's case that they were inapplicable to Kutcher based solely on his SWP membership. "The denial of compensation to plaintiff," Rauh argued, "is rendered especially anomalous by the fact that plaintiff is actually employed by, and receiving compensation from, the very Government which contends that plaintiff cannot receive compensation for earlier years."

Following the filing of the lawsuit, Rauh and the government began negotiations for an out-of-court settlement, which was reached in early June 1958. Kutcher agreed to accept about $18,000 as full and final settlement of his back pay claims, which translated into a payment to him of $13,589.94 after deductions were made for taxes, insurance, and some minor outside earnings by Kutcher during the period from October 12, 1948, to June 25, 1956, when he was suspended by the VA (Kutcher had additionally agreed to pay Rauh 25 percent of any settlement). The outside earnings were listed as $600 in unemployment compensation under the G.I. Bill of Rights, $60 from gainful employment, and $137.90 in royalties from his book. According to a March 31, 1958, letter to Weissman from one of Rauh's assistants, the government became "more and more picayune" as the details of the settlement were negotiated, as "they hate to pay anything they don't have to."

According to an April 24, 1958, letter from Rauh to Weissman, based on past rulings by the Court of Claims, the settlement had to be based on Kutcher's pay at the time of his suspension, without any adjustment for pay increases he would have received had his employment continued normally, thus explaining why the settlement was about $18,000 rather than the approximately $23,000 that Kutcher had claimed in his lawsuit. Rauh urged Kutcher to accept the $18,000 settlement "without any hesitation" because, although it was "less than the sum for which we sued, this is all that we would get if we won the suit." Kutcher wrote back to Rauh on April 29 to accept the $18,000 settlement. Rauh noted in a June 17, 1958, letter to Weissman that the Kutcher case had been "going on for almost 10 years. I can't exactly say I'll miss it, but at least I can say that I enjoyed the battle and am better prepared for the next one."

The back pay settlement led to a sprinkling of press attention for the final time in the ten-year saga of the "legless veteran," with coverage in the *Washington Post* and the Newark newspapers, among others. It also led to the closing of the Justice Department's file on the Kutcher legal case and to the dissolution of the Kutcher Civil Rights Committee. On July 2, 1958, Assistant Attorney General George Cochran Doub informed the VA general counsel that the department's file on "James Kutcher v. United States, Court of Claims No. 553-57" was "being marked 'closed' as of this date." On October 24, 1958, the KCRC and Kutcher personally sent letters to their supporters announcing the dissolution of the KCRC. In his letter, treasurer Weissman declared he was "happy" to announce that the KCRC was "going out of business because it has achieved all of its aims," as Kutcher had "regained his rights without surrendering either his ideas or right of association." Weissman said that the KCRC's final assets were $482.54, which was being presented by check to Kutcher along with the committee's files and other property. He concluded his letter by declaring, "We believe that signal victories have been registered not only for Mr. Kutcher but for civil liberties in America."

In a shorter letter, Kutcher expressed his "heartfelt thanks" and "very deep personal gratitude" to his supporters, noting that although he had met many supporters during his speaking tours, "I have never met the overwhelming number of you and never shall." Declaring that the courts "have finally sustained me on all the lawsuits" brought "against the avalanche of punitive measures" launched against him by the government, Kutcher said "I well realize that I could never have even brought these suits—and certainly not maintained the litigation for 10 years—had it not been for your support." The final financial report of the KCRC indicated that during its ten years in existence it had raised slightly over $17,000 and expended about $500 under that amount (thus yielding the money given to Kutcher when the account closed).

During the entire period between Kutcher's court-ordered reinstatement to his VA clerical post in April 1956 and the June 1958 settlement of his claim for back pay in the U.S. Court of Claims, the FBI continued to subject him to relentless surveillance. At least in the FBI's view, there appear to have been three grounds for this: (1)

in the immediate aftermath of Kutcher's federal appeals court victory in April 1956, the federal government had the right to (but did not) appeal its loss to the Supreme Court, and for a short time the VA apparently considered again instituting loyalty proceedings against Kutcher and therefore needed to be kept informed of his activities; (2) until the decision was made to settle his claim for back pay via a settlement, the same logic applied; and (3) beginning in September 1956, the FBI placed Kutcher on its Security Index (SI), a listing of individuals who would be rounded up and detained without trials in the case of a national security emergency, and FBI policy apparently required at least annual reports on the activities of all SI listees.

Thus, a July 9, 1956, report included information from a dozen FBI field offices, while a July 31 internal FBI report specifically stated that the VA had requested "additional investigation" with regard to "Kutcher's continued activity in the SWP." Apparently with the possibility of a perjury prosecution in mind, an August 2, 1956, memo from the Washington field office to FBI Director Hoover included a photostat of the loyalty oath that Kutcher swore on July 2, 1956, on the occasion of his formal reinstatement, in which, among other things, he declared that he would "support and defend the Constitution against all enemies, foreign and domestic" and did not belong to "any organization that advocates the overthrow" of the government by "force or violence." A September 24, 1956, memo from Assistant Attorney General William Tompkins informed Hoover that in response to "your request for the Department's decision in this matter," the department had "currently concluded a review" of Kutcher's activities in the SWP, an organization that has "been consistently evaluated under the criteria of the Security Index as a basic revolutionary group" and had decided that Kutcher's "active participation" in the party "clearly brings him within the requirements for retention in the Security Index."

According to a June 1957 internal FBI memo, on May 28, 1956, the VA had advised "that it was contemplated that immediately upon his reinstatement to duty Kutcher will be the subject of charges," but if this report is accurate, the VA quickly dropped this idea. This memo also reports that "supplemental investigation" of Kutcher was conducted "at the request" of the VA in June and July 1956.

A December 22, 1957, memo from Tompkins to Hoover asked for information about the SWP in connection with Kutcher's lawsuit for back pay before the U.S. Court of Claims because "in defending this action the Government may have to prove" that the SWP "advocates the overthrow of this government by force and violence." Tompkins specifically asked the FBI to provide the "usual prosecutive summary report with particular emphasis on the critical period, 1946 to the present." However, a December 30 internal FBI memo, apparently signed off on by Hoover, seemingly reflects a generalized FBI irritation with the Justice Department (the FBI felt that the Justice Department was abandoning its anticommunist campaign in the wake of adverse Supreme Court rulings), declaring that "we should not be doing Tompkins' work for him by preparing a prosecutive summary report in this matter."

A follow-up February 6, 1958, memo from Tompkins makes clear that the government was still considering fighting Kutcher's claims for back pay in court at that time. However, according to an internal FBI memo of March 12, which refers to thirty-six different informants used to report on SWP activities, the Bureau had learned by March 7 that the Justice Department had decided not to contest Kutcher's claims. This led Hoover to write Tompkins on March 12 reporting this information, asking that Tompkins therefore "advise immediately concerning the status of this matter" and reporting that further investigation was "being held in abeyance pending receipt" of a response. In reply, Tompkins effectively confirmed the FBI report in a memo to Hoover March 14, 1958, which reported that there was "now grave doubt of the wisdom of attempting a defense in this case" and approving of FBI suspension of further inquiries in relationship to it. A final FBI memo on the back pay issue consists of a letter from Hoover to the New York City FBI office dated July 11, which reported that the FBI had received information that Kutcher "has received a cash award in settlement" and thus "no further investigation will be necessary in your office in instant matter and your case may be closed."

Despite the closure of the FBI's case concerning Kutcher's status as a VA employee, the Bureau's surveillance continued, apparently on the basis of Kutcher's continuing listing on the Security Index.

Between late 1956 and early 1972, the FBI filed annual reports on Kutcher, which were always based on information obtained from both multiple informants and FBI agents, and indicated his employment status, his residence, and his various, numerous SWP-related activities, especially his attendance at SWP meetings and SWP-sponsored labor forums. In a number of instances, the reports indicate that Kutcher's employment and place of residence were verified by using various pretext telephone calls, such as pretending to be insurance or automobile salesmen, taking a television survey, inquiring about jury duty, and canvassing for the Boy Scouts (the January 22, 1965, annual report indicated that Kutcher's residence had been determined by a "suitable pretext," but also noted that he was openly listed in the New York City telephone directory!). Copies of these annual FBI reports were sent to the CSC and VA (a June 22, 1962, memo from Hoover to the FBI's New York office said that in "any contact with representatives of the employing agency" it should be "clearly understood by them that such contacts are for information purposes only and should not be construed as a pressure tactic in efforts to expedite subject's removal"). Each annual report indicated that Kutcher had been "re-evaluated" under existing Security Index criteria and that such listing was still warranted, with the basis for this usually simply given as his SWP membership.

Beginning in 1966 copies of FBI reports on Kutcher were sent to the Secret Service on the grounds that he was "potentially dangerous; or has been identified as member or participant in communist movement; or has been under active investigation as member or other group or organization inimical to U.S." (in 1972 the wording on the FBI form letter sent to the Secret Service was changed to read "potentially dangerous because of background, emotional instability or activity in groups engaged in activities inimical to U.S."). According to 1967 internal FBI memos, since 1952 Kutcher had been included on the FBI's special "detcom" (for detention of Communists) and "comsab" (for Communist sabotage) lists, but had been deleted from "comsab" after 1955 and was deleted from "detcom" on January 17, 1967, on the grounds that his former degree of SWP activity "no longer exists and the subject does not hold any leadership position in the SWP"; however he continued to be listed on the Security Index.

In fact, the FBI reports indicate no fundamental change in Kutcher's SWP activities: thus, a July 29, 1971, report indicated that during the prior three years he had attended well over 100 SWP meetings and labor forums. An internal FBI memo indicates that on April 7, 1972, Kutcher was approved for inclusion on the "ADEX" (administrative index), essentially a renamed version of the Security Index.

The first annual report on Kutcher, dated December 19, 1956, was based on at least nine informants and included such information as that Kutcher had attended "eleven SWP functions from May 19, 1956, to November 11, 1956," had contributed $125 to SWP causes, and had spoken at a Detroit SWP forum on March 23, 1956, concerning "his fight to get his job back with the VA." The December 30, 1957, annual report on Kutcher was based on thirteen informants and reported, among other matters, that Kutcher had contributed $3 to an SWP convention fund, while giving the exact dates of scores of SWP-related activities and meetings that Kutcher had participated in, including several sightings by FBI agents of Kutcher entering or leaving SWP national headquarters in New York City. The FBI's November 30, 1958, annual report indicated that Kutcher had attended twenty-seven SWP functions during the previous year and donated $150 to the party. The January 7, 1960, annual report stated that Kutcher had attended a February 24, 1959, New York City debate on "Is Marxism valid in the United States today?" and had contributed $23 to the Newark SWP on June 16, 1959. According to the January 19, 1961, annual report, Kutcher had recently visited Castro's Cuba under the auspices of the left-wing Fair Play for Cuba Committee (FPCC). The February 21, 1962, report, based on information from at least twelve informants, indicated that during the prior year Kutcher had attended a memorial meeting for a deceased SWP member, while the January 15, 1963, report declared that during the prior year Kutcher had attended "42 closed [SWP] membership" meetings, was observed leaving SWP New York City headquarters on eleven occasions, and had contributed $7.50 to the FPCC. Beginning in 1967, the annual reports indicated that Kutcher was periodically active in anti–Vietnam War demonstrations, an activity that became a high priority for the SWP and its youth group, the Young Socialist Alliance (YSA), whose activities Kutcher was also reported as periodically participating in. The final annual FBI report on Kutcher was dated March 15, 1972, and noted that Kutcher had retired from his VA position. The final entry in Kutcher's FBI file, dated August 29, 1973, reported that a review had determined that Kutcher "does not meet criteria for inclusion on ADEX as set forth in Bureau Memorandum 21-72, dated 9/12/1972."

The 1972 FBI annual report on Kutcher accurately reflected that he had retired from his VA file clerk job, which was by then paying him an annual salary of $7,186, as of January 28, 1972 (his original salary in 1946 had been $1,954). Kutcher's retirement did not come without one last flurry of paperwork related to his unusual work history. When the VA first calculated his retirement benefits, his involuntary eight-year period of suspension between 1948 and 1956 was not included as part of his pay base, apparently inadvertently, as the relevant VA files did not include a copy of his 1958 Court of Claims settlement establishing that he was entitled to the back pay that had previously been withheld. Once Kutcher brought this to the VA's attention and the needed documentation was provided, the VA recalculated his retirement base, although the process of straightening out this question consumed five months and required a thick file of correspondence involving Kutcher's lawyers and a variety of governmental officials from the VA and the CSC. Fortunately for Kutcher, in the end, the government agreed that there would be no need, as he put it in an August 28, 1971, letter to Rauh, to "go to court to adjudicate what has already been adjudicated." In the end, Kutcher was approved for a monthly retirement annuity of $299, compared to the original calculation of $244.

In 1973, shortly after Kutcher retired, the SWP filed a lawsuit demanding $40 million in damages from the FBI and other federal intelligence agencies due to decades of alleged illegal spying and disruptions of constitutionally protected activities. Soon after the suit was filed, the government revealed that FBI director Hoover had initiated a formal sabotage program against the SWP in 1961 on the grounds that it had recently been "openly espousing its line on a local and national basis through running candidates for public office and strongly directing and/or supporting such causes as Castro's Cuba and integration problems arising in the south." After fourteen years of litigation (during which Attorney General Griffin Bell was briefly held in contempt of court for refusing to release FBI files), federal Judge Thomas Griesa awarded the SWP $264,000 in 1986, finding, in a 210-page opinion, that between 1940 and 1976 the FBI had infiltrated and disrupted the party while failing to uncover any instances of "planned or actual espionage, violence, terrorism or efforts to subvert the governmental structure" or evidence leading to even a "single arrest for any Federal law violation."

Griesa reported that the FBI had instead directed all of its actions against "entirely lawful and peaceful political activities," that its investigation had revealed that the SWP expelled members who advocated "violence or disorder," and that the 8 million FBI file entries reported on the "marital or cohabitation status, marital strife, health, travel plans and personal habits" of party members. Griesa declared that FBI files revealed "little or no information bearing on national security and no information about actual or planned violence against public officials, but rather a mass of information about peaceful political activities and the private lives of individuals." Griesa added that during its "patently unconstitutional" campaign against the SWP, conducted without any "legal authority or justification," the FBI had committed almost 200 burglaries and 46 acts of "disruption" designed to create internal party turmoil, tapped SWP telephones for at least 20,000 days, and paid almost $2 million to 1,300 informers who infiltrated the organization and its youth group, the YSA (whose combined estimated membership never exceeded 3,000).

FBI documents released during the trial revealed that over 300 of the informers had become members of the two groups, including 40 who held SWP office and several who ran for election as SWP candidates. The FBI originally defended its actions because members of "subversive groups" were "presumed" to view the "use of violence as a political tool" as "inevitable" and because SWP members might "gain responsible positions not only in government but also in industry and education." However, after Attorney General Edward Levi ordered the bureau to stop spying on the SWP in 1976 following revelations of massive FBI surveillance abuses and illegal actions against numerous dissident groups and individuals (FBI documents revealed it was still then using over sixty SWP informants), FBI director Clarence Kelley conceded, "We agree it is now necessary to discontinue such investigations." As late as 1981, however, the government maintained that it could "legally investigate individuals or organizations regardless of their nature" and that the issue was not whether SWP or YSA was "guilty of a crime beyond a reasonable doubt," but whether the government could investigate "groups that openly advocate revolutionary change" even if "such advocacy might be within the letter of the law." Even after losing the case, the government argued that it had "important legitimate needs" for continuing to use the fruits of its SWP surveillance, especially with regard to "security clearance" for government employees and contractors; however, it finally decided not to appeal Judge Griesa's injunction banning such action.

Except insofar as the FBI and the SWP was concerned, Kutcher gradually faded into obscurity after winning all of his court and administrative battles in the 1950s. As noted above, he retired from his VA position in 1972. After that, a few attempts were made to revive memories about his case, but today he is largely forgotten. In 1973, the SWP's Monad/Pathfinder Press published an updated version of Kutcher's autobiography, again entitled *The Case of the Legless Veteran*, but, except for extremely brief notices in the *Nation* and the *New York Times*, it was ignored by the American press (oddly, a lengthy, laudatory account of the book appeared over twenty years later, in 1995, on an online reviewing source for history books, H-Net; it termed Kutcher an "unheralded and long-forgotten genuine American hero"). According to the World Cat electronic base, only about 150 libraries worldwide purchased the book (although this was considerably more than 34 listed for the earlier edition). In 1981, Howard Petrick, a veteran who gained an honorable discharge only after suing the government when he was given an "undesirable discharge" due to his antiwar activities while in the service, produced a film about Kutcher, again entitled *The Case of the Legless Veteran*. Petrick's film won several prizes and praise in a number of outlets, including the *New York Times* and the *Los Angeles Times*, but obtained only limited distribution, at least partly because, according to published reports, the Public Broadcasting System declined to broadcast it nationally, essentially on the grounds that it was not focused enough on Kutcher and included too much about the SWP and "McCarthyism."

The Petrick film contained little new about Kutcher other than his statement that "from the beginning" he had "never thought" he would win his struggles and that "I was just fighting because I thought the thing to do was to fight." Rauh, Kutcher's lawyer, said in the film that Kutcher's case "started before McCarthy came into it and ended after, but it was possibly the worst outrage of the whole time. I always hate to say anything was the worst. But I really believe that the disability pension hearing was the lowest point of the period." Journalist I. F. Stone termed the Kutcher case the "reductio absurdum of the whole witch hunt," as its entire "excuse" was the fear of "Soviet agents in the government, here was a Trotskyist, the most bitter and principled and unrelenting foes of the Stalinist dictatorship. . . . Yet, [the SWP] was made a target on which J. Edgar Hoover, who now turns out to have been quite a nut, quite a paranoid, wasted millions of dollars" in "infiltrating the Trotskyists."

In 1985, shortly after Kutcher was expelled from the SWP (see below), he granted an interview, published online, in celebration of fifty years of political activities (he had first joined the SP in 1935). He said that while his father had never joined a union, "he taught me that working people have to organize and rely on themselves." In 1989, shortly after Kutcher's death, an interview with him was published in a book about victims of American political repression, entitled, *It Did Happen Here: Recollections of Political Repression in America.* The only "news" in the interview was that, whereas earlier Kutcher had always said he was hit by a German mortar while getting something to eat, in this interview he relates, "I got up to perform one of the functions of nature and in the middle of that we were hit."

For a 2003–2004 law journal article and a follow-up book about Joseph Rauh, legal historian Michael Parrish interviewed Rauh about the Kutcher case before the former's death in 1992, but it included virtually no new information other than that Rauh's assistant, Daniel Pollitt, thought that Kutcher was a "slob" and that Rauh was so delighted with the Herblock cartoon about the pension disability hearing that he obtained the original drawing and hung it in his office. In a separate 1992 interview by Robert S. Peck posted on the internet, Rauh described his delight with the Herblock cartoon, while terming his victory in Kutcher's disability pension case as "like taking candy from a baby" due to the VA committee's admission that it had no procedural rules for the hearing. Rauh described Kutcher as "a man wholly without education, knowledge or anything," who was "manipulated" by the SWP into becoming the "party's best drawing card" and who would "come into the meeting with two canes, stumble up and say a few sentences that he had memorized." This description of Kutcher probably reflects Rauh's disdain for the SWP more than anything else: the overwhelming evidence is that while Kutcher unquestionably, and without question, toed the "SWP line" during his administrative and legal battles, he was not only quite articulate most of the time, but even eloquent in making his case, especially in pointing out that he committed violence only while serving in the army, that his political views were never questioned when he was drafted and had his legs amputated, and that he viewed the perceived loss of his basic constitutional rights as even more damaging than the loss of his legs.

Finally, the present author published a short history of the Kutcher case in a 2008 study of AGLOSO entitled *American Blacklist*, which argues that Kutcher "became perhaps the most famous individual victim of AGLOSO" and that his case "probably attracted more public attention and sympathy than any other single development connected to AGLOSO and thus the 'legless veteran' contributed substantially to gradually discrediting the feared 'list' that cast so long a shadow over the 'land of the free' after 1947."

Perhaps the greatest irony of Kutcher's post-1958 life was that, after having suffered and struggled so much due to his SWP membership, Kutcher, along with about 200 other SWP members (of a total membership of less than 1,000) was expelled from the party following a change in leadership and policy, in which Trotsky's theory of permanent revolution and other long-standing Trotskyist doctrines were abandoned. Although officially Kutcher was expelled in 1983 for "punching" an SWP comrade and failing to show up at a hearing about this alleged offense, it seems clear that in reality he was expelled for ideological deviationism (both Kutcher and the alleged victim denied that the punching incident occurred). Kutcher and other expelled members formed a new group entitled the Fourth Internationalist Tendency, which faded away by 1995. What was left of the SWP itself also gradually faded into oblivion after the 1983 expulsions: its presidential candidate received 40,000 votes nationwide in 1980, but only 4,000 in 2012. According to Alan Wald, a former SWP member and now a prominent historian and literary critic at the University of Michigan, "by 2011, the SWP has changed its political line domestically and internationally more often than Lady Gaga switches outfits at a performance," and it has increasingly become a cult rather than a party, purging its members via procedures that "would give even the appellation 'Kangaroo Court' a bad name."

According to a fellow SWP-expellee and friend of Kutcher, Frank Lovell, who termed Kutcher "the man who never gave up," Kutcher spent his final years "caring for his personal needs as an invalid and reading," and "never gave up his hope that somehow the SWP could be won back to Trotskyism and the traitors in the leadership exposed." At least until his expulsion, Kutcher also did volunteer work for the SWP's Pathfinder Press. Kutcher was clearly deeply shaken by his expulsion, apparently to the point of becoming physically ill. He appealed his expulsion in an anguished ten-page single-spaced typed letter to the 1984 national SWP convention, but was turned down; in it he compared the lack of due process accorded him by the SWP to his treatment by the government thirty years earlier. In his 1985 interview, he refused to talk about the expulsion, terming it a "painful subject," but reiterated his desire to have it overturned, as the SWP "is the only revolutionary party in this country, whatever mistakes it has made. That was why I didn't want to be kicked out of it and that is why I want to be readmitted." According to Lovell, Kutcher suffered another major blow when his best friend and fellow SWP expellee George Breitman died in 1986. Lovell writes that Kutcher's "body finally gave out a few days before his 76th birthday, December 26, 1988," whereupon he was taken to the intensive care unit of the Brooklyn VA hospital and "lingered in semi-consciousness until pronounced dead February 10 [1989]. In his struggle with death, as in life, James Kutcher refused to give up."

In a final irony, Kutcher, who in life furnished newspapers across the country with so many (often front-page) stories, was ignored in death. Not a single major paper mentioned his death or provided an obituary, with the exception of a tiny paid listing in the *New York Times* and a small obituary in New York's *Newsday*. The *Times* listed his brother as the sole survivor. In his autobiography, Kutcher mentioned the brother once in passing, never even giving his name. It was Max.

CHRONOLOGY

December 26, 1912	James Kutcher born in Newark, New Jersey
1932	Kutcher graduates high school, faces near decade of unemployment
1936	Kutcher joins YPSL, SP youth group
1938	Kutcher joins SWP after SP splits
1939	Congress passes Hatch Act, banning federal employment for members of groups that advocate "the overthrow of our constitutional form of government"
1940	Congress passes Smith Act, which bans advocacy of violent overthrow of the government and related matters
January 23, 1941	Kutcher inducted into armed forces after being drafted
1943	Federal appeals court upholds 1941 lower court convictions of eighteen top SWP leaders as advocating illegal overthrow of government, under Smith Act
November 9, 1943	Kutcher loses both legs to German mortar fire during Battle of San Pietro, Italy
September 27, 1945	Kutcher honorably discharged from army, given prostheses, and taught to walk with canes
August 1946	Kutcher hired as file clerk at VA
March 1947	President Truman inaugurates comprehensive "loyalty" program for federal employees in which membership in groups advocating governmental overthrow to be considered "one piece of evidence" of possible disloyalty
December 1947	Attorney General Tom Clark makes public AGLOSO listing of organizations considered dubious under Truman loyalty program; SWP is listed
August 1948	Kutcher notified by VA loyalty board of impending firing under loyalty program
September 10, 1948	Kutcher given loyalty hearing by Philadelphia VA branch board; all charges stem from SWP activities

September 17, 1948	Attorney General Clark issues new AGLOSO in which SWP is listed as advocating the illegal overthrow of the government
September 30, 1948	Kutcher granted interview with Clark
October 12, 1948	Philadelphia VA loyalty branch board finds Kutcher guilty under loyalty program due to SWP activities
October 17, 1948	LRB, the highest authority under the loyalty program, finds that firing of members of AGLOSO organizations seeking illegal overthrow of government from federal employment is "mandatory" under 1939 Hatch Act
January 4, 1949	VA administrator Gray upholds Philadelphia branch board recommendation to fire Kutcher, citing SWP membership
March 31, 1949	LRB panel hears Kutcher appeal from VA ruling
April 25, 1949	LRB affirms Kutcher firing under loyalty program and Hatch Act
June 1949	Kutcher begins nine-month speaking tour about his case
June 26, 1951	Federal district court upholds Kutcher firing
October 16, 1952	Federal appeals court overturns Kutcher firing on grounds SWP affiliation alone cannot be used to find federal employees disloyal, remands to VA for further consideration
December 1952	Under federal Gwinn Amendment banning families with AGLOSO members from federally subsidized housing, NHA seeks Kutcher family ouster from Newark apartment
April 20, 1953	VA Board of Appeals upholds Kutcher firing
April 23, 1953	VA administrator Gray endorses VA Board recommendation for firing
June 4, 1953	LRB hears Kutcher case and upholds firing
November 2, 1953	Federal district court overturns Kutcher firing on technical grounds, remands to VA
May 1954	Kutcher begins six-month speaking tour
March 18, 1955	Kutcher wins Gwinn Act eviction case in New Jersey Superior Court

June 2, 1955	After VA administrator orders Kutcher fired again, federal district court endorses finding
December 5, 1955	Kutcher wins Gwinn Act eviction case in New Jersey Supreme Court
December 12, 1955	VA informs Kutcher of intention to take away World War II disability benefits on loyalty grounds
December 15, 1955	World War II disability benefits are immediately suspended pending a hearing
December 23, 1955	Following major public uproar, World War II disability benefits are restored to Kutcher pending hearing
December 30, 1955	Amidst massive publicity, VA Committee on Waivers and Forfeitures holds public hearing on Kutcher case
January 8, 1956	VA committee restores Kutcher disability benefits, holding insufficient evidence to require their cancellation
April 20, 1956	Kutcher wins job restoration case in federal circuit court of appeals on grounds his firing was based on different charges than those brought against him
June 26, 1956	Kutcher resumes VA file clerk work after being suspended for seven years
September 1956	FBI places Kutcher on Security Index listing of those to be rounded up without legal process during a time of "national emergency"
January 16, 1957	Kutcher awarded VA ten-year service pin
June 1958	VA agrees to award Kutcher back pay for period of suspension after he files in U.S. Court of Claims
1972	Kutcher retires from VA position
1983	Kutcher expelled from SWP during political split
February 10, 1989	Kutcher dies in Brooklyn, New York, VA hospital

BIBLIOGRAPHICAL ESSAY

Note from the Series Editors: The following bibliographical essay contains the major primary and secondary sources the author consulted for this volume. We have asked all authors in the series to omit formal citations in order to make our volumes more readable, inexpensive, and appealing for students and general readers. In adopting this format, Landmark Law Cases and American Society follows the precedent of a number of highly regarded and widely consulted series.

Information about the Kutcher case is overwhelmingly available only in primary sources. The gold standard here is the collection of the KCRC, which is held by the Wisconsin State Historical Society, to whom I am indebted for an extended loan of their microfilm of their holdings, which includes hundreds of pages of extensive correspondence, newspaper clippings, legal briefs, transcripts of administrative hearings, financial records, and much else. The Wisconsin collection is supplemented by the holdings of Kutcher's close friend George Breitman in the Tamiment Library at New York University, which also includes extensive information about Kutcher's expulsion from the SWP in 1983. Kutcher's autobiography, *The Case of the Legless Veteran* (London: New Park, 1953, and updated edition, New York: Monad, 1973), of course primarily gives his point of view on things, but is reliable for factual material and reprints some important documents in its appendices. I was fortunate in being able to obtain through the Freedom of Information Act much documentation from the FBI, the Justice Department, and the VA; I also used documents from the CSC and the LRB, some of which were declassified for me, held at the National Archives in College Park, Maryland. The 1943 federal appeals court ruling in the 1941 Smith Act trial of the SWP is reported at *Dunne v. U.S.*, 138 F. 2d 137 (1943). Four of Kutcher's trials are also reported: *Kutcher v. Gray*, 199 F. 2d 783 (1952); *Kutcher v. Housing Authority of Newark*, 119 A 2d (1955); *Kutcher* v. *Higley*, 235 F. 2d 505 (1956); and *Kutcher v. U.S.*, No. 553-57 (1958), U.S. Court of Claims. The SWP 1986 legal victory concerning FBI spying is reprinted in full together with supporting material in Margaret Jayko, ed., *FBI on Trial: The Victory in the Socialist Workers Party Suit against Government Spying* (New York: Pathfinder, 1988), *SWP v. Attorney General*, 642 F. Supp. 1357 (1986).

The Proquest Historical Newspaper Database was invaluable for obtaining copies of newspaper coverage of the Kutcher case in leading newspapers across the country. I am indebted to Howard Petrick for making available to me a copy and transcript of his 1981 film, *The Case of the Legless Veteran*. An interview with Kutcher published in 1989 (shortly after his death) is published in Bud and Ruth Schultz, *It Did Happen Here: Recollections of Political Repression in America* (Berkeley: University of California Press, 1989); a 1985 interview with Kutcher is available on the web, along with material about Kutcher's 1983 expulsion from the SWP and a recollection of Kutcher by his friend and fellow-expulsee Frank Lovell, at Marxists.org/history/etoldocu ment/fit/ivtovi.htm.

Secondary literature is primarily useful for background information to the Kutcher case rather than for information specifically about Kutcher. For general information about political repression in the United States, see the present author's *Political Repression in Modern America*, 2nd ed. (Urbana: University of Illinois Press, 2001). On the post–World War II Red Scare in general, see Ellen Schrecker, *Many Are the Crimes: McCarthyism in America*, 2nd ed. (Princeton, N.J.: Princeton University Press, 1998). On the loyalty program, the best sources remain the now badly dated Ralph Brown, *Loyalty and Security: Employment Tests in the United States* (New Haven, Conn.: Yale University Press, 1958) and Eleanor Bontecue, *The Federal Loyalty-Security Program* (Ithaca, N.Y.: Cornell University Press, 1953). A very useful more recent study of the loyalty program, including a number of case studies, is Landon Storrs, *The Second Red Scare and the Unmaking of the New Deal Left* (Princeton, N.J.: Princeton University Press, 2013). Useful sources on the background to the loyalty program include Richard Freeland, *The Truman Doctrine and the Origins of McCarthyism: Foreign Policy, Domestic Politics and Internal Security, 1946–1948* (New York: Schocken, 1974); Athan Theoharis, *Seeds of Repression: Harry S. Truman and the Origins of McCarthyism* (Chicago: Quadrangle, 1971); Robert Griffith and Athan Theoharis, eds., *The Specter: Original Essays on the Cold War and the Origins of McCarthyism* (New York: New Viewpoints, 1974); and Richard Kirkendall, *Civil Liberties and the Legacy of Harry S. Truman* (Kirksville, Mo.: Truman State University Press, 2013). On AGLOSO, see the present writer's *American Blacklist: The Attorney General's List of Subversive Organizations* (Lawrence: University Press of Kansas, 2008), which includes a short account of the Kutcher case, and, on the role of Attorney General Tom Clark, Alexander Wohl, *Father, Son and the Constitution: How Justice Tom Clark and Attorney General Ramsey Clark Shaped American Democracy* (Lawrence: University Press of Kansas, 2013).

On the SWP, Constance Myers's *The Prophet's Army: Trotskyists in America* (Westport, Conn.: Greenwood, 1977), covers up through the 1941 Smith Act trial; Donna Haverty-Stacke, *Trotskyists on Trial: Free Speech and Political Persecution since the Age of FDR* (New York: New York University Press, 2015), focuses on the trial and its aftermath; and A. Belden Fields's *Trotskyism and Maoism: Theory and Practice in France and the United States* (Brooklyn, N.Y.: Autonomedia, 1988), brings the story up through the 1980s. For the 1941

Smith Act trial, see also two articles by Thomas Pahl: "G-String Conspiracy, Political Reprisal or Armed Revolt? The Minneapolis Trotskyite Trial," *Labor History* 8 (1967); and "The Dilemma of a Civil Libertarian: Francis Biddle and the Smith Act," *Journal of the Minnesota Academy of Sciences* 34 (1967). For an account of Kutcher's expulsion from the SWP, see Harvey Klehr, "The Case of the Legless Veteran," *Dissent* 33 (1986). Alan Wald's essay on the decline of the SWP in recent years is on the web at international viewpoint.org/spip.php?article2208.

The World War II battle of San Pietro in which Kutcher lost his legs is discussed in detail in Rick Atkinson's *The Day of Battle: The War in Sicily and Italy, 1943–1944* (New York: Henry Holt, 2007). A few pages on the Kutcher case are included in an article and book by legal historian Michael Parrish: "A Lawyer in Crisis Times: Joseph L. Rauh, the Loyalty Security Program and the Defense of Civil Liberties in the Early Cold War," *North Carolina Law Review* 82 (2003–2004); and *Citizen Rauh: An American Liberal's Life in Law and Politics* (Ann Arbor: University of Michigan Press, 2010). The 1992 Peck interview with Rauh is on the Internet at dcchs.org/JosephLRauh /rauh_transcript_4.pdf. For more information on the 1951 Supreme Court *McGrath* ruling and the Gwinn Act, see two articles by the present author: "The Grapes of *McGrath*: The Supreme Court and the Attorney General's List of Subversive Organizations in *Joint Anti-Fascist Refugee v. McGrath*," *Journal of Supreme Court History* 33 (2008); and "Kicking the Commies Out of Public Housing: The Rise and Fall of the Gwinn Amendment," *American Communist History* 9 (2010). A good study of the Supreme Court's growing inclination after 1956 to strike down anticommunist legal and administrative provisions is Arthur Sabin, *In Calmer Times: The Supreme Court and Red Monday* (Philadelphia: University of Pennsylvania Press, 1999). For a general study of the ACLU, which supported Kutcher's legal fight in modest ways, see Samuel Walker, *In Defense of American Liberties: A History of the ACLU*, 2d ed. (Carbondale: Southern Illinois University Press, 1999).

INDEX